ALTSCHUL'S PSYCHOLOGY FOR NURSES

NURSES' AIDS SERIES

Nurses' Aids Series

ALTSCHUL'S PSYCHOLOGY FOR NURSES

Helen C. Sinclair
BSc (Social Sciences) (Edin.), RSCN,
RGN, SCM, RNT, Head of
Department and Senior Lecturer,
Department of Nursing Studies,
University of Edinburgh

Josephine N. Fawcett
BSc (Hons) (Lond.), MSc (Edin.),
RGN, RNT, Lecturer, Department
of Nursing Studies, University
of Edinburgh

Seventh Edition

Baillière Tindall
London Philadelphia Toronto Sydney Tokyo

Baillière Tindall
W. B. Saunders

24–28 Oval Road,
London NW1 7DX

The Curtis Center,
Independence Square West,
Philadelphia, PA 19106–3399, USA

55 Horner Avenue,
Toronto, Ontario M8Z 4X6, Canada

Harcourt Brace Jovanovich (Australia) Pty Ltd,
32–52 Smidmore Street,
Marrickville, NSW 2204, Australia

Harcourt Brace Jovanovich (Japan) Inc.
Ichibancho Central Building, 22-1 Ichibancho
Chiyoda-ku, Tokyo 102, Japan

First published 1951
Fourth edition 1975
Fifth edition 1981
Sixth edition 1986
Seventh edition 1991

Typeset by Best-set Typesetter Ltd

Printed and bound in Great Britain by Clays Ltd, St Ives plc

A catalogue record for the book is available from the British Library
ISBN 0-7020-1455-9

Contents

Foreword

Elementary psychology was first introduced as a subject in the curriculum of training by the General Nursing Council for England and Wales in 1949.

The first edition of *Aids to Psychology* was published in 1951. Norah Mackenzie, the author, was a much respected lecturer in psychology and education at the Royal College of Nursing, where she introduced qualified nurses to the subject in advanced courses. She developed a course of lectures to student nurses preparing for the Preliminary State Examination, when psychology was newly included in the syllabus and she based her book on this course of lectures. Although what she wrote in 1951 is still valid, psychologists now provide much more knowledge of interest to nurses which is relevant to many aspects of their work.

When I took on the authorship of the book for its second edition in 1961 the statutory requirement was still only for six lectures, with the emphasis on the psychological development of the individual. The content of the second edition went far beyond that, to include topics which it was hoped might help the nurse to understand herself better and which might assist her in her role as a teacher or manager. It was hoped that nurses would not only study psychology because it was part of the curriculum, but that they would develop an interest in the subject and discover its relevance.

Periodic revision of the nursing curriculum has resulted in an increased emphasis on the 'reflective' nature of the process of nursing, the desirability of nurses learning to understand themselves in order to better understand their patients and fellow-workers. Increasingly lip-service is being paid to the importance of psychology. However, little evidence of this has been reflected in the wording of examination questions for first level registration of nurses.

With the introduction of Project 2000 a new system of qualifying examinations is being developed. In the new format students will have more opportunity to demonstrate their understanding of psychology in problem-solving case studies, extended essays and re-search projects. Perhaps these will show that students have found the study of psychology exciting, rewarding and relevant.

To ensure the continued life-span of textbooks it is imperative that authors are thoroughly familiar with recent advances in their discipline and with the changing needs for information, as nursing practice develops. For me it has become impossible to continue to satisfy these conditions. For the last ten years Helen Sinclair has con-tributed up-to-date knowledge in all areas of psychology. Her new co-author, Josephine Fawcett, brings a fresh perspective to the science of psychology. Her clinical nursing expertise and her active involvement with students during their clinical learning experiences renders her eminently qualified to demonstrate how psychological knowledge promotes excellence in practice.

I have not been involved at all in the preparation of this new edition. I am delighted with the book's new look. I am confident that readers at all stages of their nursing career will find it of real value.

Annie Altschul,
Emeritus Professor of Nursing Studies,
University of Edinburgh

Preface

It is 40 years since the first edition of *Psychology for Nurses* was published. With each succeeding edition, it has become increasingly clear that the study of psychology plays an integral part in nursing education. Nursing is a complex activity requiring an immense range of skills and the understanding of human behaviour and experience that the discipline of psychology offers can do much to inform nursing skills and attitudes and promote effective and sensitive care.

The book is essentially for those readers who have never studied psychology and aims to give an introduction to the subject, the different perspectives taken and how each may contribute to human understanding. However the book should offer something to those who already have a view on psychology and encourage them to think further about its relevance to nursing practice. The reference lists and further reading serve to demonstrate not only the impossibility of covering every aspect in one text but also the importance and rewards of pursuing areas of interest in further depth.

Before looking specifically at the structure of this seventh edition it is useful to point out that there is not always a clear demarcation between disciplines within the behavioural sciences. Concepts and issues addressed may equally be looked at in a sociological text. This can only be seen as advantageous in the pursuit for holistic care.

The book is now divided into sixteen chapters, the first of which gives an introduction to the subject and distinctive features of psychology and its relationship to nursing.

The subsequent chapters follow certain themes. Chapters 2–6 focus particularly on the individual and normal psychological functioning; how and why we learn, remember and forget; what influences how we perceive the world around us and how we become the personalities we are. Chapters 7–10 look at human development and the theoretical thinking that continues to influence our understanding of developmental issues. The first ten chapters thus give a sound backdrop for Chapters 11–16, the last six chapters, which look more directly at psychological issues within the nursing context.

It will be seen that the organization has been significantly altered from that of previous editions. Some of the content has been telescoped. Other content has been greatly expanded so that topics such as Stress and Pain now occupy separate chapters. This reflects our real concern that such issues are made explicit, are understood and explored. The changes do not merely reflect the adoption of a new co-author. To a far greater extent they reflect the dynamic and burgeoning nature of nursing knowledge.

There is always more to learn; our thinking in psychology and as nurses is constantly challenged not only by the development of specific research but also by our continuing observations and experience within the context of health care. We hope that in some small way this text may enhance the quality of such care.

Helen Sinclair
Josephine Fawcett

1 Psychology and its relation to nursing

Nurses are increasingly aware of the need to base their actions on a sound knowledge of scientific principles. They have always made use of scientific knowledge derived from physiology and bacteriology, for example, but only in recent years have they discoved the relevance and usefulness of psychology as one of the social sciences.

Many people use the term psychology very loosely. They do not really know what psychology is about and tend to confuse it with psychiatry, the study of mental disorder. Some people think that anyone who is good at coping with his fellow men is a psychologist. Some people are afraid of psychologists, believing that they have some special facility to see into the depths of that part of people's personality which they would prefer to conceal from others.

In the chapters which follow, it will become clear what psychology is really about and how nurses can use psychological knowledge.

It is important to remember that basic knowledge of the subject matter does not make the reader a psychologist, any more than knowledge of some basic physiology makes one a physiologist. Psychologists are scientists who, by the use of scientific research, push out the frontiers of psychological knowledge, which is then available for others to apply. Scientists construct theories based on objective facts derived from systematic observation and experiment.

Theories lead to hypotheses, which, after further

observation or experiment, will be confirmed or refuted, thus modifying the theories.

In a young science, hypotheses are more frequently refuted than confirmed. What makes psychology a science is not that facts have been firmly established, but that the scientific method is applied to the subject matter to be studied.

Human behaviour is one part of the subject matter of psychology. Psychologists are also concerned with animal behaviour and with the neurophysiological processes which accompany or give rise to behaviour. They study not only human behaviour, but also human experience, language and other forms of communication. They are interested in individual differences, be they genetically determined or occurring as a result of learning; they study how individuals and society interact, and how they behave as members of small and large groups.

No one psychologist can research into the entire range of the subject of psychology. The work of each psychologist must be restricted to one small section of the science. Some psychologists are concerned with the study of learning; some are interested in the phenomena of perception, namely the factors—or indeed laws—which govern how stimuli arriving at the sense organs are interpreted into something meaningful, and how past knowledge affects perception.

Some study the behaviour of animals; others are concerned with the study of child behaviour or development; some are concerned with investigation of the effect of early childhood experiences; and others are interested in the interaction of people with each other in small and large groups. Some psychologists are interested in social phenomena such as prejudice and stereotyping which, amongst other things, they might try to relate to personality development of the people concerned; others study people in industry.

The fact that psychologists differ in their interests, may have different ways of approaching the subject and many methods of studying and presenting the findings, has resulted in the development of a variety of psychological perspectives. Behaviourism and cognitive psychology are examples of these perspectives. Some people believe that this range of perspective must mean that nothing is known and that, therefore, everybody's guess is as good as anyone else's. This is, of course, a totally mistaken view. Different perspectives of psychology represent different spheres of interest and even sometimes different ways of interpreting the same facts. Facts there are in plenty. Nurses should aim to be informed of as many facts as possible which relate to their work and life. In additon, nurses should seek to understand how these fact were established and what predictions might therefore be possible in terms of human understanding.

PSYCHOLOGY IS THE STUDY OF BEHAVIOUR AND EXPERIENCE

There is an important distinction to be made between behaviour and the interpretation of the meaning of behaviour. In everyday life we do not always make this distinction clear. When we observe the facial expression and the movement of a person we know well, we may say that we observed him to be angry. In fact 'angry' is an interpretation we make of the behaviour he displays. If he says he is angry, his speech is part of his behaviour. His anger is his experience, which is not directly observable.

Behaviour is public and observable. Different observers can record the observed behaviour with a high degree of reliability. Experience is private. Experience, in psychological language, refers to the mental phenomena occurring directly to the individual—in Spearman's words, 'something lived, undergone, enjoyed and the like' (Spearman, 1927).

It is the study of experience in addition to the study of behaviour which makes psychology interesting and relevant to nursing. As nurses we are interested in our patients and of course other people we meet in life; in how they feel, think, suffer and enjoy. We select from the science of psychology those aspects which help us to understand human beings in the particular contexts we meet them—at home, in hospital or at work.

The scientific study of experience is more difficult than that of behaviour because experience is subjective and its investigation may depend on introspective techniques. Despite this, the study of how the world is experienced by the individual has its own validity and has been the concern of the phenomenological approaches identified by Gestalt and humanistic psychology. Humanistic psychology in particular focuses on the uniqueness of the experiencing self and sees this as more important than merely observing behaviour and making generalizations. For some psychologists, however, experience was not seen as a fit field for scientific study and in their anxiety to be rigorous insisted that behaviour was the only thing to be studied. The American psychologist Watson (1930) put forward this proposition most strongly and founded behaviourism. Behaviourists study not only human beings but also animals and the knowledge derived from these studies has contributed greatly to our understanding.

Nurses frequently have to confine their observations to behaviour. When a patient is unconscious, or too ill to speak, his behaviour is the only thing nurses can observe. On the whole, however, as nurses we would find the study of psychology dull and unrewarding if we could not include the study of experience.

The scientific method

Scientists are concerned with elucidating how certain events are related to each other. They may want to know whether one event causes another, whether other circumstances have an effect on the sequence of events, or whether there are methods that can be used to control events. An example of the sort of relationship that might be studied is whether one particular method of child-rearing unduly influences later adult behaviour. Such events may be described in scientific terms as 'variables'. Events which may cause an effect are described as 'independent variables'. Events which are affected by the independent variable are described as 'dependent variables'. In the example of the effect of childrearing on adult behaviour, the particular method of childrearing constitutes the independent variable and the later adult behaviour the dependent variable.

In order to investigate the relationships between the variables, one could use experiments, but in human psychology there are often overriding ethical considerations which make experimentation impossible. We cannot experiment, for example, in depriving children of food, or love, or even education.

Some experiments, however, have proved possible and very profitable. In the field of perception, for instance,

it was casually observed that some people allowed a
good deal of time to elapse before responding to a visual
stimulus. A number of suggestions as hypotheses were
formulated, for instance:

1.   There is always a measurable time interval between
     the moment when a light is shown and when a person
     reacts to it by pressing a button; this is called 're-
     action time'.
2.   People differ in their reaction times.
3.   Reaction time is slower if the individual being tested
     is tired or under the influence of alcohol.

These hypotheses, if true, are of interest to motorists
and to pilots for example, and to nurses, who must react
quickly to patients' signals or to danger signs.

Experiments can easily be set up to test the hypotheses. Suitable apparatus can be constructed, reaction
times carefully measured and volunteers found for the
experiments, care being taken that only one variable is
introduced into the experiment at a time, e.g. the subject
must not be hungry, cold, drunk and tired simultaneously.
Books on psychology describe many interesting experiments, carried out on people and animals, dealing with
learning, forgetting, and other mental activities, the
experiments being just as carefully conducted and as
valid as those in other sciences.

An interesting piece of research, often referred to
as the Hawthorne experiment (Roesthlisberger and
Dickson, 1939) was carried out in a factory to find out
in what circumstances production could be increased.
Five girls participated. One by one, factory conditions
were altered. The temperature of the room was increased;
rest pauses, the seating arrangement and lighting were
altered, one by one. Every single alteration in environ-

ment resulted in increased output. This experiment showed that psychologists were probably mistaken in believing that only external environment affected work to any great extent. Instead, they came to the conclusion that output rose because of the interest which was being taken in the girls' progress. The fact that change is introduced conveys to the worker the interest of management.

The findings of this experiment have led industrial or occupational psychologists into an entirely different field—that of 'morale'. Psychologists are now widely employed in industry to help raise the morale of the workers. Hospitals are finding some of this research very relevant.

Experiments with people designed to bring about a particular result are not always possible. Instead, controlled observation is used as a research method by which those already showing the characteristic to be studied are observed. In the study of disturbed behaviour, for example, no attempt of course can be made to create such behaviour, but those who are already disturbed can be studied by careful, systematic observation.

In a school, every child who had been before a children's panel (the experimental group) might be matched with a child having no record of problems (the control group). Efforts would be made to ensure as far as possible that the two groups were alike in such variables as age, sex, intelligence, social and economic standing. Having found a suitable control group with which to compare the experimental group, enquiries about the family of each child would be instituted and it might be discovered that significantly more of the children in the experimental group came from broken homes. This would provide one possible clue to the causation of juvenile problems but the relationship would not, in every case, be true.

There may be some problem children whose parents are happily married and some normally adjusted children in very unhappy homes. But, if the percentage of broken homes in the experimental group was found to be much greater than in the control group, it could be argued that the relationship was not just due to chance and therefore merited attention.

Whether psychological discoveries are made by controlled experiments or by less formal methods such as opinion surveys or self-reports about experience, care must be taken before any generalization can be made. Psychologists are always careful to specify the sample upon which their findings are based and to describe, in terms of statistical probability, the confidence with which they state their findings.

Readers of research reports are not always sufficiently careful in assessing how applicable research findings are to the different groups of people with which they deal. Psychologists cannot be held responsible for any particular course of action taken by the public or by a professional body or individual on the basis of their research. It might be possible, for example, to show in terms of probability that corporal punishment is not an effective way of changing undesired behaviour, being more likely to arouse resentment and increase, rather than decrease, undesired or even violent behaviour. Whether or not we abolish corporal punishment in the home and in schools as an official form of punishment mush be decided by parents, by teachers as a professional group and by the nation as a whole.

Again, psychologists might be able to show, in terms of probability, the relationship between visiting children in hospital and the incidence of various forms of disturbed behaviour after the child goes home. Whether or not in the light of these findings hospitals allow or encourage visiting, and parents take advantage of the facilities, is a decision to be made by the people concerned.

PSYCHOLOGY AND NURSING

Psychology is of interest to nurses because its subject matter is that of human behaviour. Nurses interact with people every moment of their working day. It is the relationships with others entered into by nurses in the course of their work that makes the job interesting and rewarding. However, some of the people the nurse meets may behave in a manner which is difficult to understand and some may not be immediately likeable. When the nurse has taken the time and trouble to try and understand such people's behaviour, she will find it much easier to gain cooperation and to deal effectively with problems which may arise. In order to do this the nurse in turn needs to understand her own behaviour and how it might affect relationships with patients.

In recent years the approach to nursing has been changing quite dramatically. This has been brought about by an increasing acceptance of the desirability to practise nursing in a more logical and systematic way. This is encapsulated in the problem-solving approach to nursing and is referred to as the process of nursing or the *nursing process*.

Any problem-solving approach basically involves a number of steps: the assessment of the problem; thinking and considering a number of possible options related to a goal; making decisions and forming a plan of action; putting the plan into action; and, lastly, judging the consequences of the actions and their proximity to the goal. These steps are generally referred to as—assessment, planning, implementation and evaluation. Many other professionals use this approach in their work, e.g. researchers and doctors, but the problems they are faced with are different from those of the nurse and so it is important to consider what is understood when nurses think or talk about nursing.

The relevance of psychology for nurses

Since the problem-solving approach can be used for health care professional activities other than nursing, it is important to consider what is understood when people think about nursing. The people who have done this systematically have constructed models of nursing. These models of nursing provide a framework for guidance to nursing practice, research and curriculum design. Discoveries in psychology as well as other sciences have influenced these nurses' thinking and an examination of the models of nursing will help to elicit the relevance of the contents of this book.

The first nurse to describe nursing was Florence Nightingale (1820–1910), and her *Notes on Nursing*, first published in 1859, provides a foundation for present day practice. She emphasized the patient's physical environment. Good ventilation, cleanliness, warmth, and the absence of noise, she suggested, provided the atmosphere which would allow natural healing to take place (Nightingale, 1980). It is hardly surprising that Miss Nightingale concentrated on physical aspects of care considering that the science of psychology dates only from the late nineteenth century. However, it should not be thought that she was unaware of psychological needs.

One of the first models of nursing was that of Hildegard Peplau. In this model nursing is viewed as an interpersonal process between the nurse and the patient in which the patient's problems are identified and mutually agreed goals are set. Peplau considers that these goals provide an incentive for the therapeutic process whereby the nurse and the patient work together to solve problems. As a result both develop cognitively and become more mature in personality development as they pass through phases and roles of the interpersonal process. During assessment, for example, the patient passes through the phase of 'orientation' where he clarifies the nature of his problem and the extent of his need for help (Peplau, 1988). As can be seen, this model adopts a developmental framework incorporating various concepts from developmental psychology, learning and memory. Equally, other models of nursing draw on major concepts within psychology to describe nursing but take a different perspective.

Another possible way of deciding what information is relevant during the assessment stage of the nursing process is to use a systems approach (Altschul, 1978). Systems do not really exist; they are created for a specific purpose. They comprise elements which have some effect on each other and which collectively do something, i.e. have an output. We think, for example, of the alimentary system as a collection of organs which act on each other and whose output is the processed food. A hospital ward can be thought of as a system, comprising patients, nurses, doctors, beds, trolleys, etc., with an output of care and cure. The elements of a system can be objects or concepts or even smaller systems—referred to as sub-systems.

We need to create a 'boundary' to identify which elements belong to the system. Any elements not in the system are in the 'environment'. It is possible to think of closed systems, which have no input from the environment, but such systems degenerate. Usually we think of 'open systems', i.e. systems which have input from their environment. Where the boundary is drawn is arbitrary, depending on the purpose for which the system is created. We can, for example, think of a system consisting only of the patient and his disordered organs, with nurses, doctors and family members in the environment. When a patient is very ill, perhaps unconscious, this may be a useful system to create. At another time we might think of a system consisting of the patient, his bed, his bedside locker, his visitors and his fellow patients. The interaction of these (e.g. the visitors who cheer him up or depress him, the fellow patients who amuse him, the bed which causes him discomfort, the bedside locker he cannot reach) all have an output of a more or less contented patient. Whether to take all these into consideration in the assessment must be decided by the nurse who knows for what purpose the assessment is made.

A system may be constructed to include the economic system of the patient's work, the social system of his home and neighbours, the psychosexual system of his family, the education system which has helped to shape him and the health care system which he has entered. For all these systems the nurse can regard herself as part of the environment, or she may wish to examine how she herself affects the patient and think of herself as part of the psychosocial system created to assist the patient make a new adjustment. If the nurse thinks of herself as part of the system she must observe and assess her own behaviour and its effect on the patient. Self-awareness and introspection are as important in some cases of assessment as objective observation and the ability to listen to the patient.

A number of nurses have developed systems models of nursing, e.g. the Roy Adaptation Model (Roy, 1980).

In this model the patient is seen primarily as adapting to an ever-changing environment. To cope with health changes a patient will use mechanisms which are physiological, *psychological* and social in origin. During assessment the nurse should obtain information about physiological needs, self-concept, role functions and interdependence (sub-systems). Roy also suggests that during assessment attention should be given to the nature and type of stimuli or *stressors* in the patient's internal and external environment which have a direct effect on his present illness or influence his response to illness.

Orem (1980), using a *self-care* model, describes nursing as having a concern for 'the individual's need for self-care action and the provision and management of it on a continuous basis in order to sustain life and health, recover from disease or injury, and cope with their effects'. Thus Orem is concerned with human needs. Assessment would be related to obtaining information about usual self-care practices, e.g. rest and activity, their relationship to health, and how they are currently affected by illness or the environment.

Some of the major concepts (e.g. need, stress and anxiety) used by these nurses are discussed in later chapters. However, systems models are also very concerned with all the interactions which take place within the system and not just the nurse–patient interaction. The chapters on attitudes, morale and communication relate to these interactions.

In Britain, the most widely accepted description of the unique function of nurses is:

> To help people, sick or well, in the performance of those activities contributing to health or its recovery (or to a peaceful death) that they would perform unaided if

they had the necessary strength, will, or knowledge. It is likewise the function of nurses to help people gain independence as rapidly as possible.

(Henderson and Nite, 1978)

Henderson and Nite go on 'In addition . . . nurses help patients carry out therapeutic plans as initiated by physicians. Nurses, also, as members of a co-operative health team, help its other members, as they in turn help nurses, to plan and carry out with patients and their families the total programme of care'. Thus they focus the nurse's attention on everyday activities such as communicating, breathing, eating and drinking. Assessment would be related to finding out the patient's degree of dependence in carrying out these activities, and identifying his needs in relation to these activities and as a result of medical prescription. Utilizing the nursing process, Roper *et al.* (1990) have developed a similar model of nursing generally referred to as the 'Activities of Living' model.

All of these nurses emphasize the importance of knowledge about what is normal in health and illness. With such a knowledge base the nurse can then make sense of the information gained on assessment. This knowledge base includes psychological functioning—the subject matter of this book.

References

Altschul, A.T. (1978) A systems approach to the nursing process. *Journal of Advanced Nursing* **3**, 333–40.

Henderson, V. & Nite, G. (1978) *Principles and Practice of Nursing*, 6th edition, p. 34. New York: Macmillan.

Nightingale, F. (1980) *Notes on Nursing*. Edinburgh: Churchill Livingstone. (First published by Harrison & Hens, 1859.)

Orem, D.G. (1980) *Nursing: Concepts of Practice*, 2nd edition, p. 6. New York: McGraw-Hill.

Peplau, H.E. (1988) *Interpersonal Relations in Nursing*. London: Macmillan.

Roesthlisberger, F.J. & Dickson, W.J. (1939) *Management and the Worker*. Cambridge, Mass.: Harvard University Press.

Roper, N., Logan, W.W. & Tierney, A.J. (1990) *The Elements of Nursing*, 3rd edition. Edinburgh: Churchill Livingstone.

Roy, C. (1980) The Roy Adaptation Model. In Riehl, J.P. & Roy, C. (eds) *Conceptual Models for Nursing Practice*, 2nd edition, pp. 179–188. New York: Appleton-Century-Crofts.

Spearman, C. (1972) *The Abilities of Man: their Nature and Measurement*. London: Macmillan.

Watson, J.B. (1930) *Behaviorism*, 2nd edition. New York: W.W. Norton.

Further reading

There are many good textbooks of psychology. They are too detailed to be read in their entirety and go more deeply into the subject than some nurses may wish to go. They should, however, be consulted for reference. Some of these contain excellent illustrations. Students should note how carefully the authors quote exact references of experimental work. Here are some suggestions.

Atkinson, R.L., Atkinson, R.C., Smith, E.C., Bern, D.J. & Hilgard E.R. (1990) *Introduction to Psychology*, 10th edition. London: Harcourt Brace Jovanovich.

Eiser, J.R. (1986) *Social Psychology: Attitudes, Cognition and Social Behaviour*. Cambridge: University Press.

Howarth, C.T. & Gillham W.E.C. (eds) (1981) *The Structure of Psychology*. London: Allen & Unwin.

Lefrancois, G.R. (1983) *Psychology*, 2nd edition. Belmont, California: Wadsworth.

The following are introductory texts related to nursing and health care.

Hyland, M.E. & Donaldson, M.L. (1989) *Psychological Care in Nursing Practice*. London: Scutari Press.

Kagan, C.M. (ed) (1985) *Interpersonal Skills in Nursing*. London: Chapman and Hall.

McGhie, A. (1986) *Psychology as Applied to Nursing*. 8th Edition. Edinburgh: Churchill Livingstone.

Niven, N. (1989) *Health Psychology: an Introduction for Nurses and other Health Care Professionals*. Edinburgh: Churchill Livingstone.

The following deal with historical development of the subject.

Brett, G.S. (1962) *Brett's History of Psychology* (edited and abridged by R.S. Peters). London: Allen & Unwin.

Flugel, J.C. (1970) In West, D.J. (ed) *A Hundred Years of Psychology*, 4th edition. London; Methuen.

Hearnshaw, L.S. (1987) *The Shaping of Modern Psychology*. London: Routledge & Kegan Paul.

Sexton, V.S. & Misiak, H. (1971) *Historical Perspectives in Psychology: Readings*. Belmont, California: Brooks/Cole.

Thomson, R. (1968) *The Pelican History of Psychology*. Harmondsworth: Penguin.

2 Motivation

In this chapter it is intended to look, briefly, at the factors involved in explaining behaviour and the changes which occur in order to understand why people behave as they do.

INHERITANCE AND ENVIRONMENT

Inheritance must first of all be taken into account. People are born with varying inherited potential and, even if environment were completely uniform for all children, their innate differences would make them experience their environment differently.

Heredity almost certainly accounts for differences in temperament, i.e. in the predominant emotional tone and the speed of reaction. It may also be responsible for intelligence and possibly for tolerance to stress. How a person responds to stress also appears to be partly determined by heredity. We are generally more concerned with the effect of *environment*, however, than with that of heredity. In bringing up children parents assume that they can influence development whatever may be their child's hereditary make-up. Similarly, when we treat patients in hospital we try to bring about change by influencing their environment.

When we try to find out 'why' a person behaves as he does we are searching for 'motives' for his behaviour. Motivation can be looked at in three different ways: (a) by looking at the person's need or emotional state *at*

17

the time; (b) by looking *backwards* at the chain of events which has led up to the present state; and (c) by looking *forwards* to see what the person's aims are. When, for example, a patient asks for a glass of water we can explain his action in the following ways.

1. By stating that he is thirsty, we are stating what is the patient's internal drive or need; explanation is solely in terms of the patient's own mental state at the time.
2. We can describe the circumstances which have led to the patient's thirst: the fact that he has had no drink for a long time, that he has lost blood, that he is perspiring profusely and has lost fluid. This is an explanation in terms of antecedents, looking backwards.
3. We can explain that he is asking for water in order to feel cooler, refreshed, or in order to keep the nurses busy. This is an explanation in terms of purpose or aim, looking forwards. This kind of explanation is often referred to as the teleological explanation.

All these forms of explanation may be useful at times. All three types can be given in answer to the question 'why'. Few people are able to recognize their own motivation when asked to account for their own behaviour. In particular, it is rarely useful to ask someone 'why' he behaved in the way he did. Motivation can be inferred, however, if one obtains replies to specific questions. For example: 'How did you feel at the time?' asks about motivation in terms of needs. 'What happened before you did it?' asks for antecedents. 'What were you trying to do?' asks for purpose.

NEEDS

Physiological needs, such as hunger or thirst, can provide powerful motivation for changes in behaviour. Maslow (1987) describes a hierarchy of needs with the innate biological needs at its base and the highest needs leading to 'self-actualization' at the apex. The latter cannot come into play until man's physiological needs have been taken care of. It is important to remember that for seriously ill patients, deficiency of oxygen or fluid may mean that the needs at the base of the hierarchy are the most urgent determinants of behaviour. Because in health and under normal circumstances these needs are easily satisfied, social motivation is more important for most people. The need for love, security and achievement, for example, provides social motivation.

It is wise to guard against trying to explain behaviour by reference to 'faculties', a method which was once popular. If, for example, a person remembers instructions easily, nothing at all is explained by saying that he 'has a good memory'. To investigate motivation for remembering we must look at interests, attitudes, ambitions and feelings of curiosity which may help him to remember. There may be a strong feeling of need for the particular information, a strong liking for the lecturer, or a feeling towards other students which makes it essential to succeed at that moment. All these are emotional states which motivate behaviour.

Emotional states give rise to physiological changes such as high blood pressure, increased blood supply to the gastric mucosa or a high pulse rate. Often people do not recognize their emotional state. It is possible to be very angry yet not to be consciously aware of it. Hidden or unconscious anger can cause a person to break something, to be sarcastic or rude, or to perspire and become flushed. Blood pressure or pulse beat may be raised without any awareness of the feelings which have caused this to happen. *Unconscious* emotional motivation is a very important driving power. We like to believe that all our actions are well thought out, rational and logical and that we are in complete control of our behaviour. In fact this is not so. Our behaviour is largely dependent on our feelings and over these we are not in control. When our feelings become too strong our ability to think clearly and logically vanishes completely: we may be blind with rage or with love, paralysed with fear, or made totally irresponsible by happiness. Our interests and attitudes also depend on feelings. What we pay attention to, what we accept or reject and what we remember as relevant at any one moment are all emotionally rather than rationally controlled. Often we are totally unaware of the emotional component of our behaviour, but even when we become conscious of the feelings which accompany our actions it may be difficult to trace these feelings back to the events from which they originate.

PAST EVENTS

The second form of explanation tries to establish how behaviour is determined by past events. In simple experimental situations it is easy to see how behaviour is related to cause. Depriving a rat of food, for example, can be shown to be the cause of the rat learning a path through a maze to find the food. Operating on the brain of a rat can be shown to be the cause of the rat forgetting skills it had previously learnt. As soon as we begin to study more complex human behaviour we find that cause and effect are not nearly so easy to connect.

1. The effect may be delayed so that by the time it occurs the cause is forgotten. For example, a mother's absence from her child in early infancy may much later make the child reluctant to allow the mother out of his sight. By that time the early separation may have been forgotten by the mother and by the child.

2. Several events in combination may produce a particular effect; each alone might not have done so. For example, sickness and separation from parents may have ill effects on a child while sickness at home may well be coped with, or a holiday away from parents may be enjoyed. Human behaviour is so complicated that we must always look for multiple causation rather than believe that one particular line of action has any one definite result.

3. It may be difficult to understand cause and effect because so much of our behaviour has unconscious motivation. As has been shown above, feelings may relate to early events, which have been forgotten by the time we are adults yet adult actions are, to some extent, determined by childhood experiences. Our attitudes to older people may be repetitions of our attitudes to mother, father or teacher; attitudes to our colleagues may resemble attitudes to brothers and sisters. Current behaviour may be determined by past experience, which we are unable to recall without special techniques. In some forms of psychiatric treatment, patients may learn to gain control over their behaviour when the link with the origin of their emotional difficulties is made clear to them.

PURPOSE AND GOALS

The third form of explanation looks to understand behaviour by reference to its purpose. People do not always know what they are hoping to achieve; their aim may be unconscious just as the origin of their action is unconscious. It may, for example, be obvious to other people that a child or an adult is trying to attract attention or that he is trying to look big. It may be obvious to others that a person is trying to dominate his family by behaving as if he were an invalid or that a mother's helplessness is designed to keep her children at home, yet the people who behave in this way may be unaware of the purpose of their behaviour.

While it would be tactless and useless to try to make people aware directly of the purpose of their action, it is often useful to indicate that their purpose is understood and appreciated. The nurse can, for example, say to a patient, 'I shall call every time I pass to see if you need anything' without pointing out to the patient that he seems to be calling in order to attract attention. A mother may be able to deal with her child's attempt to delay bedtime without having to say to him 'You are only asking for a glass of water because you want to stay up longer'.

DEFENCE MECHANISMS

Even people who have some insight into their unconscious mental state refuse at times to recognize the emotion in some of their reactions. They develop an ideal picture of themselves which they endeavour to keep intact. When feelings or attitudes do not fit in with their own idea of themselves they resort to a variety of defence mechanisms (e.g. see Freud, 1966).

Rationalization

Defence mechanisms occur in everyone to a greater or lesser extent. They are mentioned in order to assist recognition of the problems of confronting nurses and patients in understanding themselves and each other. The most useful mechanism is *rationalization*. This is a process of giving a good, logical reason for one's action, leaving out the unconscious, emotional one. The rational explanation may, of course, also be true, but it may be only a partial explanation of behaviour.

Parents say that they punish children for their own good when, in fact, they may be relieving their own anger. A nurse may explain that she forgot an unpleasant task because she was too busy. The fact that it is an unpleasant and not an interesting task which is forgotten shows the emotional cause of forgetting, though it is also true that she is busy. A patient may explain that she could not see the doctor sooner because she had to look after her children when, in fact, she was afraid of seeing him. The reasons people give for choosing their jobs or for leaving nursing are often examples of partial rationalization. The emotional reasons are difficult to express and often unconscious.

Repression

Another important mechanism is *repression*, a method of dealing with uncomfortable feelings by forgetting them (see Chapter 11). The term repression does not refer to the way we remove from consciousness all but the matter we are attending to at the moment. At any one moment, only a very small portion of one's total knowledge is conscious. While these lines are being read nothing other than their form and content is in the reader's consciousness. Many more things could become conscious if attempts were made to make them so. We could think of acquaintances, work in the wards, poetry that has been learnt, simple arithmetical operations, or a pleasant meal. All these ideas and thoughts are readily accessible.

Many things which have been equally well learnt or have formed vivid experiences are, however, forgotten. We have practically no recollection of the events of the first few years of life and, from then onwards, memory is patchy. Even some of the more recently acquired knowledge is mysteriously forgotten. A careful analysis of the difference between those things which are re-membered and those which are forgotten shows that many of the forgotten things are unpleasant and make us uncomfortable. This kind of forgetting is called re-pression. It is an active process, a pushing out of con-sciousness of those memories, and the feelings associated with them, which are hard to bear. People may forget to turn up for appointments which they did not relish in the first instance; mistakes one made in nursing patients may be forgotten, as may also any humiliating experi-ences suffered in childhood or, later, at work. Other people's discomfiture is often remembered while our own is forgotten.

The normal process of repression partly accounts for the fact that we remember only a very small selection of personal details. This helps us to keep our capacity to think and learn wide open. The total amount of repressed material, however, forms part of the unconscious aspect of the personality and may affect behaviour without the person being aware of his own state of mind. When emotions remain very strong but the events are not consciously linked with them the repressed material can become a hindrance to normal development. A child, for instance, may feel angry with his mother because she punished him. If he feels too guilty about his anger he may repress the whole complex situation. He forgets about his anger and also about the events which led up to it. The behaviour he shows is gentle, kind, solicitous, submissive. He may still be unconsciously angry and this is shown by accidental breaking of his mother's favourite things, or in his bedwetting or refusal of food.

Projection

This is a device we use in interpreting the environment around us according to our own personality. We see in pictures more than can really be justified objectively. Clouds, for example, can be made into faces or animals. We see stars in certain constellations representing bears or swans when, in fact, any other interpretation is equally possible. Mountain ranges are named according to the patterns that can be seen in them. Pictures, sounds and events are always perceived according to the mood of the moment. Interest and expectation determine what is noticed from among a much greater choice of observations and mood determines their interpretation.

All these ways of making events meaningful are *projections*. More commonly, however, the term is reserved for our attempt to deal with our own shortcomings, by seeing them in others and denying them in ourselves. When we feel guilty, e.g. about our dislike of another nurse, we complain that she is the one who dislikes us. People who are dishonest often attribute dishonesty to others. Racial prejudice is often attributed to other people in an attempt to deny it in oneself. The fact that our own attitudes are projected on to others may in turn affect other people's behaviour. If we go on thinking for long enough that a person is unfriendly that person will become unfriendly even if she did not feel that way at first. Our suspicions are then confirmed and our behaviour justified.

Identification

Our attitude to people depends largely on the unconscious mechanism of *identification*. In every situation in which we believe we understand precisely how another person feels, we identify ourselves with him. When we see a film we live through the plot as if we were one of the characters, experiencing his hopes and disappointments, his happiness and pain. Different people seeing the film at the same time may identify with different people. A young girl may come away knowing exactly how the bride felt, a young man may understand the bridegroom and an older person may understand the parents' point of view. To a certain extent, each person has seen the film differently.

While we grow up we learn the roles we are going to play in life by identification with people we try to emulate. Girls identify with their mother, later perhaps with their teacher, and later still perhaps with a film star. Young nurses identify with ward sisters or nursing officers. It may happen that a student nurse identifies rather strongly with another student nurse, who perhaps is in trouble, so that the former is unable to see the sister's point of view. There are nurses who identify so strongly with the patients that they cannot carry out treatment successfully because they share the patients' apprehension and suffering.

Substitution

Substitution of one emotional outlet for another is a common way of dealing with difficulties. Emotion may be displaced from one person to another. Anger against the ward sister may be displaced on to a more junior nurse or a patient.

Sublimation

Sublimation occurs when one satisfies one's emotional needs by devoting one's energies to some useful purpose. The unfulfilled need to give maternal care, for example, may find gratification in the care of the sick. Some lonely people give much love and care to cats and dogs when no opportunity occurs for giving their affection to human beings.

Denial of emotions

When emotions are so powerful that they become frightening one may resort to *denial* of emotions. In hospital many examples of this can easily be found among patients, relatives and nurses.

Patients may be able to tolerate their anxiety about their illness or about the family they have left behind only by appearing totally calm and unconcerned, apparently unaware of the seriousness of the situation. Bereaved relatives are often unable to cry and they sometimes say that they have no feeling at all. The optimism of some dying patients and the way patients and relatives sometimes appear as if they did not wish to be given information about the adverse prognosis of an illness is a manifestation of 'denial'. Occasionally a young mother appears not to notice that her child is deformed or mentally retarded. It is sometimes suggested that nurses protect themselves from the impact of the numerous traumatic experiences of emergencies, suffering, death and sense of responsibility by developing an unfeeling, apparently callous attitude.

The use of defence mechanisms is essential to the maintenance of normal equilibrium. Difficulties only occur if the defence mechanisms are inadequate to deal with anxiety or inappropriate to the situation in which they are used. When people's behaviour cannot be understood in terms of conscious, rational explanation it becomes necessary to investigate their unconscious motivations and defence mechanisms.

References

Freud, A. (1966) *The Ego and the Mechanisms of Defence*. London: Hogarth Press.
Maslow, A.H. (1987) *Motivation and Personality*, 3rd edition (revised by Frayer, R., Fadiman, J., McReynolds, C. & Cox, R.). New York: Harper & Row.

Further reading

Evans, P. (1975) *Motivation*. London: Methuen.
Jung, J. (1978) *Understanding Human Motivation: A Cognitive Approach*. New York: Macmillan.
McClelland, D.G. (1985) *Human Motivation*. London: New York.
Whitehead, J. (1976) *Motivation and Learning*. Milton Keynes: Open University Press.

3 Learning

Throughout life, people's behaviour changes. Sometimes this is because the body is changing; at first it is still growing and developing, and later through injury, sickness and ageing it changes again. Most changes in behaviour are the result of learning. We learn skills, attitudes and information, and we are never too old to learn.

We tend to use the term 'learning' to refer to the acquisition of new and better patterns of behaviour. Of course, strictly speaking, we could use the term 'learning' even if we get worse. If, for example, we learn to play tennis and after each period of practice we make more mistakes than before, we could say we are learning how to play badly. But it makes more sense to reserve the term for changes in a positive direction.

Learning can take place in informal settings, e.g. during coffee breaks, watching television at home, or more formally in tutorial groups, classrooms and clinical areas. In nursing there are many situations in which a knowledge of how people learn would provide insights useful to improving study and, particularly, teaching skills. A few examples are: helping patients to learn new skills; presenting information; knowing how best to ensure patients' active involvement in treatment; creating a learning environment on the ward; identifying learning experiences in clinical areas. It is with these learning situations that this chapter is concerned.

Three interacting sets of variables are important in promoting learning: the nature of the learner, the nature of the subject to be learnt, and the environment in which learning is taking place.

The learner:	Subject matter:	Environment:
Age, previous experience	Motor skills	The teacher
Intelligence and personality	Knowledge	The classroom
Emotional and physical state	Attitudes	The hospital ward
Motivation		
Learning style		
Culture		

Factors affecting learning

Individual differences among people influence learning but these are not sufficiently precise or reliable enough to accurately predict learning outcomes. Such factors as age, intelligence and personality are dealt with in other chapters. Here, individual differences in motivation to learn and learning styles will be considered.

MOTIVATION TO LEARN

All learning depends on motivation. Only if one wants to learn can learning take place and human beings want to learn for a variety of reasons. As already discussed, motivation is a complex concept. Peters (1958), a philosopher interested in education, suggests it is useful to distinguish between *extrinsic* and *intrinsic* motivation.

Extrinsic motivation is said to occur when rewards or punishment outside the learning task itself is used. It is generally found that punishment has only very transient effects and only if, by improvement, there is hope of earning praise. Encouragement and praise, on the other hand, are incentives to do well. Praise must be sincere to be effective in the long term; indiscriminate praise can be effective only in a short experiment. Other examples of extrinsic motivation might be obtaining good examination grades, the promise of a present for doing well in examinations, retaining the good opinion of others or obtaining a qualification.

It is possible to make deliberate use of people's need for support and approval from each other in the organization of educational experiences. Students working on group projects benefit, not only from the fact they are actively involved in learning, but also because they have approval at each stage from each other and because, in presenting their work, their mutual support shields them from possible criticism which might be made by the teacher. Group discussion is another method of learning in which the positive feedback from one's peers encourages learning. Conversely, students perceive the danger of not being supported by their peers as even more threatening than the disapproval of their teachers. This may be the reason why some students are reluctant to cooperate in study groups or to ask each other for help. However, once they have overcome their reluctance to expose their difficulties they quickly become convinced of the advantages of forming study groups rather than working alone without any means of knowing if they are on the right track.

Intrinsic motivation depends on seeing the learning task as interesting or relevant. Moreover it can be seen as fulfilling some inner need such as self-esteem (Maslow, 1954) or the *need for achievement* (McClelland *et al.*, 1953). It is not difficult to notice that people generally work harder at a subject that interests them. It is sometimes less clear to demonstrate that what makes a particular subject interesting is to find in it some relevance to one's own life and work. If, however, intrinsic motivation is to be expected, then it is important to show clearly the way in which the proposed learning relates to the person's daily life or work experiences. Presenting highly theoretical material for which students can see no practical application is likely to reduce motivation for learning.

Recent research assumes that people have both a positive need for achievement and a negative fear of failure. Thus people are thought to have competing tendencies towards achievement and away from failure. Where the tendency to avoid failure is greater than the tendency to strive for achievement, learning situations in which failure is either impossible, or so highly probable that self-esteem is maintained in spite of failure, will be preferred. On the other hand, where success is hoped for situations containing moderate risk will be preferred because success is more highly prized when worked for (Atkinson and Raynor, 1978). When fear of failure is uppermost then it is important to encourage and praise students. Excessive criticism may result in raising the student's level of anxiety even higher and ultimately in the disruption of learning. On the other hand, the over-confident student's motivation to learn might benefit from some criticism.

The experience of success or failure can affect students' performances differently. It can be argued that success in education leads to further success. Human learning tends to be most successful if the students themselves know what they are attempting to achieve and if, in the course of learning, they have the means of knowing the results they are achieving. All too often, especially in nursing, we omit to tell the student that she is achieving good results. Opportunities for learning in nursing are so numerous that the student cannot fail to learn something new each day, but the outcome is not always evident unless someone comments on the fact that the task has been well performed. If the patient says, or shows, that he is more comfortable or if a ward sister praises the student for her work, the student nurse will progress faster as a result. Knowledge of the results of learning, e.g. results in examinations or closed-circuit video recordings of skills, are important to the student's, or indeed the patient's, learning.

However, instead of success, some people experience only failure. Unfortunately, information about lack of success tends to be given more frequently than information about positive achievement. Most teachers will draw attention to the student's mistakes despite the fact that often mistakes are self-evident as, for example, when one breaks a piece of equipment. To remember to praise needs more conscious effort than some teachers seem to be able to make. It is well to remember how sportsmen or actors thrive on applause. Less spectacular performances should also benefit from it. Nurses should be aware of the need for knowledge of results, not only in nurse training but also when attempting to teach patients.

Where failure is the only experience, either low self-esteem may become evident or the person might reject anything to do with formal education. To avoid this situation the learner should be provided with opportunities for success, perhaps at a lower level. Success at this level will encourage learners to aim higher.

Research has shown over and over again how important self-confidence is when learning. For example Rogers (1983), in the humanist tradition, has pointed out how a student's self-concept affects his approach to learning. Encouraging a sense of self-worth, faith in one's own ability to achieve and self-directed learning will promote, Rogers argues, 'freedom to learn'.

STYLES OF LEARNING

Recent research, with students in higher education as subjects, suggests there are also individual differences in the way people prefer to tackle learning tasks. The term 'learning style' refers to a general tendency to adopt a preferred strategy when learning a given task, e.g. organizing information into categories (Pask, 1976). From this research Pask has described learning strategies as *serialist* or *holist*. Students using a serialist strategy prefer to build up a total picture by gathering details and assembling them step by step. Those using a holist strategy prefer to first gain an overview of the task and then fill in the details later. Pask labelled the style of the serialist as *operation learning*, and that of the holist, *comprehension learning*.

Moreover he described what he called 'learning pathologies' associated with each of the learning strategies. Serialists tend to get bogged down in the details and fail to see how they interrelate to build up an overall picture. Pask calls this pathology *improvidence*. In contrast the holist fails to fill in the details and tends to make generalizations from insufficient evidence. *Globetrotting* is the term used for this pathology.

Interestingly, Pask also found a third, but smaller, group of students referred to as *versatile* learners who would adapt their strategies to the requirements of a particular task. They used either serialist or holist strategies with equal facility and sometimes both. Recent arguments suggest that styles are not fixed but that people can alter strategies according to the requirements of the learning task (Gibbs *et al.*, 1982).

Psychologists interested in the processes of perception and thinking have also found individual differences in the way people tackle problems, reflecting underlying *cognitive styles*, but there is considerable difficulty in relating these various research findings about styles to one another as researchers use different tasks and research techniques. However, as Entwistle (1981) suggests, the evidence points to such wide differences in learning styles among people that it is impossible to say there is a single 'correct' way to learn, or to teach for that matter.

Although cognitive or learning styles are generally thought of as characteristic ways of learning, thinking and perceiving, the strategies people use reflect more a conscious decision having been made when faced with a particular task. Thus it seems from the research that it is possible to help individuals to learn to use a variety of strategies which are amenable to their own learning style, and to choose from them the most suitable for a given learning task.

THE FOCUS OF LEARNING

When discussing the acquisition of knowledge and skills, learning theorists generally distinguish between types and levels of learning. For example, Ausubel differentiates between 'reception' and 'discovery' learning and between 'rote' and 'meaningful' learning (Ausubel *et al.*, 1978).

Acquiring large bodies of knowledge in classrooms depends on the transmission of the major theories and concepts and on the students receiving that knowledge. However, reception learning does not imply that knowledge is just passively acquired. On the contrary, learning is much more likely to be thorough if the student attempts actively to do something with the received knowledge. Discovery learning, on the other hand, involves the student working out or solving problems and building up concepts from bits of information. It is the sort of problem-solving activity which goes on in everyday life.

Rote learning is the term used to describe a simple level of learning which relies on making arbitrary associations, e.g. between words, whereas meaningful learning requires the student to relate new knowledge to what is already known in order to achieve a deeper level of understanding.

In fact workers in the field of educational psychology have identified a number of levels of learning. Gagne (1970) hierarchically arranges eight levels of learning outcomes, from simple paired associate learning to more complex concept attainment and problem solving, and argues that more complex learning also involves learning at simpler levels. Bloom and his colleagues (Bloom, 1956; Krathwohl *et al.*, 1964) have developed comprehensive lists related to three 'domains' of learning; the cognitive domain, attitudes, and psychomotor skills. This work has prompted the behavioural objectives movement where learning outcomes are identified in behavioural terms.

As suggested earlier, learning tends to be most successful if the student himself knows exactly what he is expected to learn: Is it the learning of facts, understanding of information, or critical analysis and evaluation which is required? One of the most difficult tasks in education is to clearly delineate for the student what has to be learnt and as a result of that learning what behaviour is to be expected.

ACTIVE LEARNING

Reading material over and over again without trying to extract meaning or relating it to one's own experience will result in a rather poor level of learning. In the course of study in nursing it is essential to do something actively about the information from books or that derived from lectures. During a lecture, for example, it helps if the student listens actively and applies the information while it is being given. Some people write it down and feel the activity of writing while listening makes them active. It would possibly be more useful if they wrote only an occasional note because this might involve the greater activity of evaluating what is said, sorting it and selecting from it what appears worthy of note. If the lecture refers to some patient whom the student has nursed, it is useful to think actively of the application of the subject to the work she has seen on the ward. Throughout a lecture she should listen critically. This does not necessarily mean looking for faults, though that can be a very useful activity. A critical approach may mean admiration of the skill with which the subject is treated, or comparison of the lecturer's methods with those of others. It involves a silent running commentary on what is said. Textbooks should be read with the same critical approach; as the student reads she can actively discuss with herself the meaning of the statement, the method of explanation, and its application. Reading rapidly and actively summarizing is much more helpful than reading slowly and trying to remember.

Silent discussion with oneself is one way of learning actively. More useful still—whenever it can be done—is discussion with others. Asking questions, explaining to others, giving a talk oneself, repeating to someone what the lecturer has said, are the best ways of learning. Active methods of learning may involve trying to discover an answer to a problem oneself before the answer is given by the lecturer or by the book. This is why some lecturers begin by asking questions even though they know that the students probably do not know the answers. If the students try to find out first they are more likely to make full use of the explanation when it is given. Writing papers is an essential tool in the clear formulation of thought. The most fruitful method of learning is an attempt to communicate to others what has been learned. Reporting back, either by straightforward summary or in some more dramatic manner, such as enacting some point in a sketch or putting it into poetry, helps one to learn.

THE CONTEXT OF LEARNING

Everyone who has had experience in educational institutions will have memories of teachers they considered good and teachers they hardly considered at all, or learning experiences where the atmosphere reflected exciting activity or dull, uninspiring chores. Ramsden (1979) explored students' perception of their teaching department and how their approach to study was affected. He found that departments varied on measures of staff's relationships with students, commitment to teaching, formal teaching methods, student workload, clear goals and standards, freedom in learning, vocational relevance, and social climate. The attitudes and enthusiasm of the staff were important to the students, as were methods of assessment. Students said they worked more on courses where they got on well with their teachers and where the teacher's enthusiasm for a topic inspired them. As for methods of assessment, students describe their approach to studying as merely involving memorizing techniques, when facts or lists of main points was all that was required of them in examinations.

In nursing, Fretwell (1982) found similar characteristics which, in the students' opinion, described a good ward learning environment. The qualified ward staff were interested in the student; there were good staff–student relationships in that they gave support and help to students generally, invited questions and gave answers, worked as a team, were approachable, pleasant yet strict, and the staff promoted good staff–patient relationships and quality of care. Orton (1983) found similar character-istics in a good learning 'climate' on the ward. Although students were not asked how their approaches to studying were affected, Orton found that they were 'happy' with the ward experience.

THEORETICAL APPROACHES

Most theories have been developed from the results of experiments in controlled laboratory settings. For practical purposes it should be remembered that what is offered is a *guide* to how learning experiences might be enhanced. Like nursing, teaching is learned during practice as well as by study.

Two major theoretical approaches to learning can be discerned from the literature: behaviourist and cognitive (Hill, 1989).

Behaviourist theories

In this approach learning consists of making a new response to a stimulus to which it was not originally made. The learner's process of connecting a stimulus to a response is labelled *conditioning*. Two types of con-ditioning are described.

The first type, classical conditioning, was first described by the Russian psychologist, Pavlov. He experimented on dogs. Dogs, like other animals, automatically salivate (unconditioned response) when they eat or smell food (unconditioned stimulus). Pavlov rang a bell (conditioned stimulus) when food was offered to the dog and before long he was able to show that it was possible to produce salivation (conditioned response) by ringing a bell without giving any food at all. After a period of ringing the bell without offering food the newly acquired pattern of salivation stops (extinction). To maintain the conditioned response, it is necessary from time to time to give food paired with the sound of a bell. This is described as reinforcing the conditioned response.

Watson, a psychologist of the behaviourist tradition, showed that it is possible to demonstrate conditioning techniques with children in the same way as dogs. He conditioned his own child to become afraid of furry animals by frightening him with a loud noise every time he played with a previously beloved pet rabbit.

Pavlov and the behaviourist psychologists have studied in detail how conditioning depends on the time interval between the unconditioned stimulus and the new stimulus and how the conditioning process is affected by reinforcement. For ethical reasons only certain conditioning experiments with human beings can be carried out in laboratories. It is possible to condition a blinking reflex to stimuli other than movement near the eye. It can also be shown that people differ in their responsiveness to conditioning, perhaps due to inherited differences. In everyday life it is probable that quite a lot of conditioning takes place.

Aldous Huxley describes in *Brave New World* how, in his fantasy, children could be conditioned against the use of books. His method is well described though not foolproof. It is possible that some isolated, strong dislikes or phobias have accidentally occurred by this process.

Methods of conditioning which rely more specifically on the way in which the reward is obtained are called *operant conditioning* (Skinner, 1938). In this form of conditioning the appropriate behaviour brings about the reward. For example, a pigeon can learn to release a pellet of food by pressing the correct lever. The more often it presses the lever the more reward it obtains and it can be shown that it learns to work very fast indeed. It can be seen that this form of conditioning involves the active participation of the subject.

Behaviour modification

Operant conditioning is now a method used extensively in a form of treatment called behaviour modification. Patients with behaviour disorders have successfully learned socially acceptable behaviour within a relatively short time. Mentally retarded children have learnt skills for daily living such as the use of the toilet, dressing and undressing, when previously they had been thought incapable of such progress.

There are many behavioural modification programmes which have been developed and used for patients with particular problems, for example, chronic pain (see Chapter 16).

Such programmes require very thorough and careful implementation. First, it is important to have a very detailed study of the patient's behaviour before teaching begins, not only to be able to set realistic objectives but also to determine what specific reinforcers should be used for each individual patient.

Second, it is important to plan the reinforcement schedule and keep to it very conscientiously. At first it is usual to reward every success immediately. Later, intermittent reinforcement may be planned, for example every third success. The nurse who carries out the treatment may need to carry with her the selected reinforcers, e.g. Smarties for children or for adults tokens which can be exchanged for a desired reward.

In order to be able to give a reward, one must be sure the appropriate behaviour will occur, at least occasionally, perhaps by accident. (If it never occurs, one cannot reinforce anything.) It is sometimes necessary to lead gradually to the desired behaviour, at first perhaps being satisfied with an approximation to it. For example, if a child never urinates in the potty, it may be necessary at first to reward sitting on it, even if it is not actually used. This process is called 'shaping' behaviour.

One preparatory step towards using reinforcement is to analyse how complex the desired behaviour is. To eat soup with a spoon, for example, has many subskills, such as sitting down long enough, putting the hands on the table and not into the soup, holding the spoon by the handle, and lifting the spoon in the correct direction. Any one of these activities can be separately rewarded, without waiting until a whole plateful of soup has been eaten without making a mess.

One of the most important aspects of behaviour modification which nurses need to learn is to ignore inappropriate behaviour. This is not at all easy, because in all their training nurses learn to give attention to patients whenever they perceive a need for care. If a patient wets or soils his clothes, for example, it is, in most circumstances, right to attend to the patient promptly, kindly and caringly. However, such attention may well act as if it were a reward and thus serve to reinforce the inappropriate behaviour of wetting and soiling the clothes. To teach the patient proper toilet habits, one has to reinforce elimination in an acceptable way and ignore the unacceptable behaviour. Even to display disapproval might reinforce unacceptable behaviour.

A systematic attempt to change behaviour by making new associations with pleasurable stimuli may help to overcome a disabling problem. Patients have been helped by this method to overcome disabling fears of open spaces or other phobias. Some success has also been recorded in the treatment of alcoholism by establishing a conditioned link between nausea and drinking alcohol. This is described as aversion therapy.

Behaviour modification is sometimes criticized on ethical grounds, particularly when aversion measures are used. However, even the use of positive reinforcement should be carefully monitored because it may be necessary to deprive the patient of some of the care he would otherwise obtain, in order to make the use of rewards effective.

Cognitive theories

The psychologists taking this approach are more concerned with what goes on in the mind when learning is taking place. Of great interest to cognitive theorists are aspects of learning such as how we learn new concepts, solve new problems, process and structure knowledge. Psychological processes such as perception, thinking and remembering are their central subject matter. Historically, the origins of this approach can be traced back to the *Gestalt* psychologists at the end of the nineteenth century.

The Gestalt school of psychology was particularly interested in the way in which insightful learning and problem solving depended on the spontaneous awareness of the relationships of things. The German word Gestalt means 'form' or 'configuration'. Gestalt psychologists, essentially concerned with perception, pointed out that awareness of form is an immediate experience. Perception of the total form occurs instantaneously, e.g. we perceive the figure of a square instantaneously—we do not build it up from four lines and four right angles. We arrange things into patterns and groups until they fit into a scheme we can understand. Gestalt psychologists stressed that our behaviour is always determined by the way in which we see and understand things, rather than by the objective reality of the situation. Our interpretation of environment depends on our attitude, our aim, our previous learning. We make the present fit in with our own frame of reference and the situation becomes meaningful according to our own previous knowledge.

Since the Second World War many new ideas have been introduced from developments in other sciences studying information processing, e.g. cybernetics and computing. The study of complex human learning demanded much more sophisticated methods, and educational psychologists have taken the study of learning much more into the classroom, though laboratory settings with human subjects are also used by researchers.

INVESTIGATING LEARNING

Experiments have been carried out to investigate how learning takes place and how study can be effective. The difficulties of experimenting with human beings are quite considerable. If they learn too fast one cannot observe the learning process. If one experiments with learning material which is familiar to some subjects but not to others, results cannot be compared. If, for example, one were to experiment with the learning of poetry one might find that one person already knows the particular poem; another, though not familiar with this poem, knows many others and learns poetry as a hobby; a third person knows no poetry at all and dislikes the idea of learning it. The method of learning used during the experiment would contribute less significantly to success than previous experience.

It is therefore important to carry out learning experiments with tasks which are equally unfamiliar to all subjects. The material must lend itself to measurement and must be learnt sufficiently slowly to make observation of progress possible. Recent research by educational psychologists into how students learn (see, for example, Entwistle and Ramsden, 1983) relies on self-reports from students about their approaches to learning as well as controlled experimental techniques.

Experiments in learning skills have yielded some useful knowledge. Skills like typewriting, tracing patterns while looking into a mirror, or fitting various parts of equipment together, have been studied. These lend themselves to experimentation because learning is obvious and can be measured by timing the total performance. A graph can be plotted showing how much more quickly each attempt was completed than the previous one. An alternative way of measuring learning is followed when a fixed amount of time is allowed and one measures how much of the task was completed: for example, how many words were typed in a period of ten minutes. Another method is to count mistakes and observe their reduction in successive trials.

These experiments have shown that learning takes place fairly rapidly at first and that there follows a more gradual progress. Fitts and Posner (1973) have described three phases in the acquisition of a skill: the *cognitive phase* when the learner is trying to understand the task and develop a strategy; the *associative phase* when the stimulus response connections are made; and the *autonomous phase* when the patterns of response are refined. Learning to drive a car is a clear example of this process. The learner driver attends to an explanation of gears, clutch and steering. The learner is then involved in responding to new stimuli: the movement of the car, the feel of the steering wheel, the view of the road. The learner obtains feedback information from what he is doing and this feedback in turn guides and shapes responses. During this phase the learner is thinking about and conscious of every movement he is making. Finally the whole process of using controls becomes one: gears are changed correctly, clutch, brake, accelerator and steering wheel are used without conscious awareness. The driver is now free to learn more complicated manoeuvres.

Skills in nursing are probably learnt in the same way. The first bed bath takes a very long time. Every action, every move is conscious. Skill in handling water, soap and flannel, rapidly increase; and, after practice, the procedure is carried out sufficiently automatically to enable all the attention to be devoted to the patient. It is important to practise nursing procedures often enough so that a level of skill is reached which then allows the nurse to give full attention to the patient's comfort and need. We have used the example of giving a bed bath deliberately for several reasons. Once such a skill is mastered there is a tendency to forget the demands of its acquisition. Hence the necessity to appreciate the time it will take for a new student nurse to acquire a skill which a trained nurse might view as relatively simple and automatic. Another reason is the tendency to underestimate the skills required to give what might be considered to be 'basic nursing care' and consequently such care is often placed in the domain of the less experienced nurse. Patients often comment on being lifted and made comfortable; pillows arranged and sheets made smooth, noting how differently they experience such nursing when carried out less skilfully by a 'novice' compared to an 'expert' (Benner, 1984).

The giving of an injection can exemplify the difference between a polished performance and the early attempts at learning the skill. It is not only a matter of differences in speed. The skill appears to consist of a sequence of small steps in the motor performance—steps which can be practised individually and then put together into a complex task. A number of factors appear to apply more specifically to learning skills than to other forms of learning.

Firstly, although we refer to 'motor skills', the task is in fact a sensorimotor one. The learner must pay attention to stimuli: some from his environment, e.g. from the patient's facial expression or posture; some from the tools he is using; and some from within the nurse herself. Recognition of appropriate stimuli, and learning to exclude those which are not appropriate, takes time.

Secondly, any complex skill consists of a number of subskills. It may be that one of the subskills is particularly difficult to perform and learning of the total skill cannot progress until the subskill has been mastered. Some student nurses, for example, have particular difficulty in manipulating the syringe when drawing up medication fluid. They cannot progress with the procedure until this has been mastered.

Thirdly, the smoothness of the skilled performance arises because attention is paid to the next stimulus while the motor task related to the previous stimulus is still taking place. The skilled nurse, for example, is already rechecking the prescription sheet while she attaches the needle to the syringe. The learner is, at first, only able to attend to one stimulus and respond to it at that time. To anticipate the next move the way the skilled person does, practice is necessary.

Lastly, in all motor performances, minor errors occur which require correction. If one has moved the piston up a little too far one pulls back a little to correct this. Awareness of one's own performance is referred to as 'feed-back' and feed-back leads to correction. Hardy (1980) discusses how the teacher is involved in augmenting the student's feed-back when learning nursing skills. The unskilled person tends to over-correct, with the result that the performance appears jerky. Tiredness also has this effect and so do drugs and alcohol, as was shown in investigations on drivers and pilots. It seems that, in spite of the fact that student nurses often find it impersonal, skills need to be practised in a laboratory situation before they are carried out on patients.

Very often a sudden increase in learning occurs just before the end of the practice period. When a learning experiment is carried out warning is sometimes given that time is nearly up: 'Only two minutes to go'. This usually results in a sudden spurt of rapid progress. Everyone is aware of the amount of learning which can be fitted into a very short space of time before examinations. There is usually some guilt feeling about doing so much in so short a time, having done so little before. This is not justified. In fact the long period of apparent inactivity is probably a consolidation of learning necessary to enable rapid progress to be made at the end. Some people feel that cramming before examinations is not real learning. It is real in the sense that it marks a steep rise in learning but here consolidation needs to occur later. To facilitate learning it is well worth while to provide periodic goals in the form of formal assessment and feed-back. Obviously they would lose in value if assessment occurred too frequently and spacing of goals should depend on the age of the student and on the subject matter.

DISTRIBUTIVE LEARNING

In many learning experiments, particularly those where the material to be learnt is long lists of words or nonsense syllables, it has been found that the beginning and the end of the list were learned most easily. Moreover if any of the material was markedly different from the rest; for example, if any of them were presented in red, while the rest were black, these were remembered easily. If any of the syllables are accidentally meaningful, for example if one of them belonged to the learner's own car number or telephone number, these too will be learnt quickly. Learning, then, spreads from the quickly learnt parts to the parts immediately in front and behind and so on until it is complete.

Similar ways of learning are often observed in real situations. The first and last lectures of a course often stand out, and so does any lecture given by a visiting lecturer or a substitute. If any lecture happens to be particularly relevant to the work the student is just doing in the ward, or to a patient she happens to be nursing, it is much better remembered.

In any one lecture the opening remarks and the summary at the end are the really important parts. Any anecdote told in the middle is also likely to be remembered because it stands out. If a one-hour study period is divided into six ten-minute periods with intervals, much more learning takes place than if the hour is undivided. This is referred to as *distributive* learning. It is believed to be more effective than intensive or *massed* learning. This applies to many other learning situations. At school, for example, four periods of mathematics per week are better than two double periods or one whole morning. The timetable for student nurses is usually so arranged that each subject is taught on every day rather than a whole day being devoted to a single subject. Some people believe that a course of lectures spread over perhaps 12 weeks is more useful than if all lectures are given in four weeks and for that reason they find study days more effective than study blocks. Private study should be distributed over several periods in preference to a few long sessions. One hour's study every day is better than two days of staying up all night. It is more effective to study a little of each subject every day than to devote one evening to anatomy and physiology, another to community health and yet another to psychology. There is, of course, an optimal study period for each type of subject matter. Where a large amount of preparation is necessary, for example if apparatus has to be set up as in bacteriology or for physiological experiments, or in practical nursing, it becomes uneconomical to make the class too short. Lectures are better used if they are as short as possible. Each student must find her own best rhythm for study, but, however convinced an individual may be that she studies best by sticking to one subject for many hours, it is at least worth trying to divide the total period up into several shorter ones and to distribute them more evenly over the weeks or years.

GLOBAL AND PART LEARNING

There is a marked difference in the rate of learning according to the method by which the total amount is tackled. In some experiments subjects were encouraged to learn a page of nonsense syllables by reading through the whole lot and learning the whole page. In other instances the page was divided into several parts, each part being learnt separately. The former method is called *global learning*, the latter, *part learning*. Global learning tends to be more effective than part learning. Although many subjects believed they could succeed better if they learned a few lines at a time they did, in fact, learn more easily when they treated the whole page as one. In learning poetry the method of learning one verse at a time leads to an association of the last line of the verse with the first line of the same verse instead of leading on to the next. The result is that the first verse is very well learnt, the rest much less so and that there is a risk of getting stuck and having to restart instead of being able to carry on when prompted. It is particularly true that a meaningful whole is more easily learnt than separate parts which do not appear to have any meaning in relation to each other. The whole poem, not its separate verses, has meaning. Even with nonsense material, wholes are learnt better than parts; difficult parts need special practice later.

To apply the principle of global learning to the study of nursing it is important to consider how big the 'whole' subject should be to make a suitable unit for learning. Lecture courses can be so arranged that the first lecture gives a survey of the total subject to be covered and the last lecture gives a summary of the course. Any individual lecture can in the first few minutes give an outline of the subject as a whole. Textbooks are sometimes so arranged that the first chapter gives an indication of the total subject matter of the book. Each chapter has an introduction giving an outline of the whole chapter. In this way each part is seen in relation to the whole. It is worthwhile beginning a new subject, anatomy and physiology, for example, with a very simple outline of the total functioning of the body. Reading a very simple book, like those written for children, which can be read through as a whole before detailed study of any part takes place, can be helpful. Most students find it difficult to learn any part of physiology when it is first attempted. After a study of the whole body the study of any one part falls into place and becomes quite easy.

References

Atkinson, J.W. & Raynor, J.O. (eds) (1978) *Motivation and Achievement*, abridged edition. London: Hemisphere.

Ausubel, D.P., Novak, J.D. & Hanesian, H. (1978) *Educational Psychology: A Congitive View*, 2nd edition. New York: Holt, Rinchart and Winston.

Benner, P. (1984) *From Novice to Expert*. California: Addison-Wesley Publishing Company.

Bloom, B.S. (ed.) (1956) *Taxonomy of Educational Objectives: Book 1. Cognitive Domain*. London: Longman.

Entwistle, N. (1981) *Styles of Learning and Teaching*. Chichester: Wiley.

Entwistle, N. & Ramsden, P. (1983) *Understanding Student Learning*. London: Croom Helm.

Fitts, P.M. & Posner, M.I. (1973) *Human Performance*, 2nd edition. London: Prentice-hall.

Fretwell, J.E. (1982) *Ward Teaching and Learning*. London: Royal College of Nursing.

Gagne, R.M. (1970) *The Conditions of Learning*, 2nd edition. New York: Holt, Rinehart and Winston.

Gibbs, G., Morgan, A. & Taylor, E. (1982) Why students don't learn. *Institutional Research Review* 1, 9–32.

Hardy, L.K. (1980) Keeping up with 'Mrs. Chase': an analysis of nursing skill learning. *Journal of Advanced Nursing* 5, 321–327.

Hill, W.F. (1989) *Learning: A Survey of Psychological Interpretation*, 4th edition. London: Methuen.

Krathwohl, D.K., Bloom, B.S. & Masia, B.B. (1964) *Taxonomy of Educational Objectives: Book II. Affective Domain*. London: Longman.

Lewin, K. (1935) *A Dynamic Theory of Personality*. New York: McGraw-Hill.

Maslow, A.H. (1954) *Motivation and Personality*. London: Harper and Row.

McClelland, D.C., Atkinson, J.W., Clark, R.A. & Lowell, E.L. (1953) *The Achievement Motive*. New York: Appleton-Century-Crofts.

Orton, H. (1983) Ward learning climate and student response. In Davis, B. (ed.) *Research into Nurse Education*, pp. 90–105. Beckenham: Croom Helm.

Pask, G. (1976) Styles and strategies of learning. *British Journal of Educational Psychology* **46**, 128–148.

Peters, R.S. (1958) *The Concept of Motivation*. London: Routledge & Kegan Paul.

Ramsden, P. (1979) Student learning and perceptions of the academic environment. *Higher Education* **8**, 411–428.

Rogers, C.R. (1983) *Freedom to Learn for the 80's*, 2nd edition. Columbus, Ohio: Merrill.

Skinner, B.F. (1938) *The Behaviour of Organisms*. New York: Appleton-Century-Crofts.

4 Remembering, forgetting and perceiving

APPROACHES TO THE STUDY OF MEMORY

Learning depends, among other factors, on memory, and the way in which new material is first apprehended or perceived. Any task of memory involves the individual in being able to attend to information, perceive, transform, and store it for however briefly, and then retrieve it from memory. Disruption at any of these stages is referred to as forgetting.

It is now about 100 years since Ebbinghaus first pioneered experimental research into human memory. He designed very simple rote learning tasks and was his own subject in many of his experiments. He learned long lists of nonsense syllables. These syllables are formed by picking out vowels and consonants and putting them together in such a way that they have no meaning: GEZ, LEB, SIL, KAS, would be acceptable syllables; SUN, DOG, BUT, would be excluded because they have meaning. Nonsense syllables can be arranged to form lines and groups of lines to be learned like poetry. They can be presented visually, read and studied, or they can be projected onto a screen one at a time, or exposed in an apparatus for a measured length of time, or read aloud to the subject. These experiments enabled Ebbinghaus to come to some general conclusions about learning and memory, e.g. as Figure 1 shows, we forget at a rate which decreases with time.

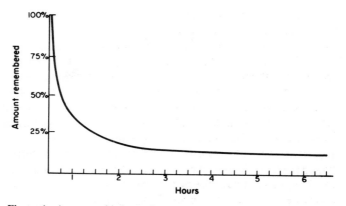

Figure 1. Amount of information recalled over an increasing period of time.

However, the drawback in Ebbinghaus' approach was that it applied only to simpler forms of learning, e.g. rote learning. Complex human learning and memory rely heavily on meaning. Bartlett (1932) suggested that what he called 'effort after meaning', i.e. a desire for understanding, was required for good memory. So instead of using nonsense syllables in his experiments he used meaningful material such as stories or pictures, emphasizing that it is memory as used in everday life which should be studied. Like the study of learning, since the end of the Second World War research into memory has been influenced by the information processing model.

The evidence from the research carried out by neurobiologists as well as psychologists, and from the study of clinical disorders of memory, suggest that there are two major memory stores: one for fleeting conscious memories referred to as primary or short-term memory, which is distinct from another, large capacity long-term memory.

The act of making a telephone call will provide a useful means of illustrating this distinction. After looking up a telephone number in a directory, we can retain it in short-term memory long enough to dial. Should one be interrupted during these actions, then the number is likely to be forgotten and will have to be looked up again. If it is a number which is important or useful to remember then some technique, such as repeating it over and over again or attaching some meaning to it, is required in order to commit it to long-term memory. This transfer from short-term memory to long-term memory is vital for learning.

COMPONENTS OF MEMORY

In fact modern psychologists taking the information processing approach describe three components of memory.

1. *Sensory memory*: after information reaches the senses it is briefly registered in the sensory store. Some of this information is successfully passed to the short-term memory store. For example, the visual image obtained when looking at the telephone number will enter the sensory store, and be selected from other incoming information for processing.

2. *Short-term memory* holds information longer than sensory memory and has a limited capacity. It has been suggested that approximately seven items can be held in short-term memory (Miller, 1965). Processing strategies allow information to be *chunked* either in terms of meaning or organization, improving the efficiency of short-term memory storage capacity. For example, 1965 as a date is one item

or chunk of information rather than four separate items or digits. After a short period (estimates vary from a few seconds to a few minutes) the information is either lost from memory or passed on to the more permanent store, long-term memory. Baddeley (1976) describes short-term memory as 'working memory' as, he argues, some temporary storage is required for such tasks as mental arithmetic, reasoning or problem solving.

3. *Long-term memory*. It has been suggested that long-term memory has virtually unlimited capacity. However, the process of 'remembering', or the bringing back into consciousness relevant items of information accurately and speedily, is rarely achieved with perfection. Information about meanings, concepts, properties and events are stored over a long time. This stored knowledge is organized into what are referred to as *schemata*. Bartlett used the term schema to describe a whole complex or structure of knowledge about a particular topic.

WAYS OF REMEMBERING

Unless information or knowledge is important or relevant, transfer from short-term memory into long-term memory is unlikely to take place. As soon as any knowledge becomes superfluous it tends to be forgotten. If the student works for examinations only and cannot see the usefulness of her knowledge in her work then most of what is learnt is forgotten immediately after the examination.

The association of new material with that which is already familiar or with something which is striking to the individual will increase the chance of remembering it. A student's learning can be helped by explaining how linkages can be made, making analogies and using various techniques to highlight important points.

Another way of encouraging remembering is referred to as *rehearsal*. Repeating information over and over again and beyond the point of the first accurate recall is termed *over-learning*. We do this when learning poetry or parts in a play. However in rehearsing information, a person might elaborate this process by linking the information to, for example, visual images. Luria (1969) describes an extreme example of a man who used imagery to remember vast quantities of meaningless material. Mnemonic devices are used specifically to aid recall, e.g. short jingles which are used to remember the names of the cranial nerves or the number of days in each month of the year.

FORGETTING

There are a number of theories which have been proposed to account for forgetting. Memories are said to fade away or *decay* over time, or as the result of *interference* by other events. It is extremely difficult to test the first theory on human beings as it is almost impossible to exclude interference. Although some experiments have found that learning just before going to sleep aids retention, it is suggested that even if lack of interference is a factor, physiological consolidation of the memory-trace most certainly is another (Baddeley, 1983).

Interference from other information processed either just before learning or just after learning can affect recall. *Proactive interference* is said to occur when previous learning disrupts new or target learning (the learning to be tested). On the other hand when subsequent learning inhibits the target learning, *retro-active interference* is said to have taken place. When the materials to be learnt are very similar a greater amount of forgetting occurs than when the materials are very different.

The timetabling of lessons in various educational settings is designed to reduce forgetting due to inter-ference. Very dissimilar subjects follow each other, e.g. in schools, a language might follow mathematics, or in colleges of nursing, practical nursing then anatomy. In her own study the student can use time in such a way that the greatest possible variation occurs. A period of reading may be followed by writing or discussion, a variety of subjects being studied in succession.

Forgetting is often associated with the learner's emotional state. Everybody tends to forget unpleasant, painful experiences. Freud suggested that this type of forgetting has its origin in the *repression* of events as-sociated with anxiety discussed on p. 23. Repression is not a conscious process. It may be a way of coping with unpleasant experiences and with any less desir-able personal characteristics. Not only the unpleasant experiences are forgotten but also the anger, sorrow and humiliation which accompanied the experience. If learning becomes associated with an emotionally un-pleasant activity, forgetting is much more pronounced. This may be why punishment is not, in the long run, effective in promoting learning.

The forgetting of unpleasant, worrying events is sometimes evident when a history is taken from a patient. Some of the most significant events in the patient's life may be completely forgotten. A serious illness, a stay in hospital, or the causes of his parents' death may not be recalled by the patient. Even prompt-ing by a relative may not lead to recall. Without under-

standing about repression it would seem surprising that
such important events could be forgotten.

Repressed material is not necessarily permanently
forgotten; it may be inaccessible to conscious recall at
one time and may be remembered quite spontaneously in
a different context. In fact, conscious effort to remember
may make it more difficult. Free association of ideas
may suddenly lead to the recall of something which
appeared to be completely forgotten and which, when
remembered, arouses considerable emotion. Repressed
material is recalled when current events and circumstances evoke a connection and when an emotional
state makes it possible to remember. When anyone is
depressed or hears depressing news all past recollections
may suddenly assume a depressing nature. All kinds of
examples of the sad things that have happened to the
individual himself, to others, to the world are suddenly
remembered. When the mood is good, funny or amusing
incidents, jokes and success stories are remembered.
It is well known that visitors to patients sometimes
indulge in recollections of all the sad and unfortunate
experiences which they remember suddenly when the
association with hospital, sickness and death brings
those memories to the fore. Patients do not always
find stories of other people's suffering, operations,
treatments and misfortunes at all comforting. Nurses
may have to help visitors to remember positive, encouraging and hopeful topics of conversation by their own
cheerful, optimistic attitude to visitors. The visitors
in turn help the patient to think of cheerful events in
response to their mood.

Repression of unpleasant, painful thoughts occurs
not only about the past but also about the future. For
many patients the problems related to their return
home, resuming the role of the breadwinner and the

position in the family usurped by someone else during their illness, are so difficult that they rarely emerge in consciousness.

The patient may appear to forget his family and his work and remember only events which occur in the hospital. His conversation is about the ward, the nurses, other patients, the food he is served, the activities of doctors, nurses and other staff. He appears to forget all he is told about his own home and family. Children in hospital show this to a very marked degree. They appear to forget their parents soon after arrival in hospital, may not talk at all about home but become visibly distressed when mother visits. It may be that the thought of home would be too painful and is therefore repressed.

Rehabilitation is very difficult as the patient has been unable to think of his future life. It only becomes possible to help patients once they consciously worry about specific problems or difficulties, but no help can be given while the patient has apparently forgotten all about his troubles. Repression of painful material is a useful defence mechanism, allowing the patient peace of mind and relaxation. It may serve as a temporary amelioration of difficulties in so far as it makes the patient behave as if they did not exist. To overcome difficulties, however, the patient has to be helped to face them. In the long run, protection from the recall of unpleasant thoughts is not in the patient's interest.

Memory and brain damage

The activity of remembering is only possible if the brain is healthy and intact. When the brain is damaged by accident, operation, drugs and toxins, memory is impaired. The degree of forgetting is related to the location and extent of brain damage. Forgetting takes place most rapidly immediately after learning, before consolidation has taken place and much more slowly later on. Because of this the the material most recently learnt is most completely forgotten after head injury. Past memories remain intact. After accidents causing unconsciousness there may be complete loss of memory for the events leading up to the accident. Patients who suffer from concussion may have forgotten what they were doing at the time of the accident. On recovery from electro-convulsive therapy, epileptic convulsions, or an anaes-thetic, the patient may forget where he placed his belongings, what was the last meal he ate, or which part of the ward he is in.

Some forms of brain damage interfere not only with recall but also with the ability to understand and learn what is going on. Old patients, or patients who suffer from confusional states during heart failure or fever, appear to suffer from loss of memory for recent events while retaining vivid and detailed memories of their dis-tant past. Their inability to remember recent events is very largely due to their lack of attention and con-centration and consequently a failure to fully grasp and learn what is happening around them. Accuracy of remembering depends first and foremost on perceptual integrity and on the quality of learning which occurs in the first place.

PERCEIVING

Some people have the ability to see every detail instan-taneously. They succeed in taking in a complete picture at once as if they were storing a photograph somewhere inside them. Later, when trying to remember, it is as if they were looking at the photograph and reading off details they might not consciously have noted at all. This process is called 'eidetic imagery'. It is a rare ability, useful to anyone on whose accuracy of evidence one has to depend. It occurs more commonly in children and in some artistic people. Most people perceive only inaccurately what is happening and their ability to remember reflects faults in perception in an exaggerated way. *Perception* is the interpretation of sensory stimuli which reach the sense organs and brain.

The eye is capable only of distinguishing shape, movement and colour. When we say that we can see a table, or Uncle Jack, or a boat on the horizon we make use of the sensations, remember other similar sensations and give a meaningful explanation of them by referring to objects and people.

Perceiving is a learned activity. To perceive it is necessary to remember previous experience and to recognize the new sensory stimuli as identical or similar to stimuli previously experienced and named. When the infant first experiences the sensory stimulus which an orange, for instance, presents, he sees a coloured round image. Similar images are produced by the moon, a large ball or a rattle. The infant repeatedly experiences the same sensation of roundness but he learns to discriminate between the different objects. He learns to handle the orange, get an idea of its size, put it in his mouth and learn about its texture. He smells it, bites it and learns about taste, throws it and learns what weight it has and how much damage it can do. Eventually, he hears the word orange frequently used in connection with the object and learns that it can be cut and produce a good drink and that his mother does not like him to play with it. When he then *perceives* an orange all his knowledge about oranges is used to interpret the visual impression.

About the moon that initially produced a similar image, he learns different information. The moon cannot be reached or played with and knowledge about it remains remote. The ball and the rattle are recognized by the noise they make, the texture when they are pressed or sucked, and their hardness. Their size is known by handling them, and their distance, when they are first seen, is realized by the effort required to reach them. Playing with them is approved of and encouraged.

By the time the infant can name the four different objects which produce the same round, visual image he is making use of a wealth of information without necessarily being conscious of it. All this information allows for the development of accurate perception of external objects.

From an assortment of seperate perceptual events we begin to extract characteristics they have in common and then use a symbol, e.g. a word, to refer to the objects with which we associate these common properties. Such symbols are called 'concepts'. Concepts are not static. Once we begin to use a concept our perceptions are organized in new ways. The concept helps us to 'generalize', i.e. to try to apply the concept to new and different perceptual patterns, and then to 'discriminate', i.e. to eliminate inappropriate objects from the class embraced by the concept, by becoming aware of specific perceptual patterns on which to base the classification.

When something entirely new appears we can only describe it as being 'like something else'; it is possibly like a composite picture of a number of previously known things. We perceive the new thing by comparing it with what is already known. At the moment of perception an effort is made to make the experience meaningful. This 'effort after meaning', mentioned earlier, determines the way in which the experience is later remembered. If, on first acquaintance, a man looks like 'Uncle Jack' he is remembered to be like him. When asked for details later the colour of his hair is given as dark, like Uncle Jack's; he is remembered as having a moustache like him, being about six feet tall, of medium build. His eyes, mouth, smile, movements are recalled as resembling those of Uncle Jack. In fact the more the new acquaintance is thought about the more like Uncle Jack he appears to be. Often when the new acquaintance is seen again one fails to recognize him because in reality he may be very little like Uncle Jack while the memory of him has become more and more similar to Uncle Jack.

Distortion

Perception depends always on one's degree of understanding at the time. As everybody who perceives the same thing has different previous knowledge, different expectations and attitudes, different standards of comparison, no two people ever perceive the same event in precisely the same way. In remembering what was perceived, distortions occur according to the importance that has been attached to the various parts of the perception in the first instance. In some ways it is remembered as being more conventional than it really was; in other respects unusual details, which had been noticed, are exaggerated on recall. Different people's reproductions of the same situation in paint or drawing or in story form are totally different.

Bartlett (1932) has demonstrated the process of perception and the distortion in remembering by a series of experiments. He drew a pattern, for example, which had certain features of a cat but otherwise was a very unusual design. The first person to be shown the picture was asked to draw it from memory and pass his drawing on to the next person who, in turn, drew it from memory. The features resembling a cat became more and more cat-like until in some series a completely conventional drawing of a cat was produced, often with cat-like details totally unwarranted by the original picture. Other reproductions stressed some of the unusual features of the design and these were accentuated. Both the familiar features and the unusual ones had become exaggerated.

Simlar distortions occurred in the retelling of a rather involved, illogical story. Familiar elements were retold in more and more familiar versions. The story became shorter, more logical and more commonplace. A few details seen to be incongruous became more absurd and irrelevant.

It is very important to remember the distortions which occur in perception and in subsequent remembering when the reliability of evidence is considered (Loftus, 1979). What is seen at the time depends on what the observer expects to see, on his attention and on the meaningfulness of what is perceived. How much of it is remembered, and how accurately, depends on the distortions which take place in the effort to understand. It also depends on a person's emotional need to forget unpleasant aspects, particularly as they affect him. It is very easy for him to accept suggestions as to what he has perceived and then to believe it to be his own perception. After being shown a picture for a short period the subject can be asked to describe what he has seen. When he has enumerated all he can remember, some of which is almost certainly wrong, he can be asked such questions as: 'Did the woman in the picture wear a hat?' or 'How many bottles did the milkman carry?'. Even if there was no woman or milkman in the picture many people are prepared to give the number of bottles and to swear that the woman did wear a hat. They later remember the woman and the milkman perfectly clearly. If they are shown the picture again they are genuinely surprised to find how different it is from their recollection. It is well known that distortion occurs when people give evidence in court (Leippe *et al.*, 1978). Counsel for defence or prosecution make use of this knowledge when they wish to throw doubt on the reliability of evidence of a witness.

Nurses have to learn to perceive situations accurately and guard against distortion in reporting. Signs and symptoms of the patient, his facial expression, posture, abnormal colour, or observation of pulse, of excretions or discharges cannot be accurately perceived by the new student because she does not know what to expect when she looks at the patient. When she knows something of the illness she notices symptoms which she has learnt to look for. Her observations become meaningful. The more experienced, well practised and knowledgeable she is the more detailed the perceptions become. Because observations become more meaningful they are better remembered and reported. Unusual or unforeseen events, such as accidents or sudden changes in the patient, are less well perceived because the necessary 'set' to make perception meaningful is lacking. It is all the more important for the nurse to give a running commentary to herself at the time, making details of observation conscious and writing a statement immediately, before distortions can occur. One can train onself to observe by noticing what belongs together, what is out of place, what changes are taking place and what explanation of them might be given.

Selective responses

Enabling nurses to perceive details and remember accurately depends on knowing what is relevant. The new student cannot distinguish, among a mass of details, those which are relevant to the patient's illness. The more experienced nurse is able to select perceptions relevant to the patient's illness. There are obvious advantages in being able to select what is important, but also dangers, because knowing what to look for makes it possible to neglect observations which appear irrelevant yet may be significant. This is why a fresh look at the patient, the unbiased report of a new nurse, the observations of another doctor or the comments of visitors may bring to light some symptoms which had been overlooked. Sometimes the fact that the patient's illness has been 'diagnosed' interferes with observation. Only those things which are relevant to the named illness are noticed. Other symptoms or complaints may be ignored and a better understanding of the patient's illness prevented. Transfer of the patient to another ward, or the introduction of new staff, may lead to a completely new way of looking at him. The publication of articles describing a new syndrome often leads to many observations of the condition, because attention has been drawn to particular symptoms or patterns of symptoms. Equally an attitude of optimism and hopefulness leads to observing improvement which might go unnoticed in a more pessimistic setting.

There are certain stimuli to which we appear to respond more readily than to others. Some noises cannot be ignored; some patterns of sound are noticed with more pleasure than others. Some visual stimuli tend to call for response more readily than others. This may be due to the significance attached to past learning.

The good form of squares and circles and symmetry are perceived with satisfaction, so much so that there is a tendency to fit what we see with our preference for good form. Figures which are well rounded and close are more pleasing than irregular shapes with parts missing. 'Gestalt' psychologists paid particular attention to the need for completeness, wholeness and closure. Our need to see figures as if they were complete leads us to ignore faults at times. We see this shape ⊓ as a square and remember it as a square without paying attention to the missing lines. When we do notice that a piece is missing the gap is magnified in our perception and recollection because it is disturbing to feel that the figure is incomplete. When nurses observe symptoms they tend to observe all the symptoms which should be there, although some may be missing.

When observations do not fit into a good pattern we have a tendency to make up a pattern. We remember numbers in groups, make up rhymes, make noises into tunes. Similarly we try to classify observations. The greatest satisfaction is gained when everything is neatly organized and named. Our tendency to organize perception into a clear pattern is so great that we sometimes feel satisfied when order is established, without realizing that the organization into pattern may stem more from us than from the material we perceive. We feel satisfied when we know the name of a disease but categorization alone does not necessarily reflect full understanding. In fact, there may be many conditions grouped together under one name. Nurses often believe that they know more about the patient when they know the diagnosis. In fact they have only satisfied their need to categorize and in order to know more about the patient it may be necessary to forget the classification and look again at all the details which can be observed.

The need to classify, to see things as complete, to close the issue, is much greater in some people than in others. The activity of creating order from a wealth of apparently unrelated perceptions is a valuable step in acquiring scientific understanding. However, to see clear patterns where they do not really exist, to demand simple structure always, and to see things only in clear categories, leads to an excessively simplified perception of a complex situation; it prevents reassessment and regrouping of perceptions and means that a great deal of material may be ignored. Learning consists both in the activity of creating clear, classified patterns which serve as a framework for further perception and learning, and also in the process of reconstructing existing patterns, reassessing and breaking down established patterns to recreate afresh.

All people engage in attempts to reach clear structuring of their perceptual world and to defend the understanding of their concepts from the disruptive effect of new perceptions which do not fit in. Festinger (1957) studied what he termed 'cognitive dissonance' (see p. 268), a kind of disharmony one experiences when new information makes it difficult to persevere in one's attitude and beliefs.

Image and reality

When we perceive the world around us we always have to make some judgements on rather scanty evidence. Often we do not even know why we judged as we did. Size and distance of objects, for example, are related to each other. We know how big people are. When we see them as being very small we judge them to be a long way off; when they look big we think they must be close by. We use a 'frame of reference' of well-known objects and judge new impressions by comparison. We assume, for example, that the walls and window-frames of a room are vertical and judge people's position in space by reference to the room. If the room is distorted we tend to misjudge the size, distance and shape of objects and people in it. When the know the shape of an object, for example when we know that the table top is square, we continue to see it as square whatever the position of the eye, and therefore the image on the retina, may be in relation to the object. We tend to see colour as constant even if the light changes.

There is always the possibility of error in perception. We usually compensate for errors by using several senses at the same time. We do not rely entirely on sight to judge size and distance, but also use touch and hearing. We verify the perceptual experience by handling the object and doing something with it. Very often, however, errors in perception do occur; these are called 'illusions'. Some of them are universally experienced; some are personal errors resulting from private expectations and attitudes. Some visual illusions can easily be demonstrated and examples may be seen in Figure 2. Perception of size is often determined by the importance attached to the person or object. Children nearly always see and remember their teacher as being tall and big. Villages, towns, and places known in childhood appear bigger in retrospect than they really are. Holidays appear longer than they really were.

Sometimes it is difficult to know how much error there is in perception, particularly if there is no means of checking by a different approach. In familiar surroundings it may be easy to recognize shapes or noises. If the frame of reference is removed it may be impossible to perceive accurately what is going on.

Many patients find it very difficult to distinguish

R

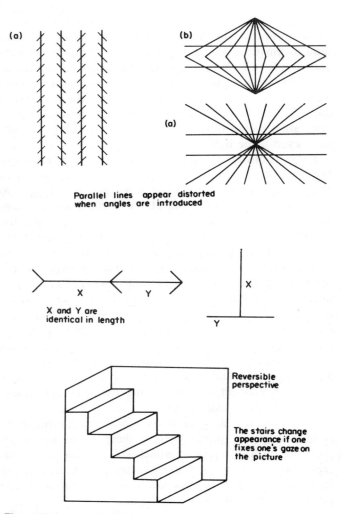

Figure 2. Some examples of illusions.

clearly what they see and hear in hospital. Where everything is strange and new there are no fixed impressions
against which to measure the reality of perceived events.
This is made worse by any defect in vision or hearing
the patient may have. It is a terrifying experience to be
unable to orient oneself clearly. It cannot be stressed
too much how important it is to help a patient to learn
about his environment by making use of every possible
sensory device. Showing, allowing the patient to touch,
to handle and to use equipment, explaining, talking
about the tools used to carry out a procedure, con-
firming the patient's perceptions when he is right, and
correcting them when he is mistaken, are essential to
good nursing. Particular attention must be given to
a patient whose eyes are bandaged, who cannot hear
clearly, who is only partially aware of his environment
because of sedation, or whose position in bed makes it
difficult for him to observe what is going on.

Perception is the necessary raw material of thought. If
a person is deprived of sensory stimuli it becomes very
difficult for him to think cleary. Images of previous perceptions become so important that it is hard to know for
certain what is reality and how much comes from one's
own reconstruction of past perceptions. Normally we can
clearly distinguish between images and reality because
images belong to one's self only. In the absence of sensory stimulation images become so powerful that they
begin to be taken as reality (Hebb, 1961).

There are some mentally ill patients whose own images
are so powerful, even when they perceive reality, that
they fail to distinguish between reality and images. The
term 'hallucination' is used for perceptual experiences
which do not arise from sensory stimulation. It is never
possible to be sure whether a patient is misinterpreting
a stimulus and has an illusion, or whether he experiences

a perception for which there is no stimulus at all—an hallucination. Some patients are able to describe their hallucinations very clearly, either in words or by drawing pictures of them.

Perceptual thresholds

We often manage to have fairly accurate perceptions even though the stimulus is very weak or present for only a very short time. We refer to the perceptual threshold when we try to measure how long an exposure is necessary before a picture or word is recognized, how bright the light has to be before we can see, how loud a noise must be to be heard. The threshold differs for different people. Activity of the sense organs plays a part. Apart from that, the individual's general state of readiness and awareness determines the threshold of perception. When a person is tired or ill the threshold may be high and many things he would normally notice remain unseen or unheard. Certain drugs, however, heighten perception. Aldous Huxley described the changes in perception which occurred when he had taken the drug mescaline. Some people, who have become addicted to drugs, have perhaps done so because they enjoyed the greater awareness of stimuli under their influence. The threshold for hearing may be lower when other senses are not used. Blind people can learn to make use of auditory information which is not noticed at all by sighted people. Patients, seemingly unconscious and unable to communicate, may, in fact, hear perfectly (Ashworth, 1979).

The threshold differs for familiar and unfamiliar stimuli. Those stimuli which cause emotional distress differ from those which are neutral. Nurses sometimes become unaware of noises which are clearly perceived by and are very irritating to patients. The sounds of a trolley being set up, of monitor alarms and 'bleeps', may be very disconcerning to the patient and not noticed at all by the staff. Conversation between nurses or between doctors is often heard by the patient to whom it refers, just as anyone may hear his own name mentioned against the general background noise of undifferentiated talk. Patients have a tendency to believe that preparation for treatment or discussion of prognosis or diagnosis refers to themselves and, therefore, hear and see clearly some things which in isolation give rise to misunderstanding and unnecessary anxiety.

Subliminal perception

Although conscious perception occurs only when sensory stimulation has reached the threshold of perception, a certain amount of information can be conveyed by noises or visual stimulation just below the threshold of the individual. This is referred to as 'subliminal perception'. It can be demonstrated that words of a given length, printed sufficiently clearly and largely, can be read when they are flashed momentarily on a screen. At that point words which have no particular emotional significance can be clearly recognized. If words which cause anxiety—referring to death, violence, suffering or sex—are interspersed with neutral words it is found that they cannot be recognized at that level of exposure. The threshold of perception for these words is higher than for neutral words. However, measurements of blood pressure, breathing and perspiration show that an emotional response has occurred. This indicates that some perception must have taken place below the threshold. This can also be demonstrated if a person is asked to say the first thing that comes to his mind every time something is flashed on the screen. Even if he is not quite able to read the word on the screen the association which comes to mind is usually relevant.

The fact that some perception occurs even below the threshold of conscious awareness has been used in advertising in some countries. If the name of some merchandise is flashed on the cinema or television screen so fast and so feebly that it is not consciously recognized it is not possible to resist such advertising deliberately. Therefore such methods may be more effective than the overt use of advertising. Most people consider that 'subliminal' advertising is immoral and publication of results of subliminal advertising has caused a good deal of indignation. For practical purposes it is useful to remember that a patient may not be consciously distressed by whispered words or brief glances at his charts but subconsciously it may result in alteration in emotional state and behaviour.

Projection

The way in which people perceive the world around them is clearly dependent on themselves as much as on the sensory stimulation provided. Previous experiences, readiness to listen, attention, interest and physical health may make a lecture or demonstration perfectly clear to one student while another student, whose background, attention and interest differs, may come away from the same lecture with a totally different impression of what has been said. Much of what is perceived in any given situation is in fact put into it by the perceiver. The external world is reconstructed and interpreted to fit it with the personality of the person who perceives. He is 'projecting' into the situation much of his own personality. Clearly, the more precise the external stimuli the less room for projection; the more vague the external circumstances the more projection can take place.

It could be argued that a much clearer picture of each student's individual understanding might be gained if her characteristic way of perceiving the world could be known.

PERCEPTUAL ALTERATION IN HOSPITAL

Most people can recognize the sense of heightened awareness or what could be described as perceptual vigilance that accompanies any new experience, be it the impact of first viewing the beauty of a mountain range, the bustle and noise of a huge and anonymous city or such things as a child's experience of the first day at school or a nurse's first day on a busy and strange hospital ward. Every detail is noted and given significance. Often the perceptions, when reflected upon, are found to have been exaggerated or even distorted in some way; buildings appeared bigger, noises louder and even people encountered larger than life. If this is so, consider someone newly admitted for the first time to the strange and potentially stressful environment of the hospital ward. Deprived of his independence and his health compromised, he must now contend with strange activities, strange people and perhaps even stranger smells and sounds. In many ways all the normal life events have to be redefined or reinterpreted. His perception of other people and the significance they hold for his well being and personal goals are suddenly very different. In terms used by *existential psychologists*, whose main concern is the person's unique experience of existence, the newly admitted patient's *phenomenal* world (the world as it appears to him) has suddenly changed and his ability to predict events, automatically understand the behaviour of others or direct his affairs may well be shaken. In such a situation, it is for the nurse to appreciate not only the obvious physical needs of her sick patient but also, therefore, his disrupted world and what this may mean to him. It may well add an unwanted dimension to his loss of independence. If the nurse is able to recognize this, the sensitive nursing care such an appreciation can generate may do much to help restore or maintain his dignity and self-esteem.

In time, of course, we all get used to those novel experiences that initially demanded such attention. We *habituate* to stimuli once the novelty is over and, hopefully, replaced by comforting familiarity. Nurses describing patients as having 'settled in' are observing this process.

Recognizing the potential problem of perceptual disruption in a newly admitted patient and acting upon it in a sensitive and individualized way can do much to bring about a sense of well being in a patient that is independent of the management of his particular physical problems.

References

Ashworth, P. (1979) Sensory deprivation. *Nursing Times* **6**, 294.

Baddeley, A.D. (1976) *The Psychology of Memory*. London: Harper & Row.

Baddeley, A.D. (1983) *Your Memory: A User's Guide*. Harmondsworth: Penguin.

Bartlett, F.C. (1932) *Remembering*. Cambridge: University Press.

Festinger, L. (1957) *A Theory of Cognitive Dissonance*. Evanston. Ill.: Row Peterson.

Freud, S. (1939) *The Psychopathology of Everyday Life*. Harmondsworth: Penguin.

Hebb, D.O. (1961) in Solomin, P. *et al.* (eds) *Sensory Deprivation*. Cambridge, Mass.: Harvard University Press.

Leippe, M.R., Wells, S.L. & Ostrom, I.M. (1978) Crime seriousness as a determinant of accuracy in eyewitness identification. *Journal of Applied Psychology* **63**, 345–351.

Loftus, E.F. (1979) *Eyewitness Testomy*. Cambridge, Mass.: Harvard University Press.

Luria, A.R. (1969) *The Mind of a Mnemonist*. London: Cape.

Miller, G.A. (1965) The magical number seven, plus or minus two: Some limits on our capacity for processing information. *Psychological Review* **63**, 81–97.

Further reading

As well as Baddeley (1983), mentioned above, the following books are useful:

Cohen, G., Eynsenk, N.W. & Levois, N.E. (1986) *Memory: A Cognitive Approach*. Milton Keynes: Open University Press.

Gruneberg, M.M., Morris, P.G. & Sykes, R.N. (eds) (1978) *Practical Aspects of Memory*. London: Academic Press.

Schiff, W. (1980) *Perception: An Applied Approach*. Boston: Houghton Mifflin.

5 Personality

People are all different and generally proud of their uniqueness. The unique characteristics each person develops in the course of his life is referred to as personality.

It is important for nurses to study the concept of personality because it helps them to understand themselves, each other, and their patients. Personality may determine success and failure in nursing, the ability to make friends and to adapt to different working conditions. Personality influences the kind of work one enjoys and the interests one develops. Personality is one factor which affects the way one copes with pain, illness and crises.

Intuitively, one tends to believe that uniqueness cannot be studied. Each person's unique personality structure consists however of the same characteristics which other people also possess, but in different quantities and different combinations.

The study of personality represents an attempt to investigate these individual differences. (For a detailed discussion of the theories of personality see Hall and Lindsey, 1978.)

There are a number of approaches to the study of personality. Some psychologists investigate how personality develops and changes. This approach is described as the *dynamic approach* to personality. The dynamic approach emphasizes that personality can develop and change. Some psychologists are interested in describing people and in attempting to measure certain personality characteristics. This approach may be referred to as the *factor analytic approach*. The factor analytic approach, by contrast, emphasizes the enduring constant characteristics rather than the tendency to change. One of the controversial issues in psychology is whether or not a stage is reached in adulthood when personality becomes stable. Both approaches are useful, but they are based on very different assumptions.

If selection of an employee is considered it can be seen that the prevailing view can be influential in determing selection procedures. If it is believed that personality does not change, selection will consist of finding people of the appropriate personality and consequently, a means whereby personality can be measured and assessed (see Chapter 6). Occupational psychologists attempt to solve problems of staff selection and occupational guidance by trying to obtain personality profiles of people who are successful in their jobs, and to match these with the personality characteristics of people whom they advise about the kind of career for which they are suited.

On the other hand if the view is that personality is dynamic, capable of development and change, selection criteria using personality tests will be relatively less important. Finding ways of developing desirable characteristics in employees assumes much greater importance.

Another approach is the *personal construct approach*. Psychologists interested in this approach are less concerned with describing or with tracing the origin of the personality structure than with the way a person makes sense of his experiences. They pay particular attention to the way in which people see similarities and differences in their environment and base their behaviour on predictions arising from these comparisons (Kelly, 1955).

We will attempt to outline the different ways of thinking about personality by looking at the problems of describing the personality of those who are deemed to be good nurses.

PERSONALITY TRAITS

The most common way to describe the nurse is to enumerate a number of qualities she possesses. Such characteristics as patience, honesty, perseverance, conscientiousness, thoroughness, initiative are often mentioned. These are referred to as *personality traits.*

Personality traits have been described most extensively by Allport (1937, 1966) who arrived at a list of several hundred. Such a large list is not very useful for practical purposes. Other psychologists have tried to see whether a particular group of traits often occurs together. They have described clusters of personality traits, or 'personality factors', or 'dimensions of personality' (Cattell, 1950; Eysenck, 1953). We shall refer to this again when we look at personality tests.

A trait is a tendency to behave in a consistent manner in various situations. The knowledge that a person possesses a particular trait makes prediction of her behaviour possible. A nurse who is thorough, for example, carries out a variety of tasks with thoroughness. She is thorough in her studies, in her routine ward duties, in her attempt to get to know patients, in her dealings with ward management and in her own personal affairs. If she is asked to carry out a job it can be predicted that she will do it thoroughly, whatever it may be.

Of course the question of whether a nurse has a particular trait can be verified only from observation of her behaviour; thus, to say that she is thorough simply means that she has been observed to demonstrate this trait repeatedly in the past.

Some personality traits have been carefully investigated in order to find out whether the use of a single word, describing a trait, corresponds to some unifying characteristic of personality. Honesty, for example, has been the subject of study in a large sample of children (Harthshorn and May, 1930). They were given every possible opportunity to cheat and behave dishonestly in many different situations. During school-work they had the opportunity to cheat by looking up the answers or by copying from others. They could cheat in their report of the results or of the time they took over individual items. They also had the opportunity to steal or to tell lies. It became obvious in these investigations that honesty or deceit were not in fact single traits. Some children cheated in their work, but not in their handling of property. Some gave false reports but worked without cheating; some told lies about their work, but not about their behaviour. Some children may cheat at school but not at home.

Most of the traits we look for in nurses have not been as carefully examined, but it is probable that they, too, are more complex than would appear. It may well be that a nurse who is thorough within the ward environment may have a very casual approach to her own personal surroundings. It is necessary to ask, not simply whether or not a nurse possesses any given trait, but rather how much of it she has, in what circumstances she displays it, and whether the trait is specific to particular circumstances or fairly generalized.

TEMPERAMENT

Another way of describing a suitable or unsuitable personality is to refer to *emotional state* or *temperament*. Such characteristics as moodiness, emotional instability, and being easily upset are less desirable qualities. Cheerfulness and an even temperament are more desirable in the nurse.

Temperament is the term used to refer to the way in which emotions are expressed and experienced over a long period of time. Mood describes the emotion prevailing for a short period.

At the moment of hearing bad news, for example, a person feels sad. This may be only a brief experience of an emotion but if sadness persists it is called depression. This mood may last all day or several days or weeks. Some people become depressed at frequent intervals. They tend to feel happy and elated at times and then plunge into a depressive mood. This is their temperament; it is one of mood swings sometimes called cyclothymic.

Classification of personality according to temperament has been attempted many times. It has always been recognized that temperament is in some way connected with bodily structure and particularly with neuroendocrine function. The ancient Greeks described four personality types to which they attached, if somewhat inaccurately, a biological basis. People who were described as phlegmatic, i.e. calm unemotional people, had large amounts of mucous secretion, a true observation of the parasympathetic activity in a relaxed calm state! The angry, irritable person, frequently losing his temper, was thought to have excessive secretion of bile and was described as choleric. The optimistic, excitable person was thought to be full blooded—sanguine—and the unhappy, depressed person was associated with what was described as black bile—melancholic.

Kretschmer associated different temperaments with body build. He thought that a schizoid temperament— a reserved, shy, withdrawn, emotionally shallow personality—is most often found in asthenic people, i.e. people who are long and thin in body build. Cycloid temperament—mood swings from elated to depressed and emotional lability—he associated with pyknic body build, a short and stocky physique.

Shakespeare seemed to have similar ideas; in *Julius Caesar* he says:

> Let me have men about me that are fat;
> Sleek-headed men, and such as sleep o'nights;
> Yond Cassius has a lean and hungry look;
> He thinks too much; such men are dangerous.

The American psychologist Sheldon (1942) describes a similar association of temperament with body structure but divides bodily types according to the development of various tissues during the growth of the fetus.

The fertilized ovum splits until a ball of cells is formed which then arranges itself into three layers. The outer layer is called ectomorphic; the middle, metamorphic; the inner one, endomorphic. As the embryo develops the ectomorphic layer forms mainly skin and nervous system; the metamorphic layer, bones and muscle; the endomorphic layer the internal viscera. Sheldon believes that temperament is associated with the predominance of any one of these layers.

There is very little to show whether any particular temperament makes one person more suited to nursing than any other temperament. People whose mood varies are sometimes difficult to get on with. Student nurses may find it a strain to have to adjust to the mood of the ward sister. The temperament of the nurse certainly has some effect on the feelings of the patient. However, it would be wrong to say that this is a bad thing. On the whole it is easier to feel strongly about people whose emotions are strong and who express their emotions. Excessive placidity may become very disconcerting.

In adjusting our behaviour we often take into account what emotional reaction it is likely to provoke in others. If other people's emotions are quite erratic it becomes difficult to take them into account; if emotional response is absent, guidance is missing. Some patients assume, for example, that the nurse's mood is related to what they themselves have said or done. Equally the patient may find the nurse's mood unusual or inappropriate. Nurses are expected to be temperamentally 'on an even keel'. Any deviation in the nurse's mood is sometimes thought by the patient to relate to what he himself has said or done. This may be because the patient expects the nurse's emotional response to be to his own actions and may not consider other possible explanations. For example, it may have been the case that the nurse's own circumstances have influenced her mood.

Some people may be temperamentally more suited to nursing than others, but, except in extremes, it would be very difficult to select candidates according to temperament. Temperament is inclined to change somewhat with age. Adolescents are frequently moody. In middle aged women, probably associated with hormonal changes in the menopause, mood swings again frequently occur. In women this may become most troublesome. Disorders of endocrine glands, for example the thyroid, are also often accompanied by changes in temperament.

PERSONALITY TYPE

Another way of describing a nurse's personality consists in referring to *personality type*. There is an overlap between descriptions of temperament and type. Certain temperaments are believed to be associated with body types, as already referred to.

Descriptions of a person as shy, reserved, keeping himself to himself, or, on the other hand, descriptions of hearty, easy-going people who are the life and soul of the party, good mixers, popular, are descriptions of the introvert and extrovert personality types, respectively. These terms were first used by Jung (1923) and introvert and extrovert characteristics have been described by many psychologists.

Introverted people do not behaviourally react very much to other people's feelings. Their own interests and activities are not directed towards others. They require relatively little external stimulation to maintain personal equilibrium. Extroverts require constant stimulation and search out activity and dislike their own company. Most people are not entirely introverted or extroverted but exhibit characteristics of both types.

There is no special merit in being either introvert or extrovert. Some extroverts, by virtue of their love of activity, are excellent company and give valuable contributions to society. The morale and tone of a nurse's home, sometimes the atmosphere of a ward—certainly the success of a party—depends on the number of extroverts there. On the other hand, extroverts are often inclined to show off, to put themselves in the limelight and to depend on other people's approval so much that they become irritating or overpowering.

Introverts sometimes make other people uncomfortable because they appear too little concerned with what is going on. On the other hand, their thoughtful comments and emotional support, when they are able to give it, can be extremely valuable to their colleagues and to patients. Again it seems as if, in nursing, there is room for botii types except perhaps extremes in either.

The most common way of describing personality characteristics is to refer to *attitudes*. The concept of *attitude* is discussed in Chapter 11 but at this point it serves to reflect upon how, during a nurse's professional career, some attitudes may alter and develop while others may remain unchanged. In terms of the various approaches to the study of personality one has to be aware of the stability of certain characteristics, e.g. those that brought the individual to become and remain a nurse, and yet also to be aware of the dynamic nature of personality that will allow for change and development within the person. In this way it can be seen that these views of and approaches to the study of personality are not necessarily mutually exclusive.

PERSONAL CONSTRUCTS

The personal construct approach to the study of personality was first described by Kelly (1955). Kelly suggested that the best way to find out about a person was to ask him. His theory of personality was based on tests of self-concept whereby a person was allowed to express his own view of the world rather than answer questions that may be based on another's (e.g. a psychologist's) view of the world. Kelly considered that an individual's personality arose from the way he constructed the world around him. This in turn depended on how he interpreted experiences and anticipated events.

From this basic idea Kelly went on to develop a technique known as the 'repertory grid' which was used to explore an individual's personal constructs of the world around him. The 'constructs' were seen as bipolar, e.g. black/white, good/bad, kind/unkind and the individual is asked to describe people, objects or emotions, which Kelly called 'elements' in terms of such constructs. Ideally the constructs were of the individuals own making and not supplied by the psychologist carrying out the test. In order to elicit a construct rather than suggest one, the triad method was employed. The person might be presented with three elements, e.g. mother, daughter and son, and asked to say in what way two are alike and different from the third. It may be that two, say mother and son, are tidy and daughter is untidy. In this way the bipolar construct tidy/untidy has been elicited and can then be used to describe other members of the family or even friends and colleagues. In determining how someone sees members of his immediate family he may be asked to place mother, father, sister etc. on a number of bipolar constructs so that by these careful methods the individual has created a description of himself. There are many variations within Kelly's basic system, all of which require careful scoring and special statistical analysis to determine and evaluate someone's major constructs. Kelly believed that his methods could reveal constructs and views, and therefore aspects of personality, of which the person himself might be barely aware.

A similar approach to the study of personality underlies Osgood's interest in the measurement of meaning (Osgood *et al.*, 1957).

Osgood obtains a picture of personality from the way a person attributes qualities to the elements chosen from his environment. Osgood believes that one can intuitively place any concept somewhere in a dimension defined by adjectives which denote opposite poles. For example, the concept of mother can be placed somewhere between warm and cold, between hard and soft, between strong and weak. The arrangement of objects, people and events in the emotional qualitative matrix denotes the uniqueness of one's personality.

The personal construct approach is increasingly used to research such problems as the socialization of students into the nursing profession (Davis, 1983), or the difficulties experienced by ward sisters in the interpretation of their role (Runciman, 1983).

INTELLIGENCE

Intelligence is the one aspect of personality more extensively measured than all the others. Though it is difficult to define intelligence, it is clear that it has something to do with the ability to learn. Children who are mentally handicapped and who learn very slowly are said to have a low intelligence. It is a matter for argument whether they learn slowly because of their low intelligence or whether to say that a child has a low intelligence is simply another way of saying that he learns slowly.

There is some evidence that heredity is an important factor in determining intelligence. Ability depends on the intelligence of parents and grandparents. Identical twins tend to resemble each other more in intelligence than do brothers and sisters or non-identical twins. The fact that identical twins raised apart are a little less alike than those brought up together shows that environment plays some part in the development of intelligence.

How big a part is played by heredity and how much intelligence is influenced by environment has been hotly debated. Eysenck (1971), basing his writing on earlier work of A.R. Jensen, suggested that American Negroes are genetically less well-endowed than American Whites. This view came under attack from many psychologists, some of whom hold extreme views, denying the existence of innate differences of ability. They point to the fact that social class, with the accompanying educational privileges it bestows on children during the early years, is highly correlated with scores in intelligence tests, and believe that greater equality of opportunity would result in levelling up of intelligence. The more moderate critics of Eysenck's view accept that variations in ability are at least partly attributable to genetic influences. They suggest, however, that the brain is susceptible to external influences and believe that the psychologists' efforts could be more profitably spent in finding methods of social and cultural enrichment in order to eliminate individual differences rather than devising selection procedures designed to perpetuate the social class differences in intellectual endowment. In the next chapter some methods of measuring intelligence will be described. None of these measure directly the innate aspect of intelligence. This can only be inferred from the actual performance in daily life. Hebb (1949) has suggested that one can think of innate intelligence as 'intelligence A'. This potential intelligence with which a person is endowed cannot be measured. 'Intelligence B' is the effective intelligence measurable by tests. It is the result of modification of intelligence A by environmental influences which can start during intrauterine life and continue during the critical periods of child development.

Intelligent parents, on the whole, have more highly intelligent children than dull parents. While it would appear that heredity is involved, it was noticed that some children, whose environment had changed, dramatically improved in intelligence scores. Children moved from orphanages to foster homes, for example, or from bad homes to good ones, made rapid strides and showed much higher scores in later tests. It should also be noted that although parents and children are similar in intelligence, children tend to be nearer average than their parents. Outstandingly brilliant children can be born in any family just as severely mentally handicapped children can be born to very intelligent parents. It is possible for people of varying intelligence to reach similar levels of attainment, though the brighter person tends to take a shorter time than the less intelligent. The brighter person can do it unaided; the less intelligent may need help. This has important implications for all fields of education, not least for nursing education. The learning expectations of the brighter student may be greater than those of the less gifted. Discouragement of the slow has to be avoided and the stimulus of competition must not be sacrificed.

In everyday life, people of various levels of intelligence must be able to live with each other. Perhaps particularly in nursing, an awareness of the difficulties of the less intelligent and a natural acceptance of the abilities of those of high intelligence are important. How the nurse communicates with patients of differing levels of intelligence and education is an important consideration in the planning of care.

References

Adorno, T.W., Frenkel-Brunswick, E., Levinson, D.J. & Sanford, R.N. (1950) *The Authoritarian Personality*. New York: Harper.

Allport, G.W. (1937) *Personality: a Psychological Interpretation*. New York: Holt, Rinehart and Winston.

Allport, G.W. (1966) Traits revisited. *American Psychologist* **21**, 1–10.

Cattell, R.R. (1950) *Personality*. New York: McGraw-Hill.

Davis, B. (1983) Student nurses' perception of their significant others. In Davis, B. *Research into Nurse Education*. Beckenham: Croom Helm.

Eysenck, H.J. (1953) *The Structure of Human Personality*. London: Methuen.

Eysenck, H.J. (1971) *Race, Intelligence and Education*. London: Temple.

Hall, C.S. & Lindsey, C. (1978) *Theories of Personality*, 3rd edition. New York: Wiley.

Harthshorn, H. & May, M.A. (1930) *Studies in Deceit*. New York: Macmillan.

Hebb, D.O. (1949) *The Organisation of Behaviour*. New York: Wiley.

Jung, C.G. (1923) *Psychological Types*. New York: Harcourt Brace and World.

Kelly, G.A. (1955) *The Psychology of Personal Constructs*. New York: Norton.

Osgood, C.E., Suci, G.J. & Tannenbaum, P.H. (1957) *The Measurement of Meaning*. Urbana: University of Illinois Press.

Runciman, P. (1983) *Ward Sister at Work*. Edinburgh: Churchill Livingstone.

Sheldon, W.H. (1942) *The Varieties of Temperament*. New York: Harper.

Further reading

Hampson, S.E. (1988) *The Construction of Personality*, 2nd edition. London: Routledge & Kegan Paul.

6 Psychological testing

Having discussed some of the ways in which psychologists have tried to describe personality, we shall now look at the tools which can be used to measure personality characteristics in order to be able to compare people with each other. Some of these tools consist of highly structured tests, to which numerical scores can be assigned. Other tools are unstructured and require subjective interpretation by the tester. No one tool can give a full picture of personality.

When one needs a fairly accurate profile of someone's personality, for example in order to give advice about a suitable career, or in order to understand psychological problems a patient is trying to cope with, one tends to rely on a combination of methods to obtain information.

Let us take as an example how one tries to obtain a personality description of a student nurse before and during her training.

OPEN REPORTS

These are most widely relied on. The assumption that ward sisters know which of their students are progressing well is, on the whole, well justified.

One method of writing reports consists of using blank paper and writing whatever appears to the writer to be important. This method will highlight the student's faults and merits and its overall tone gives an indication of the student's general ability. Details, examples and episodes may be mentioned. There are some serious drawbacks to this method. First it is possible to leave out statements about large areas of the student's performance. This happens either deliberately about unfavourable characteristics on which the sister prefers not to report, or it may happen unwittingly about all those aspects which are unspectacular yet may be the essential ingredients of a good nurse. Another drawback is the emphasis every sister places on those aspects which to her appear to be of particular importance. One sister may always comment on tidiness and punctuality; another one never thinks of mentioning these but always refers to an ability to teach others or to cooperate. This bias makes comparisons of successive reports difficult.

Halo effect is a further drawback of this method of reporting. Any one outstanding characteristic may influence the opinion of the reporter to such an extent that the whole report is coloured by it.

RATING

Some of these difficulties can be overcome if the report is made in the form of a rating scale.

The reporter is not given an entirely free hand. Instead she is given a number of headings and asked to state the degree to which the characteristic is present in the student.

In an open report, for example, the sister may mention that the student is not always punctual. This may mean that she arrived late on one occasion, or, on the other hand, it may mean that the student is unpunctual so often that it had to be mentioned in the report.

If the method of rating is used the question of punctuality must always be filled in because the heading already appears on the paper. The sister may be asked to rate each item on the report on a five-point scale, meaning that the nurse is:

1. always punctual.
2. usually punctual.
3. average in punctuality.
4. frequently unpunctual.
5. always unpunctual.

On some report forms the questions are all set out and the sister ticks the answer which applies. This makes it possible to give detailed examples of what is meant by the rating, for example:

1. Her work is always accurately done without any need to supervise.
2. She usually works accurately, occasionally asks for guidance.
3. She works well with only cursory supervision.
4. She works well only when supervised.
5. She does nothing at all unless closely supervised.

This kind of reporting makes it necessary for the sister to think about every aspect of the nurse's work, even those she would otherwise have thought unimportant. Rating will give a fairly clear picture as to whether a student is average, above or below average, or quite outstandingly good or bad.

Although this has been discussed here in relation to the personality assessment of the nurse, the method of reporting under pre-set headings and with some idea of rating has much to recommend it in reporting a patient's progress, and particularly on the behaviour, attitudes and interests of mentally ill patients. The same sort of rating method is profitably used in the assessment of pain.

INTERVIEWING

This is the most popular of all methods yet it is probably not the most effective. Many people believe, quite erroneously, that they can accurately assess a person as soon as they engage him in conversation. Appearance, bearing, speech can be noticed. Questions can be asked about attitudes and interests and many answers allow the interviewer to gain some knowledge of the interviewee's emotional approach. Interviewing can be very effective provided it is well prepared and the questions asked cover a wide area in order to make possible an assessment of all aspects of personality.

There are great drawbacks, however, in this method. Interviews take place in stressful circumstances and great skill is needed to put the person who is interviewed at ease. The interviewer's body language, gestures, eye contact, facial expression, attitude of approval or disapproval may influence the answers (Argyle, 1973, 1975). It is difficult to avoid asking leading questions and people often try to give the answer they think may be the expected one. Only a very long interview could give a comprehensive picture of personality. In business, interviews are sometimes conducted over lunch and the more relaxed atmosphere and unbusinesslike setting make it possible to cover ground far beyond the immediate questions of work. On the whole, while some people are shrewd interviewers the method has little to recommend it. When interviews are used to select candidates for a job, this may help the candidate more than the employer in enabling the former to see the place of work, ask questions and feel more at ease by the time work begins. Interviewing techniques can be greatly improved by training and by introducing structure into the interview.

The Seven-Point plan (Roger, 1974) is possibly one of the most widely known formats for job interviewing. It provides a framework within which interviewers can work and suggests the following areas should be explored in the context of matching the candidate with a job.

1. Physical characteristics or abilities which are important to the job, e.g. good health, vision, hearing and speech.
2. Attainments which include education, personal and professional background and an assessment of how well the candidate has done in these areas.
3. Overall general ability, especially general intelligence and cognitive skills.
4. Special aptitudes, though at an interview for selection to nursing this is especially difficult as a young person needs time to develop special aptitudes, though social skills are important.
5. Interests and how they are pursued which are occupationally significant, e.g. intellectual, physical and social pursuits.
6. Personality attributes such as self-perception, reliability, sociability.
7. Circumstances which might be important in relation to the person's life and aspirations.

PERFORMANCE TESTS

Some personality characteristics can be assessed by specially designed tests. Accuracy, speed, perseverance, manual dexterity are some of the personality characteristics for which tests have been devised. If high scores on certain tests are obtained by students who later prove themselves to be successful and low scores are obtained by those who give up training or prove to be poor nurses, the tests are said to correlate highly with success or to have a high predictive value.

So far no tests have been found to predict satisfactorily success in nursing as distinct from success in examinations. Barbara Lewis and colleagues investigated this problem at the University of Manchester Institute of Science and Technology (Lewis, 1980, 1983). She suggested that her research had relevance for the development of future recruitment and selection procedures'.

More research is needed involving the use of 'test batteries', i.e. a large number of varied psychological tests. These will have to be used on large numbers of new recruits to nursing. Recruits must be in nursing long enough to make it possible to know which nurses are successful on the wards and in the school, which nurses are poor and fail to make the grade. The test battery results should then be statistically analysed.

By such methods, useful tests are sometimes found which, however, may not appear to have any obvious connection with the ultimate tasks. A test consisting almost bizarrely of holding one leg up a few inches above a chair was shown to have a high correlation with success in some jobs. It emerged that this test served to measure the characteristic of perseverance. Clearly it is difficult to imagine anyone predicting the validity of this test.

MINIATURE SITUATIONS

It is sometimes said that the only real way of knowing how suitable a person is for a job is to let her try it for a while. There are many reasons why this practice is not desirable in selecting student nurses. It is expensive, disrupts people's plans and is most distressing to those who are not successful. Instead it may be possible to devise miniature situations which resemble the real tasks a nurse may have to carry out. Her manual skill, speed, ingenuity might be tested by asking her to move or clear away some equipment. Her ability to work with others can be tested by giving a group of candidates a group project to carry out. This may reveal who assumes leadership, with how much authority they state their views, how easily they cooperate with others or how submissive they are.

Emotionality can be tested by giving conflicting instructions, criticizing performance, stressing the importance of failure. Some tests of this kind have been successfully used in the selection of officers in the Services. They have also been used in the selection for psychiatric nursing, particularly where participation in group therapy will be required. It is known that some nurses find it too stressful to speak openly about psychological problems in the presence of others. If a group discussion is included in the selection procedure, a foretaste of what will be required later may help a nurse and her potential employer to make the right decision about her suitability for the job.

QUESTIONNAIRES

This is by far the most common tool in personality measurement. Questionnaires are quick to apply. A great deal of information is rapidly available. The subject simply reads through the questions and puts the appropriate mark against each. Some questions require the answers 'yes' or 'no' and space is left for the expression of doubt. There are questionnaires in which the subject is required to underline statements with which he agrees, cross out those with which he disagrees, leaving blank those about which he feels doubt or indifference. Answers to questionnaires can be readily checked and scored objectively, rendering interpretation of responses by the tester superfluous.

Examples of questions used in personality inventories or questionnaires

Questions	Answers	
1. Are you inclined to keep quiet when out in a social group?	Yes	No
2. Are you more interested in athletics than in intellectual things?	Yes	No
3. Do you adapt yourself easily to new conditions?	Yes	No
4. Do you have frequent ups and downs in mood?	Yes	No
5. Do you usually take the initiative in making new friends?	Yes	No
6. Would you rate yourself as a lively person?	Yes	No
7. Do you prefer to work alone rather than with people?	Yes	No

Many people feel that reliance cannot easily be placed on the answers given in self-rating. The desire of the subject to put himself in the best possible light always influences the answers. More serious still is the fact that the same question may lead to very different interpretations. A personality inventory, for example, may ask, 'Do you feel diffident when you meet strangers?' As it is impossible to know how diffident other people feel and as everybody feels diffident at times, any one person

Examples of self-rating type of questionnaire

In your own opinion, which of the following words apply to you? Underline them and use two lines for emphasis. Put a cross, or two crosses, through any that do not apply. Leave the rest blank.

hardworking; businesslike; energetic; steady; lively; impulsive; easygoing; unobservant; aimless; untidy; ambitious; pushful; determined; serious; self-reliant; quiet; shy; hesitant; sensitive; moody; discontented; cheerful; self-confident; popular; a leader; tactful; critical; rebellious; solitary; worrying; humorous.

may quite honestly say 'yes', though he only rarely feels diffident; or answer 'no' because he does not always feel diffident. If questions are carefully worded and well selected, however, questionnaires can have a very high degree of validity. In fact it is not really necessary to examine the meaning of the answer at all. The value in questionnaires lies in comparing the answers many people give to the same questions. Some personality characteristics such as neuroticism, introversion and extraversion can be assessed with considerable success by the use of questionnaires.

From the answers people give to questions in personality inventories it is possible to draw a 'personality profile'. This shows to what extent various personality characteristics are present. Each characteristic could be plotted on a ten-point scale, for example, and a person's profile might look something like the one shown in Figure 3. Some personality inventories have been so extensively used that norms for the general population are now known and also the characteristic profiles for various subgroups within the general population. In order to use personality inventories in selection pro-

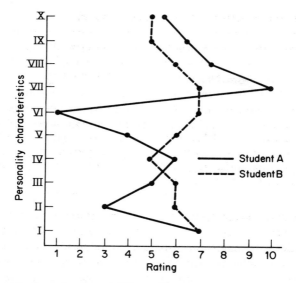

Figure 3. Example of personality profiles.

cedures it is necessary not only to compare personality profiles of nurses with other occupational groups, but also of successful and unsuccessful nurses, profiles of young nurses and older ones, of student nurses, staff nurses and ward sisters and of nurses who have specialized in some field of nursing, e.g. in psychiatric nursing, theatre nursing or intensive care work.

The following are some of the personality inventories which have been used in research in nursing but so far this has not led to any conclusive results.

The Eysenck Personality Inventory
This is a short questionnaire and measures two personality scales only—extraversion and neuroticism (Eysenck, 1970).

R.B. Cattell's 16 P.F. Test (Personal Factors)
This test measures 16 personality factors, including dominance and emotional stability (Cattell, 1965).

Minnesota Multiphasic Personality Inventory
This contains more than 400 self-descriptive statements and the subject is asked whether these statements are true or false if applied to himself. The scales on this test measure adjustment to family and to people of other races, and emotional stability as compared with groups of mentally ill people.

PROJECTIVE TESTS

These tests make use of people's tendencies and willingness to make up stories about things they see. When shown an ink blot, for example, people see butterflies, dancing girls, pictures of skeletons, or many other images. When a vague picture is shown depicting, for example, two people, a story can be invented about their relationship to each other, their difficulties and troubles. The stories people make up about pictures reveal something about their own personality; they project onto the picture feelings and thoughts of their own. The projective tests most commonly used are the *Rorschach Test* and the *Thematic Apperception Test*. In nursing, suitable pictures might be devised to test attitudes to patients, work or hospital.

INTELLIGENCE TESTS

There are large numbers of well-tried intelligence tests which can be employed to give an estimate of a person's intelligence. Some are particularly useful for children, others for adults, yet others for the elderly. Some tests can be administered in groups, others need to be given individually. Many of the tests are variations of the ones first developed by Binet at the beginning of the twentieth century. Some tests require the ability to read and speak the language in which the tests are conducted; others rely entirely on non-verbal material, e.g. shapes, patterns, colours and figures. The test items cover a very wide range of skills, for example, the British Ability Scales contains 24 tests. Many tests have been devised for children such as the Stanford–Binet, the Wechsler and, more recently, the British Ability Scales (Elliot *et al.*, 1977).

Since it is impossible to compare mental and chrono-logical age with each other in adults, comparison is simply made with other people who have carried out the test and the results are given in percentiles not as intel-ligence quotient. The 50th percentile means brighter than 49% but less bright than 50% of all people of the same age. The 95th percentile means brighter than 94 out of every 100 people.

Supposing any particular test has 60 items and each correct answer scores 1, the total score of any one subject could range from 0 to 60. In fact, of a random selection of people, more than half might score 25 to 35. On a graph the scores would be distributed as shown in Figure 4. This kind of distribution of scores is called a 'normal distribution' or a normal curve. The range of scores which includes roughly 68% of all subjects is termed the 'standard deviation from the mean'. The score which occurs most frequently is referred to as the 'mode'.

The normal distribution is frequently observed in the measurement of human characteristics. Height and weight are normally distributed. Examination results,

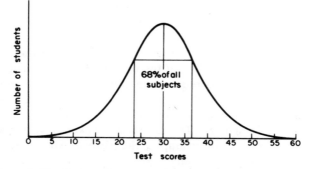

Figure 4. Distribution of scores in a test with 60 items.

too, tend to be normally distributed if the total number of candidates is large enough.

Weight of men or weight of women would each be normally distributed. If the scores of men and women are put together there is a 'bimodal' curve, i.e. there are two humps, as shown in Figure 5. Whenever a bimodal

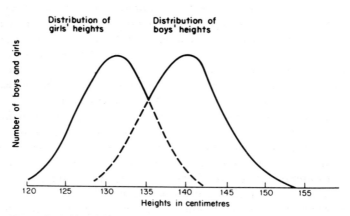

Figure 5. A bimodal curve.

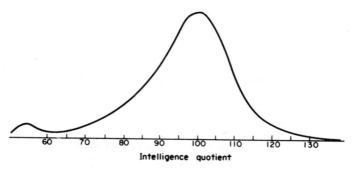

Figure 6. Intelligence score showing second mode.

distribution is discovered it means that two groups are involved rather than one: weights of boys and girls, or of Scandinavian and Chinese people, weights of walnuts and hazel nuts coming out of a bag of mixed nuts, all would show bimodal distribution.

Intelligence scores of the total population are, on the whole, normally distributed. This shows that there is a measurable characteristic common to human beings. There is no clear evidence of any difference between men and women or between people of different races. However Eysenck and Kamin offer differing views on the origins of 'intelligence'.

At the lower end of the scale, among the people whose score is low on IQ tests, there appears to be a second mode. This suggests an intellectual impairment for different reasons e.g. acquired brain damage. (Figure 6).

Tests are valid only for those people on whom they were standardized. Tests tried out on children only, for example, are not valid for adults. To devise a test which is widely applicable it is necessary to standardize the scores on groups of children, young people, old people, town and country people, representatives of every kind of trade and profession. Standardization means that the grading of the scores is based on a knowledge of how large numbers of people actually performed the test. A test standardized in England cannot be automatically applied, for example, in the United States of America.

Reliability and validity

A good test must be reliable and valid.

Reliability means that repeated administration will give the same result. This is like a thermometer which would be expected to show the same reading on successive occasions if circumstances had not altered.

Often with intelligence tests there is a very slight improvement after the first test; this is the result of becoming familiar with the situation and the type of information required. After the initial practice, however, no further improvement occurs if the test is reliable. For this reason some tests have a short practice test to precede them. Other tests are divided into two similar sections and one of each can be given on successive occasions.

Reliability merely means that the test score itself can be depended on. The test must, however, also be *valid*; that is, it must actually measure something real, beyond itself. It is possible to imagine a thermometer which is so reliable that it always reads 100°C; however, it would not be valid because it would take no notice of changing conditions outside itself. There is reason to believe that intelligence tests are valid, that there is some real quality which they measure although it is still difficult to discover the nature of intelligence.

Analysis of intelligence tests

Spearman (1927) attempted to analyse some of the tests in use. First, he tried to find out what kind of activities are involved in intelligent behaviour. Secondly he devised a method of comparing scores of various test items statistically by a method called factor analysis.

He decided that two main activities constitute intelligence:

1. The discovery of a relationship.
2. The discovery of which other things have relationships which are similar, thereby possibly discovering new facts.

For example:

Black is to white as Night is to . . .

The first task is to find the relationship between black and white. These are opposites. Next, find another word which has the relationship of opposite to night: the answer is *day*. This kind of activity might be called finding analogies, or forming first deductions, then inductions.

Examples of this process could be given from a wide variety of test items. For example: 1, 3, 5, 7 . . . next item 9. The relationship between these is a difference of 2; the next figure which has such a relationship to the previous figure is 9.

Another example:

Pot . . . Top   Dog . . .

These are related by reading backwards; the next word is *God*.

By means of mathematical calculations Spearman was led to assume that intelligence consists of a general factor, which he called 'g', and special factors called 's'. The higher the 'g' the better the performance on all types of tests and the greater the ability to learn.

The specific factors are shown by the fact that people do better in certain groups of tests than in others. For example, one person with a high general intelligence may do particularly well in all the tests involving numbers and less well in those involving words. There are special abilities of verbal facility, number sense, space, mechanical ability, musical ability, manual dexterity.

Different tests vary in the degree to which they measure 'g' and the type of 's' they are meant to measure. Usually it is wise to give a battery of tests which, between them, measure a wide variety of 's's. If only a single test is used it should, if possible, measure mainly 'g'.

Binet's test consists of such a wide variety of items that most 's' qualities are probably covered. Raven asserts that the 'g' factor in his 'Matrices' is very high. This is a test consisting of patterns and designs which are related to each other in special ways. No verbal ability is needed for this test. Raven's Progressive Matrices have been used quite extensively in student nurse selection.

On the whole, people who have a high general intelligence do better in whatever they choose to do than people with low general intelligence. It is a fallacy to believe that people who are good at Latin, for example, must be bad at sewing. They may have more special verbal ability than manual ability; but even so, the high general intelligence will allow better performance at sewing than will be evinced by a low general intelligence with relatively high manual dexterity. In fact, however high the special ability, a low general intelligence only allows low level performance. Naturally, interest and encouragement may lead the less intelligent person to develop his skills; discouragement and lack of interest may lead the more intelligent to neglect them. But, however unfair it may seem, it is none the less true that high intelligence makes it possible to perform well all round.

There are some people, whose scores on intelligence tests are not particularly high, but who are capable of outstanding, original contributions in their sphere of interest. There are others, whose intelligence, as measured on some tests, is very high, but who perform badly on certain test items because they give solutions which are unconventional, unorthodox and not allowed for in the standardized scoring. The term 'creative intelligence' is used to describe the ability to think along original lines rather than in a manner which is convergent with the thinking of others. It is therefore possible for a person of average intelligence to obtain a very much higher score when his creative ability is measured.

Most tests of intelligence tended to contain 'closed items'. That is, a set of predetermined answers were given from among which the correct answer was chosen. This demands convergent thinking. So 'open' tests were constructed to tap divergent or creative thinking. A number of tests are now commonly used, e.g. 'Uses of Objects' and 'Word Association' tests, to attempt to measure creativity.

In the performance of any one task there are usually more than two factors operating. Some are group factors acting over and above the specific factors. Speed, fluency, verbal facility, for example, affect any specific ability which may be shown in a test.

Conduct of intelligence tests

Intelligence tests should always be administered under carefully controlled conditions. The candidate should be comfortable; instructions should be given exactly as prescribed and timing strictly adhered to.

Tests start with easy items and gradually become more difficult. Later items often follow logically from earlier ones. The subject who works systematically through a test can often solve problems which, taken out of context, may appear excessively difficult. Tests should range beyond the ability of the subjects to be tested. The candidate is therefore often told before he begins that he may not be able to complete the test in the time allowed.

Though in all intelligence tests the aim is to exclude items which rely for their solution on previous education or experience, this is very difficult to achieve. All those tests, for example, for which printed instructions are given, depend on the ability to read. Language comprehension is taken for granted in most tests. How difficult a particular question is to the subject who tries to answer it inevitably depends on the experience that subject has had.

The search for 'culture-free' tests, i.e. tests which do not depend on prior educational and social experience, has so far not been very successful. Even performance tests in which no printed language is used have proved to be culture bound, because even the understanding of diagrams and patterns depends on previous learning.

It has been thought that intelligence declines with advancing years—from early adulthood very slowly, after middle age slightly more rapidly. This decline is, however, very gradual and not noticeable except on testing (Figure 7). However more recent evidence suggests that intellectual potential is stable throughout adulthood until the sixth or seventh decade. If there is age-related decline, it is manifested mainly with very difficult tasks demanding maximum performance (Baltes *et al.*, 1979). A rapid decline in intelligence occurs only

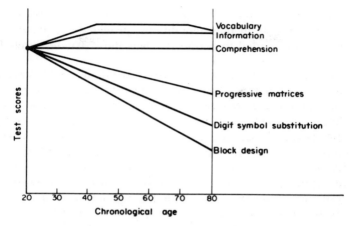

Figure 7. Performance in certain subjects slowly deteriorated between the ages of 20 and 80.

when the brain is damaged, by such things as tumours, injury, drugs, toxins, chronic infections, alcohol, or the effects of vascular disturbances.

In severe cerebral deterioration a decline in intelligence is noticeable. The altered behaviour and interaction which occur are described as dementia. One of the characteristics of dementia is the decline in those abilities which involve judgement, discrimination and remembering instructions. Intelligence tests can be used to exclude mental handicap or dementia before a diagnosis is made of some other illness. In some mental disorders the patient's behaviour may be so disordered that dementia is suspected. In schizophrenia, for example, the patient's logic is all his own and other people find it difficult to follow his reasoning. His actions may appear to lack meaning and not to be based on ordinary good judgement. In depression the patient may be inactive, uninterested, apparently lacking understanding. Yet intelligence tests in these conditions, provided the patient can be persuaded to cooperate, will show that his intelligence is in no way impaired.

Intelligence tests often help to diagnose mental handicap as distinct from emotional disturbances, especially in children. Mental handicap should be diagnosed as early as possible in order to begin special training early. Intelligence tests could also be used when children's disturbed behaviour at school is not fully understood. Children of low intelligence may respond to the pressure of school and their parents' ambition with resentment, rebelliousness, or complete discouragement and apathy. In the education and training of mentally handicapped children it is particularly important, not only to assess the overall level of intelligence, but also to investigate specific areas of relatively high and low achievement.

There is some danger that those concerned with the upbringing of mentally handicapped children may be satisfied with too low a level of achievement, assuming that low intelligence prevents the child from making further progress. Many children are unnecessarily handicapped because of the low expectation people have of them and they fail to achieve their potential.

Children with very high intelligence may find the work too boring, cease to pay attention and then begin to do badly at school. It is always of interest to find out why children, or even some grown-up students, fail in their studies in spite of high intelligence. This may be due to emotional trouble which interferes with learning. In child guidance, student selection and occupational guidance it is important to assess how effectively the individual uses his intelligence or whether other factors impede performance.

Analogies
Underline the correct answer.

Up is to *down* as *high* is to . . .	Book, Sky, Low
Fire is to *hot* as *ice* is to . . .	Water, Solid, Cold
Cause is to *effect* as *disease* is to . . .	Reason, Death, Life
The day before yesterday is to *the day after tomorrow* as *Saturday* is to . . .	Sunday, Monday, Wednesday

Opposites
Where the words mean the same or nearly the same underline *same*, where they mean the opposite or nearly the opposite underline *opposite*.

Dry . . . Wet	Same, Opposite
Dirty . . . . Unclean	Same, Opposite
Haughty . . . Arrogant	Same, Opposite
Relinquish . . . Cede	Same, Opposite
Munificent . . . Parsimonious	Same, Opposite

Reasoning
(a) Find the two letters or numbers which continue the series.

30, 50, 70, 90, ...
Z, A, Y, B, ...
¼, ½, ¾, 1, ...

(b) Underline the two words which do not belong to the same category as the rest.

Hat, Boot, Head, Shoe, Glove, Hand, Dress, Stocking.
Apple, Plum, Rose, Orange, Apricot, Cabbage, Cherry.

Digit symbol substitution

1	2	3	4
	1°	C	+

2	1	4	3	2	4	1	3

Figure 8. Some examples from intelligence tests.

References

Argyle, M. (1973) *Social Interaction*. London: Tavistock.

Argyle, M. (1975) *Bodily Communication*. London: Methuen.

Baltes, P.B., Brinn, D.G. & Thomie, H. (1979) Concept of Development and Life Span Developmental Psychology. In Baltes P.B. & Brim O.G. Jr. (eds) *Life Span Development and Behaviour*, Vol. 2, pp. 282–312. New York: Academic Press.

Cattell, R.B. (1965) *The Scientific Analysis of Personality* Harmondsworth: Penguin.

Elliot, C.D., Murray, D.J. & Pearson, L.S. (1977) *The British Ability Scales*. Windsor: NFER.

Eysenck, H.J. (1970) *The Structure of Human Personality*, 3rd edition. London: Methuen.

Eysenck, H.J. & Kamin, L. (1981) *Intelligence: The Battle for the Mind*. London: Pan.

Lewis, B.R. (1980) Personality profiles for qualified nurses: possible implications for recruitment and selection of trainee nurses. *International Journal of Nursing Studies* **17**, 221–234.

Lewis, B.R. (1983) Personality and intellectual characteristics of trainee nurses and their assessment. In Davis, B.D. (ed.) *Research into Nurse Education*. London: Croom Helm.

Roger, A. (1974) Seven-Point Plan. London: NFER.

Spearman, C. (1927) *The Abilities of Man: Their Nature and Measurement*. London: Macmillan.

Further reading

Anastasi, A. (1990) *Psychological Testing*, 6th edition. New York: Maxwell Macmillan.

Sternberg, R.J. (1985) *Beyond IQ: A Triarchic Theory of Human Intelligence*. New York: Cambridge University Press.

7 Development in infancy and early childhood

THE CONCEPT OF DEVELOPMENT

There are two overlapping terms which are often used interchangeably—namely growth and development—which frequently give rise to much confusion and ambiguity. *Development* is the more inclusive term, and behavioural change is usually referred to as developmental when it follows a sequence related to age. *Growth* refers to an increase in amount of a certain characteristic, and is most easily applied to physical characteristics, e.g. height. It is less easily applied to behaviour, although one may perhaps speak of intellectual growth when, for example, a person can solve more problems of the same type as those which were being solved earlier.

Approaches to studying development

There are many ways of approaching the study of child development. Some observers have made specific contributions to our knowledge of physical, especially neuromuscular, development; others have paid attention to intellectual development. Some psychologists have taken a special interest in the study of emotional development and personality. Earlier studies of emotional and social development tended to rely on information gained from older children or adults reminiscing about their childhood experiences. Currently, psychologists study development by directly observing children's behaviour in its normal setting or under experimentally controlled conditions. More and more sophisticated techniques are now available which allow more detailed observation of the behaviour of children. Thus, the field of child development, especially in the past three decades, has become a prestige area for researchers to work in, and a great deal of activity is taking place, with the literature on the subject proliferating.

Similarly, in nursing, before the 1960s, little emphasis was placed on child development in the curriculum. Since then however, the importance of learning about human development has been recognized. In attempting to build up good patient–nurse relationships, the nurse may benefit from understanding her own behaviour as well as her patient's. However, a person does not behave or act in a vacuum. One is affected by, and makes one's mark on, a world of objects and people, and it is to the world of the child which we will first turn.

The family

In order to examine child development, we must look at the arena in which it takes place. Most commonly, children develop and grow within the family setting. Thus, we are concerned with the child's world of people: of mother, father, brothers, sisters, grandparents, other relations and friends or even enemies. The objects with which the child is involved are everyday objects: household objects, toys, books and objects in the out-of-door setting.

Family life in Britain, however, is not a static entity. Indeed, the pattern of family life is changing in many ways. Geographical and occupational mobility frequently means that young families move into areas where they do not know anyone. Separated from relations and former neighbours, young parents feel isolated and have no one they know sufficiently well to turn to for advice in times of family crises.

Divorce is now being resorted to more frequently and, since marriage is still popular, some households may contain the children of two families. There is also an increase in the number of single-parent families.

In examining child development we generally think of the child growing up in a world of stable relationships and of material sufficiency, where there is enough food, clothes, toys, books and outings available to him. But what about the child who lacks some, or all, of these things, in other words who is deprived? Developmental psychologists are very much interested in this question and examine situations where children are most vulnerable to the effects of the environment. It has been suggested that, for example, chronic illness in parents, family disharmony or discord, multiple mothering, e.g. in residential nurseries, and lengthy-hospitalization can lead to long-term harmful effects for the child. It has been found that there is a strong association between divorce or separation of the parents and delinquent behaviour of the children. However, is it the divorce or separation *per se*, or the tension at home preceding the divorce or separation which results in the delinquent behaviour? It seems from studies (see Rutter, 1981) that it is more likely to be the latter—the child being vulnerable during periods of family stress. Similarly, it should be noted that children are just as vulnerable when their parents are ill as they would be if they were ill themselves.

INFANCY

The period of child development discussed in this section is from birth to around the child's second birthday.

Although various aspects of development have been separated to allow discussion, it should be remembered that they are highly interdependent.

Perceptual development

Perception refers to any process by which immediate awareness of what is happening in the environment is obtained. Information is gained about things which directly impinge on the senses. The world is perceived by seeing, hearing, touching, smelling and tasting. Other resources which are used by the older child and the adult when perceiving are memory and knowledge, and these resources can, in turn, direct the use of the senses. The newly born baby, however, does not have such resources and this means that babies cannot use the perceptual system in the way adults can. The child uses the senses to learn about the world: what his mother looks like, or what different foods taste like, etc. But he is limited in many ways. For example, he cannot move around to look at things as he lacks the ability to walk.

As a starting point when examining perceptual development, it is important to know what a baby's capacity to perceive is. For many years psychologists thought that a baby at birth perceived a world which was meaningless and tended to describe it as a flickering world filled with shadows. Recent studies have shown that a baby has more ability than was at first thought.

If the newly born infant is examined, a number of reflex actions can be elicited. When the finger, for instance, is placed into the palm of the baby's hand, the hand closes in a grasping movement. It is so firm that the force of the child's whole weight would not loosen the grasp. If the cheek is touched, the baby turns his head toward the stimulus; this response is known as the rooting reflex and

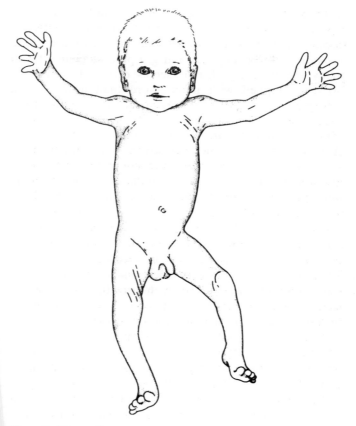

Figure 9. Moro reflex.

enables the baby to find the nipple of the breast. The Moro reflex can be elicited in response to a sudden loud noise or by suddenly withdrawing support. The child will momentarily extend his usually flexed limbs and may cry (Figure 9). A walking response can be elicited if the baby is supported, in order to be upright, and has his feet placed on a flat surface. These responses normally disappear in the first few months of the baby's life. True walking and reaching out and grasping of course begin many months later. But it seems certain that a baby arrives equipped with much more than a few reflex actions.

Hearing or auditory perception

As adults, we use some cues which enable us to locate sound accurately. Sounds which are directly ahead arrive at both ears at the same time. Displaced sounds arrive at different times. For example, sounds coming from our left side will arrive at the left ear before the right ear. Similarly, the sound will be louder in the left ear than in the right ear. However, the distance between the ears of a baby is smaller than the distance between the ears of an adult, as the head is much smaller and indeed its size increases continuously with growth. Some of the difficulties in testing the ability of very young babies to locate sound might be understood if it is considered that, in order to demonstrate hearing ability, one must use other abilities, e.g. turning round, pointing and so on, and some of these abilities the young baby just does not possess or they are poorly developed. This makes testing difficult. What has emerged from studies, however, is that young babies can locate sound, but not accurately (Bower, 1977a).

Tucker (1982) describes how it is now possible to test the hearing of very young babies. However, the technique is not yet generally available and testing still relies on fairly crude measures, e.g. at about 6 weeks the child will still to a bell or mother's voice and turn his eyes to the sound source, and will look round when spoken to (Barber *et al.*, 1976).

Seeing or visual perception

We see a three-dimensional world from a two-dimensional retinal image. Psychologists have argued that the world seen by a newly born baby is flat, like a two-dimensional image. Since depth is the third dimension, how then do adults perceive depth? There are a number of visual cues which are used. Because we have two eyes which converge to focus on an object, we get information from the convergence. For example, as a finger approaches the face in a straight line the eyes converge, so the nearer the finger is to the face the greater the convergence angle. Convergence angle, therefore, declines with distance. Similarly, because the two eyes are side by side they each get a slightly different view of the world. When moving objects are seen, when looking ahead, the object nearer to the person seems to move faster than the object further away in the distance. Finally, as objects move nearer the observer, the image of them on the retina expands correspondingly. The same thing happens if the observer moves towards an object—there is retinal expansion. Additionally, there is information available from secondary cues, such as those used by artists, to indicate the relative positions of objects in depth.

It is known that young babies can focus on an object about 20–25 cm (8–10 inches) in front of their faces. Recent studies have indicated how difficult it is to test the young baby's ability to perceive distance. Numerous behavioural indicators have been used in experimental conditions. One famous study required that the child was able to crawl (Gibson and Walk, 1960). The child was placed on a glass-topped table. On one half of the table a piece of check-patterned linoleum was fixed just underneath the glass, and, under the other half, the linoleum was 1 m (3.5 feet) below the surface of the glass. A visual cliff was therefore created at the midpoint. The child who could crawl refused to move on to the part of the glass with the linoleum 1 m below it, demonstrating that children of crawling age (7 months to 1 year) could perceive depth. Other studies with babies only a few weeks old have used behavioural responses such as the eye blink. Defensive behaviour composed of three components—eye widening, head retraction and hands brought up to the face—was used in a number of experiments, and seems to indicate that 1-week-old babies do indeed perceive depth (Bower, 1977b).

Touching, tasting and smelling
The newly born infant does seem to know what part of his skin is being touched. He can be seen to rub his nose with his hand in order to get rid of an irritant or attempt to withdraw from a painful stimulus, for example an injection. Not much is known about the sense of taste in the young baby, except that he seems to prefer sweet things. Similarly, the sense of smell in the young baby is thought to be present. The child responds to noxious odours, although he quickly becomes habituated to the smell and then fails to respond. One interesting study demonstrated that very young babies had a preference for the smell of their own mother's breast-milk-soaked pad over one belonging to another mother (MacFarlane, 1977).

Perceiving people
Until now the discussion has been about the baby in a world of objects, but of course the child lives in a social world. As mentioned earlier, many young babies can focus on objects about 20–25 cm in front of the face. Probably, the 'object' most frequently appearing at this distance is the mother's face. When the baby is alert he is actively visually searching the environment. Most

fascinating of all to him appears to be features of the human face, the eyes being the most important of all. Also, this same sensory selectiveness seems present when the sense of hearing is considered. A study has shown that babies between 3 and 8 days of age are particularly responsive to human speech (Condon and Sander, 1974).

Learning to perceive

If the child has to learn to use his sensory apparatus, he must be provided with things to see, hear, touch, taste and smell. How important the sight and sound and touch of human beings are to the child has already been mentioned, and will be discussed more fully later. A baby lying in a cot in a visually impoverished environment has little chance of learning to use sight. On the other hand, passively providing a large number of brightly coloured objects, or having the radio playing loudly all day, will do little to help the child, and indeed sudden over-stimulation can be harmful. The child must actively use his senses in order to learn. Even in the first months after birth, the infant follows a moving object with his gaze and sometimes, before he is able to grasp the object, he reaches out and is able to turn his head to follow the object until it has gone out of his field of vision.

At about 6 months of age the child is able to pick up bricks, spoons or any other object within his reach and very soon he learns more about their size and texture by putting them into his mouth, and by touch. By banging the objects he uses his hearing to learn about the noises they make. He learns to use his sense of taste as different foods are introduced into the diet, but it should be remembered that the young child does not know that some nasty-tasting substances, e.g. bleach, can be harmful.

The use of the sense of smell can be encouraged by getting the child to sniff various odours, e.g. flowers.

It is necessary for his development that he should be allowed to explore, not only with his eyes, but by finding out what he can reach, how much effort is required and all the possible uses to which things can be put. Even adults really know about objects only when they have used them in various ways. The need to find out how things can be used is ever present. The young child's need to handle everything he sees, to bang and throw, to suck and bite, to listen to various noises, should be satisfied in a safe environment if he is to learn and become a lively, inquisitive child.

Motor development

The study of the child's ability to use his muscles in his environment seems to be a much less daunting prospect compared to the study of perceptual development. The motor behaviour of the child can be easily observed and, therefore, fewer inferences need be made. Many studies have been undertaken in order to make systematic surveys of children's behaviour at various ages. Muscle activity has been observed in detail, and development from generalized movement of the body as a whole to the detailed movement of finger and thumb has been listed, described and photographed. Development of eye movements and of posture have all been studied. Similarly, eating habits, sleep and elimination have come under scrutiny. Some of these studies were carried out by Gesell, at the Clinic of Child Development, Yale University (see Table 1).

When hundreds of babies have been observed it is possible to state at what precise age 50% of the babies have mastered any particular skill. The age is then taken to be the norm for the particular activity. It is an average figure obtained by taking into account the slowest and

Table 1. Norms for development (described by Arnold Gesell).

16 weeks:	Eyes focus on mother or dangling toy
	Turns head on hearing noise
28 weeks:	Sits alone
	Reaches out for toy
	Grasps with palm of hand
	Begins to articulate sounds
40 weeks:	Can grasp toy between fingers and thumb
	Pulls himself up and stands holding furniture
	Imitates syllables
52 weeks:	Creeps about freely
15 months:	Begins to walk
	Speaks a few words—da, no
18 months:	Bladder control almost established during the day

the most rapidly developing children. No parent should worry because his child's performance is below or above the average. Variations within normal limits are great. It is only when a child differs so greatly from the norm that some help is obviously required that the nurse should draw attention to it. More frequently the nurse may have to explain to parents that norms, or milestones, are merely rough guides, not absolute standards of perfection (Table 1). The speed at which motor skills are achieved does not predict the rate of development of intellectual skills.

Parents may indicate their sense of responsibility for the child's progress by asking many questions about development. They may, for instance, wish to know how much of a child's future is determined by heredity and how much by the environment they will be able to provide. They may also wish to know how actively they should help their child to learn and how much of the child's development is simply due to maturation rather than to learning.

All these are difficult questions to answer and the

nurse's greatest contribution may lie in encouraging
parents to express their fears and beliefs rather than in
making authoritative statements.

Human beings, unlike most animals, take many years
to reach adulthood. During these years the body develops
and changes take place in behaviour, both these following a characteristic sequence. The rate of development is
partially determined by heredity; partly, however, it is
affected by the extent to which the child's needs are met
at each stage of development.

At each stage of development the child is able to learn
a variety of skills. His actual achievements then depend
on the cultural influences which have been brought to
bear on him at the appropriate stage of development. On
the whole, it is useless to attempt to teach any particular
motor skill before the appropriate stage of development
is reached. Recent research has shown that early stimulation and teaching can have remote beneficial effects, but
premature training can be wasteful and even harmful if it
results in frustration and reduced motivation to learn.
The child cannot be taught to walk before he has reached
the appropriate stage of maturity. When he is able to
learn, progress, or fine tuning, depends on the amount of
interest taken by his parents.

Cognitive development

When watching children at play, parents or other observers frequently comment that they would love to know
what is going on in the child's mind. Before the child is
able to speak he is unable to convey his experiences, and
knowledge about his thinking must rest on inference. It is
only relatively recently that inferences about cognitive
development have been based on direct observation of
young children.

Intelligence testing and learning
Psychologists using a quantitative approach are likely to ask such questions as 'How much intellectual ability does a particular child have compared with other children of his age?' In order to attempt to measure these abilities a number of tests have been devised. However, much controversy surrounds the question of whether or not infant intelligence tests are useful. The evidence seems to indicate that infant tests are not accurate, nor do they predict future performance in intelligence tests. Such things as imitating, ability to fit blocks into matching shapes, to build block towers, and point to parts of the body, are tested. The young child's lack of verbal skills is probably the greatest difficulty, but it is also very difficult to gain his cooperation.

The qualitative approach to cognitive development
This approach to the study of cognitive development includes the development of cognitive processes and the accumulation of intellectual content. Cognitive processes comprise such functions as perception, thinking, reasoning and language development. Intellectual content, on the other hand, is the result of these processes, in other words it is the knowledge content of the child's mind. In the qualitative approach the emphasis is on examining the different levels of understanding children are capable of at different ages. Understanding involves firstly codified knowledge or concepts, and secondly it involves ways of thought, or, as they are sometimes referred to, rules of thought. The child is not just a miniature adult. His way of thinking is determined by his concepts, and his level of understanding. Development involves advancement of understanding.

Our present day understanding of intellectual development in children is largely due to the massive amount of work, produced over many years, by the famous Swiss psychologist, Jean Piaget. His studies have become classics in the literature of child development and have been the stimulus to much research since the 1960s. Piaget describes intellectual development in terms of stages which are invariant, i.e. the child cannot reach stage 2 before stage 1 is attained. However, there is considerable flexibility in the ages at which the children reach the stages. He identifies the various stages according to the level of thought. Four major periods of development are described.

1. Sensory motor period—birth to about 18 months to 2 years.
2. Preoperational period—2 years to 7 years.
3. Concrete operational period—7 years to 11 years.
4. Formal operational period—11+ years.

In this section we are concerned with the first period of development. During the first stage of the sensory motor period, which lasts from birth to about 2 months of age, the child is primarily modifying some reflex actions. If the sucking reflex is taken as an example, then modification would include the adjustments made by the baby when he is 'fitting' his mouth to the shape and size of the nipple or teat. Piaget refers to such adjustment as *accommodation*, i.e. the effort the child makes to fit his behaviour to the environment. With practice, the child distinguishes which things in the environment are suckable and will suck vigorously at a nipple or teat which gives milk but reject something which does not when he is hungry. Dealing with the environment by making it fit with one's own existing mental structures, Piaget refers to as *assimilation*. Accommodation and assimilation are described as the invariant intellectual functions by which an individual interacts with the environment at various levels of development.

From about 2 to 4 months of age the child begins to combine his modified reflex actions in various ways. For example, if by chance the child puts his fingers into his mouth, he sucks and finds it pleasurable. If the fingers drop out of the mouth, the child will attempt to put them back again, suck and gain pleasure, and so on. This behaviour Piaget refers to as *primary circular reactions*. The sequence of behaviour involves combining and coordinating sucking behaviour with finger moving behaviour. Although this is an advance over the first stage, the child is not aware of the fingers as, for example, parts of the body, but only as suckable objects.

During the third stage of the sensory motor period, from about 4 to 8 months of age, the beginning of intentional action is observed. It is during this stage that the child begins to expand his world to include objects in the environment and the child manifests what Piaget calls *secondary circular reactions*. For example, if the child lying in his cot accidentally kicks a suspended toy, it moves and the movement gives pleasure, so the child kicks the object again and so on. Here the child's kicking activities and his watching activities are brought to bear on an object in the environment in a highly selective and directed manner.

In the few months before the child's first birthday (Piaget's fourth stage) the behaviour again changes. Here, intention precedes action and this is seen when the child will try to remove barriers in order to get at or expose a favoured object, e.g. a toy hidden beneath a cushion. This degree of coordination is also noticeable when the child begins to imitate actions performed by an adult, e.g. waving goodbye.

Following the child's first birthday, he begins to show

evidence of seeking out and creating novelty rather than just repeating actions discovered by accident. The child actively explores his environment of objects to discover their features and properties. It is during this time that the child discovers the 'joy of being the cause'. Thus he begins to grasp some concept of cause and effect. Observable during this period are what Piaget refers to as *tertiary circular reactions*. Here the child will demonstrate such behaviour as dropping things, for example over the side of his pram. When the behaviour is examined in more detail it will be seen to include grasping, moving arm, letting go, watching and listening (for noise when object hits the floor). When the object is retrieved the child repeats the behaviour, but also varies the sequence by using different objects, varying the height of dropping and so on. The child thus begins to understand that he can manipulate and control parts of the environment by his own actions.

The sixth stage Piaget suggests marks the beginnings of thought and children of this age, 15 months to 2 years, can perform certain mental experiments. The child begins to work out actions in his head before trying them out in reality, and for Piaget this can be performed without the use of language. Thus Piagetian theory argues that thought develops before language. However, the child's thinking at this age is very limited and is tied very much to the present.

Concepts of the sensory motor period
If our knowledge of the world is examined, it can be understood in terms of certain concepts, e.g. concepts of objects, space, causality and time. During the sensory motor period, the child develops the concept of object permanency. This involves the idea that an object still exists when it is out of sight. Thus, if the child's reactions

to the disappearance of objects are examined, the development of object permanency can be seen.

During the first two months of life there seems to be no particular response to an object which disappears. Between 2 and 4 months of age the child will track or follow an object with his eyes, gaze at the place where the object disappears but will make no attempt to search for it. Similarly, between 4 and 6 months of age, if a child is interested in a toy and the toy is partially covered by a cloth, he will attempt to reach out to get the toy, but makes no attempt when the toy is completely covered, i.e. out of sight, out of mind. At about 7 months of age the child will manage to retrieve a hidden object. However, children under 18 months of age still make

Figure 10. The child still searches under cloth A for the hidden toy moved under cloth B—stage 4 of Piaget's object concept has not yet been achieved.

mistakes in finding the hidden object or toy. Thus, if two cloths are used and a toy is hidden under cloth A, the child will retrieve it. If, however, the toy is first hidden under cloth A and then moved and hidden under cloth B, the child will still attempt to find the object under the original cloth, A, despite the fact that the displacement of the object was clearly visible to the child and indeed the outline of the toy under the cloth clearly visible to the observer (Figure 10). By the age of 1 year to 15 months, the child will be able to retrieve the toy from under either cloth, but cannot cope with invisible displacements of the object until about 18 months of age, when the child can find the object no matter where or how it is hidden.

Very young babies seem to have difficulty in understanding relationships in space between one object and another. They have difficulty with relationships such as 'on', 'in', 'in front' and 'behind', and it is not until about 18 months old that they demonstrate understanding of these concepts.

Social and emotional development

When discussing social and emotional development there are numerous aspects which will be highlighted. The human baby is born into a world of people, of social relationships. Social behaviour is, therefore, all important, as are the mechanisms involved in its development. Social interaction patterns are currently receiving much attention by psychologists.

To begin at birth, the assumption is made that the newly born baby is socially incompetent. However, this does not mean that the baby has no potential or capacity at birth to become social. What then is the capacity which will allow the child to develop social skills? It

appears that there is already a built-in behavioural repertoire, e.g. in the newly born baby's crying he possesses a
powerful signalling system through which he exerts an
effect on the people around him.

Crying

A newly born baby will cry in a number of different
situations. Sudden loud noises or sudden withdrawal of
support may elicit crying. When the child has not been
fed, not had his nappy changed for a number of hours, or
is pricked by a pin, an adult may say that the child is
hungry, in discomfort or in pain. These latter statements
are, strictly speaking, unjustified. It is not really possible
to know what a baby experiences. Hunger, discomfort
and pain are states of conscious experience which generally are communicated to others in words. Babies cannot
speak. Their only method of communication at this stage
is crying. In everyday language it is, of course, quite
acceptable to attribute to the baby feelings which are
believed to be experienced when we are short of food,
wet or cold, or pricked by a pin. In psychological language,
however, it is important to distinguish clearly between
behaviour which can be observed and the inferences or
interpretation of that behaviour, which may be wrong.
Nurses have to do this frequently. For example, when
the nurse hears a baby producing a very high-pitched cry
it reasonably could be inferred that the baby has some
degree of cerebral irritation. Thus, we observe behaviour
and make tentative guesses, not only with babies but
with any patient who is unable to speak: such as the
unconscious patient, or the patient who has lost his speech
due to cerebral haemorrhage or laryngeal damage, or the
patient suffering from depression or schizophrenia, who
will not speak.

Is there then, anything distinguishable about the baby's

cry which may allow us to differentiate between a hunger cry, a pain cry, or a frustration cry? One study (Wasz-Höckert *et al.*, 1968) looked at this question and used tape recordings of what were categorized as (a) the birth cry, (b) the pain cry, and (c) the hunger cry (the cry produced at birth, the cry produced when the child was pricked sharply, and the cry produced when the child had not been fed for 4 hours). When the tape recordings were played back to listeners, the cries were identified repeatedly with great accuracy by mid-wives, children's nurses and parents. Spectographic analysis of the types of cry revealed that these cry signals could be identified.

Nevertheless, it is misleading to suggest from this work that babies are born with a number of clearly-defined, recognizable cry signals. Thus, parents have to decide why the baby is crying on the basis of other information. Indeed, on many occasions parents are at a loss to explain crying, especially persistent crying in the evening. But, if crying happens after the child is fed, parents often attribute it to 'wind'.

Yet, crying, more than any activity in early life, brings the parents or nurse to the child's side and he will receive attention. This attention may vary from feeding, or nappy changing, to being picked up, cuddled or spoken to, all of which tend to quieten the baby. During the child's first year, the amount of crying gradually reduces and it is used increasingly to convey meaning, being directed at specific people nearby in order to produce a social response.

Smiling and babbling

The development of smiling is extremely important. It is a very powerful signal produced by babies which generally guarantees social attention for the child. A smile can be produced by a baby anytime after birth, but the earliest

smiling seems to convey little in the way of social awareness. It is at about 4 to 6 weeks of age that the baby's
smiling changes dramatically. The smile broadens and
the eyes light up. Mothers often describe feelings of
pleasure at the sight of their smiling child. The smile is
immediately rewarding to the parents.

Babies of about this age, as has been suggested earlier,
appear to show some preference for human faces, especially the eyes. But it seems that the child's smiling at
this stage is unselective. He will smile as readily at the
faces of strangers as at the faces of members of his
family. At about 6 months of age, however, the child will
become more selective and smile more readily at familiar
faces than strangers' faces.

As the smile becomes more warmly expressive babies
begin to coo and gurgle to the sound of voices and the
sight of the human face. When the baby smiles and gurgles
the mother responds by smiling and making some vocal
reaction. As she pauses, the baby responds once again
and a whole sequence of social interaction or 'conversation' takes place. Schaffer (1977) points to the importance
of the establishment of interpersonal synchrony as a
primary task of early development. This development
of 'phasing' or 'fitting in of behaviours' between the
baby and the mother is largely dependent on the kind
of opportunities which the mother provides for social
interaction. Sensitivity of the mother to the child's state
of arousal is also highly significant, for the same stimulation can elicit smiling and gurgling when the baby is in an
alert state, but when in another state he is likely to
respond by crying. Thus, a baby's response is not only
determined by the adult but also by the baby himself.

As the child develops over the first year of life, the
coos and gurgles gradually give way to distinct sounds of
consonants and vowels and, by about 6 months of age,

the child will repeat his own accidental sounds, e.g. ga, ga, ga. At about 9 to 10 months of age the child will be heard to repeat or imitate sounds he has heard others make.

Stimulation

The available evidence indicates that children need social stimulation in order to develop social responsiveness. But the word stimulation is too broad a concept and must be examined in more detail. It should be evident from the above discussion that, for example, *timing* is important. Giving the child time to respond to stimulation is crucial. Similarly, it would seem that the *quality* of stimulation the child receives, rather than the amount, is an important factor. It is not general, constant, background noise the child needs, but rather a form of stimulation which is directed towards, and is meant for, the child in particular. The *regularity* and *variety* of stimulation are also important. Not only is all this crucial for the development of social relations, but it is also important for cognitive development. Expressive behaviour is thus fostered when parents stimulate their baby and respond promptly and lovingly to his signals. Stern (1977) has shown that mothers vary in their ability to establish a social dialogue with their child. It requires the mother to accommodate to the child's rhythm of behaviour—to 'fit in' in a mutually satisfying way leading to synchrony.

Attachment

When one examines the behaviour of the mother and the child shortly after birth, one perplexing question often arises. Is there a special relationship between the baby and his mother (known as bonding or attachment) which is crucial for both? One approach to looking at this question is to look at the effects of separation of the baby from his parents at birth, e.g. the necessity to put the child into a special care nursery for medical reasons. Klaus and Kennell (1982) claim that the first 24 hours are crucial to the bonding process and argue for the importance of early close contact between mother and baby to the fostering of bonding. This work has prompted much attention in maternity hospitals to the environment, and making opportunities for close physical contact between parents and their infants. Where separation is unavoidable, e.g. when the baby is very small or ill and requires admission to a special care nursery, visiting by parents and the touching or handling of their baby are encouraged.

On the other hand, the evidence seems to indicate that babies do not form *special* attachments to familiar people in their world until after 6 months of age and the process of developing bonds extends over a period of many months. Thus parents who adopt children need not fear that their relatively late arrival in the life of a baby will be detrimental to the bonding process.

There seems to be a variety of factors which contribute to the development of special attachments. Babies display attachment to people by seeking to be close to them, by striving to gain attention and approval, and by becoming distressed when separated from them. Bowlby (1969) emphasizes the importance of certain responses in children, such as sucking, clinging, following, crying and smiling, in the formation of attachments, since they attract attention and bring people close. Schaffer (1977) places the emphasis on the baby's initial attraction to people rather than objects, followed by his learning to distinguish between different people, and finally his ability to form lasting, emotional attachments to specific individuals, and his rejection of other, strange individuals. What seems to be crucial here for prompting attachment is the social attentiveness of the parents, rather than their physical care.

Another question which frequently arises when attachment is considered is whether attachment has to be to one person or if it is possible for the child to form multiple attachments. Studies indicate that babies seem to focus their attachment on one person at first, usually the mother. But this first attachment is quickly followed by other attachments, e.g. to father, siblings, grandparents. At about 18 months of age most children have formed multiple attachments. However, it is important to recognize that the infant is an active participant, and Dunn (1977) suggests that the child's main goal is to strive to maintain a balance between the need for a loving relationship and the desire to explore the world outside it. Ainsworth (1979) and her colleagues have found that securely attached children use mother as a base from which to explore the world. Thus attachment is a necessary prerequisite for toleration of separation.

Fear of strangers and separation anxiety
Although some young babies may be seen to demonstrate a sort of freezing behaviour when approached by strangers, in that they will be absolutely still while gazing at the stranger, this behaviour has not the intensity with which fear of strangers is demonstrated at about 8 months of age. However, there are many variations. For example, a baby sitting on his mother's lap is unlikely to show fear when approached by a stranger, but if the mother is present but not holding him, he may well show fear of the stranger.

Separation anxiety usually refers to the anxiety a child feels when separated from his mother, or usual caretaker. The child usually protests loudly, and he is likely to reject any attempt at comforting by others. When the separation is prolonged, the child will usually become quiet, apathetic and withdrawn. When the mother or caretaker reappears the child may cling to her, but at the same time ignore or reject her attentions.

Development of self

The infant's increasing knowledge of his surroundings is accompanied by the beginning of an awareness of his own separate identity. As he begins to move about his cot, knock his body against the sides, play with his own limbs, put his toes and fists into his mouth, he is learning about his own boundaries—becoming aware of his own 'body image'. For a long time to come he will develop his body image through play so that, although his size and shape are constantly changing, he is constantly aware of himself.

To have an accurate body image, activity of the body in relation to the environment is essential. Skill in games and grace of movement are the results of accurate body image. Some children, whose movements are restricted, whose opportunity for play is curtailed, or who suffer from disorder of the nervous system, have difficulty in acquiring an accurate body image. Some idea of the magnitude of the infant's task can be gained when we realize how difficult it is for adults to change their body image. A deformity or disfigurement, for example, is very difficult to accept. Patients who lose a limb or whose limb is in plaster often find it difficult to change their body image.

Some psychologists believe that the process of learning to distinguish the 'self' from the 'not self' is very important in development. A very young infant cannot distinguish clearly between himself, his mother and the food she provides. As he grows he perceives his own identity, and develops an image of self and a sense of his own worth as a human being.

Knowledge of growth and development, as described in this and subsequent chapters, may be helpful to nurses who have any dealings with children or with young parents. Another reason for learning about development is the belief of many psychologists that early childhood events partially determine what kind of adult personality will finally emerge. It is interesting to find out how much people remember of their early experiences. Some psychologists claim that special techniques of psychoanalysis enable people to recall events from the earliest months of life. Because the infant has no speech, no thought in terms of adult concepts, it must be assumed that his early experiences are recalled in the realm of feeling.

EARLY CHILDHOOD

Developing physical skills

During the first year the infant's progress is more rapid than at any other time. Careful observation of photographs and films taken at regular intervals and detailed records of behaviour are now available, showing how muscle control progresses, in what order the infant learns new movements and when coordination takes place between eyes, grasping movements and movements of hands towards the mouth. When this stage is reached the infant is ready to explore his environment in play. Motor development of the child between 2 and 5 years of age appears much less dramatic and more gradual than development during infancy. One of the major achievements of the young toddler is toilet training.

During the first year of life elimination occurs automatically. Bowel action depends on the food the child is taking and on his general health. Sometimes, while the infant has chiefly milk, bowel action is so regular that observant mothers manage to prevent nappies being soiled, but as soon as mixed feeding begins, or whenever the infant is slightly unwell, bowel action becomes irregular. Toilet training is not possible until sphincter control is established and until the child is able at least to understand, if not use, language.

The bladder empties by reflex action whenever it is full and learning can only begin when the child can learn to recognize fullness of the bladder and communicate to someone his need for help before reflex emptying occurs.

Most people learn to control bowel and bladder at some time during childhood. The anxiety so many parents experience in their attempt to speed up control is quite irrational. Because parents believe that they should train their children in toilet habits as soon as possible they show strong emotional reaction to the child's elimination. When the child is constipated his mother becomes worried. She is pleased when the bowels function properly, yet upset when the child makes a mess or plays with faeces. These emotional reactions are difficult for the young child to interpret.

The child may not understand why his mother is sometimes pleased when he passes urine and at other times the reverse. The association between place and action of elimination can only be formed if it is possible to make the two events coincide. Generally it has been found that children are clean soon after nappies are left off, because at that moment it becomes possible to catch the child in the act of elimination. It is easier to train a child in the summer months and much easier when he is able to walk.

Bedwetting often occurs for some time after training has been established in the daytime. This is partly due to the very long night and it may help to toilet the child late in the evening. Usually the child wets at the moment of waking. When he moves from cot to bed and is old enough to get out and reach the toilet by himself he usually begins to have a dry bed and is proud of it.

There is no need to worry if a child is later than is usual in establishing toilet training. Psychologists believe too rigid toilet training to be positively harmful. Frequently the child reverts to enuresis later in childhood.

Other advances in physical skills are in climbing, balancing, hopping, skipping and throwing. Climbing and balancing have an emotional content—fear of falling. Climbing is usually first observed when children try to climb on furniture or up stairs. When children are walking, mounting the stairs is usually done in the upright position, but without alternating steps. Descending in the upright position usually develops slightly later and it may not be until the child is about 4 years old that he will use alternate steps. Hopping and skipping require more advanced motor coordination and appear later in the pre-school years. Feeding activities also reflect developing motor coordination and by 2 years of age most children can feed themselves. Cups, spoons and forks are used in most instances, effectively, if somewhat clumsily, but using a knife for cutting or spreading is more difficult in terms of motor coordination and the child may not master its use for a further few years. Undressing, then dressing, at least in part, are achieved by the child before 5 years of age, but some accomplishments, e.g. tying laces, may take longer.

Thinking and reasoning

Cognitive development during the pre-school years is accompanied by the acquisition of language. The young child becomes less dependent on perceptual skills and his cognitive abilities become increasingly differentiated from motor abilities. The child now enters what Piaget calls the period of preoperational thought, when the child prepares for the period of concrete operational thinking.

The beginnings of representational thought enable the child to go beyond his early actions of the sensory motor period, to develop the ability to contemplate and reflect. He develops the ability to consider the past as well as the future. As discussed earlier, he can now understand the permanence of objects but has not fully developed the concepts of space, time, causality, weight, number, form, colour and size. It is during the pre-school years that the greatest strides in mastering these concepts take place.

Piaget maintains that the concept of space is constructed by the child by his acting on objects in space. By 2 years of age the child has in his vocabulary such words as 'up', 'in', 'out' and 'go away'. By the age of 5 years, he is capable of walking simple routes, e.g. to the local school. Objects in space can now be understood as related to one another and he can now take into account the movement of objects, independent of his own actions.

At the beginning of the pre-school years, the child still lives very much in the present. Thus the toddler finds it very difficult to wait. 'Now' appears to be the only word he uses to indicate time. He will begin to relate time to concrete events in his immediate experience, such as teatime or bedtime. By about 2 years of age he is beginning to understand simple time sequences such as having a drink of juice after medicine. Next the child is able to distinguish between morning and afternoon, but it is not until the age of about 4 or 5 years that the child can distinguish between past and future. One little boy, for example, who was told, 'Tomorrow we go to see granny', asked, 'Is today tomorrow?'.

But, even by 5 years of age, the child is fairly tied to the present and he is just beginning to be interested in clocks. It may not be until about 7 years of age that the child can appreciate the time of day. From this it can be seen that, for example, the toddler will not understand that mummy is coming to visit at say, 6 o'clock, but may understand if the coming visit is related to his everyday routine events, e.g. teatime.

The concept of causality is also poorly developed. The child of this age tends to think that events which happen together cause one another to happen. This type of thinking is referred to as *phenomenistic* and is the basis of superstitious belief. For example, the child operating with this mode of thinking may associate pain and fear with a white coat because he had received an injection in the past by someone in a white coat.

Another characteristic of the young child's thinking is his belief that inanimate objects are alive (referred to as *animism* by Piaget). Because the child tends to model the world on his own experience, he believes objects can feel pain or cold or fear, as he does. He also believes that everything has a purpose. It is argued that children's questions about the 'why of things' should be answered in terms of purpose and intentions rather than lengthy factual explanations. For example, the answer to the question of why the sun shines should be something like 'to keep us warm' rather than an exposition of the facts of heat and light.

The young child is now developing the ability to reason, but his reasoning tends to be done in relation to striking features of the environment rather than through the use of logic. Piaget devised a number of experiments to test the child's ability to reason. The famous beaker experi-

Figure 11. The beaker experiment.

ment will help to illustrate what are sometimes referred to as 'conservation tasks'. The child is shown two wide beakers, of the same size, filled with, for example, lemonade, to the same level. The child is then asked if there is the same amount to drink in each. When the child is satisfied that there is, the experimenter pours the lemonade from one of the wide beakers into a tall narrow beaker in full view of the child and then asks if there is the same amount to drink in the wide beaker as in the tall beaker (Figure 11).

The child who responds by saying that one of the beakers contains more or less than the other, Piaget would claim, lacks the ability to conserve. If, on the other hand, the child responds by saying the quantities are equal or the same, he has demonstrated conservation and is able to reason logically that as nothing was added or taken away the quantities must be the same despite the fact that the appearance has changed. Once the child is able to reason, for instance that the number of a set of objects must remain the same although its arrangement is altered, and that the original arrangement can be obtained by reversing the movements which caused the alteration of the arrangement in the first place, he is said by Piaget to have reached the stage of concrete operational thought—usually at about 7 years of age. Piaget's ideas on conservation have aroused considerable interest among developmental psychologists and much research has resulted. Some recent findings seem to indicate that young children, at least from the age of 4 years, are not as limited in their ability to reason as Piaget has claimed. Rather, it seems that young children try to make sense of situations (the experimental situation) before turning their attention to what is being said, and thus make mistakes (Donaldson, 1978).

Language acquisition

The development of language in the years before school age is impressive and cannot be isolated from the child's intellectual development. As was discussed earlier, babbling precedes the production of a specific language. From the first single words, so eagerly anticipated by parents, the child progresses to elaborate and complex verbal productions.

Recently psychologists have taken the view that language arises from a need to communicate and has its origins in early child–parent interaction. As mentioned previously, early interactions between child and parents are significant in the development of attachment. It is argued they also have significance for communication and are a precursor to language (e.g. see Trevarthen and Hubly, 1978).

Speech

Shortly after birth infants are highly responsive to the sound of the human voice and are able to discriminate speech from non-speech (de Villiers and de Villiers, 1979). Throughout the first nine months of life a form of communication between child and parent(s) can be readily observed. In this social dialogue the child is exposed to a variety of complex signals, one of which is speech. It can be observed that parents seem to make a disproportionately greater contribution to the dialogue. Even so, the idea of 'turn-taking', so essential to easy conversation, requires the parents to be sensitive to the child's need for time to respond. It has been shown that mothers vary in their ability to establish a dialogue with their infant (Stern, 1977).

The production of speech

As described earlier, at about 2 to 3 months of age infants begin to make babbling sounds. These babbling noises, which so delight every mother, increase in frequency, become repetitive and suddenly begin to sound like 'mama' or 'dada' at about 9 months to a year. Some children babble in sequences using changing intonation rather like sentences. When listening to parents talking to their young children it is noticeable that they speak more slowly, in shorter and simpler sentences delivered at a higher pitch, and placing more stress on words than is normally found in adult conversation.

One very large question has stimulated theoretical argument: what is the relationship between babbling and the child's first words? One theory holds that two particular processes are important. The first is that parents selectively reward speech which approaches the adult mode of speech. Rewards consist of receiving attention, smiles, or responses to speech words and none to other sounds. Imitation is the second process; the child imitates the speech which is heard. Certainly young children are good mimics of their parents' utterances as well as behaviour in general. However, this explanation is at best incomplete for it fails to account for the observation that when children begin to speak in sentences they produce completely novel ones—indeed some which are not used at all in adult speech. Such children's phrases as 'he getted it' or 'his is gooder' suggest that children are extracting rules from what is heard in adults' speech and are applying them to compose their own utterances. One theory proposes that children are born with a language acquisition device (Chomski, 1976) to account for this observed fact.

These approaches have tended to concentrate on how a child builds up words and sentences and have examined the errors which children make in syntax. More recently, the focus of investigation has turned to examine the function of speech.

Children's speech
Why do children talk; what meaning is attached to their talk? These questions have firmly placed the nature of

children as well as the nature of their talk at the centre of research investigation (Garvey, 1984). Thus studies of children's speech take place in natural contexts where children can be heard talking: in play schools, nurseries and in the family setting. It is the idea that children speak to communicate, to convey meaning, to comment on their environment as ongoing action which is important. Halliday (1973) identified seven different functions of children's speech (see Table 2).

When the child has learnt to pronounce words he begins to enjoy using language. He repeats all he hears, talks to himself or any audience he can find and begins to widen his vocabulary by asking questions. He appears to be very inquisitive at this time, but a little observation shows that the questions may not be as searching as they appear to be at first. He rarely listens to the answer and no answer really satisfies because the question is not meant to be interpreted too literally. He may, for instance, ask for names. This is partly a way of keeping the adult's attention; partly it is an experiment with sound. New words are joyfully accepted.

Some children begin to speak rather later than others. This may not have any serious significance if the child appears to develop normally in other ways and is not unhappy. Some children omit altogether the period of

Table 2. Seven functions of speech based on Halliday's (1973) classification.

Function	Meaning
1. Instrumental	To get things
2. Regulatory	To get others to do things
3. Interactional	To maintain contact with others
4. Personal	To express individuality
5. Heuristic	To learn and describe environment
6. Imaginative	To pretend and create
7. Representational	To inform

meaningless sounds, of baby talk, or repetition of single words. When they begin to talk they surprise everybody with their clear articulation, large vocabulary and accurate grammer. It may be that they practise silently or when they are unobserved. There are, however, many reasons for delay in speaking which should be investigated.

Some children manage to communicate without speech so well that they do not find it necessary to use it. Position in the family can affect speech development in a variety of ways. Older children may learn to speak early because the mother has plenty of time to speak to them. Younger children may learn more slowly, often because their mother is busy and has less opportunity to speak to them. On the other hand the reverse may happen; older children may find they can prolong babyhood and retain their mother's attention by not speaking; younger children may learn more rapidly if the older children help to teach. The words used in communication constitute only one part of the total message which passes between people. Tone of voice, gestures and intonation provide the rest. Occasionally the words convey a different meaning from the tone of voice. Mother, for example, may call the child 'darling' yet indicate by her intonation that the child is not very dear to her at that moment. Children may sometimes have difficulty in learning to speak because of the conflicting messages they receive, or they may learn to respond to tone of voice rather than to the words, e.g. if the child fails to comply with instructions until the mother shouts.

Children whose general development is slow and whose intelligence is below normal begin to speak rather late. If the child makes no attempt to repeat words or play with sounds by the time he is 2 or 3 years old this delay should certainly be investigated. Some children are slow to learn to speak simply because no one takes the trouble to speak to them.

Children learn to speak sooner if they have an opportunity of hearing speech at face level. The child, who is held on mother's arm while being spoken to, or while mother sings songs or nursery rhymes, associates speech with all the other pleasant experiences of being loved and nursed. Speech from a distance does not seem to become significant to the child.

Children who grow up in institutions are in much greater danger of not learning to speak at the proper time. At home a child hears the same sounds made repeatedly by the same person. There is consistency in tone of voice, in vocabulary and in the occasions when certain words are used. In hospitals or children's homes a great number of nurses may be attending to the child, all of them too busy to speak, or, if they do speak, may be unable to provide known conversation.

Nurses who care for small children need to know the importance of speaking often to these children, making sure that the child learns to associate words with all his activities. When the child begins to speak he should be encouraged by being given a quicker and more accurate response to his needs than if he has to try to make them known without speech. Children love to play with adults who sing nursery rhymes to them, help them to repeat verses, and tell stories which have striking repetitions of words. They insist that precisely the same words be used on every occasion and gradually begin to join in at appropriate points. Mothers who read to their children, tell them stories and sing songs to them, teach them rhymes and give them books to play with, help their children to acquire, even early in life, a vocabulary which enables them to learn faster and make greater progress later on at school. It has been shown that children who

are deprived of this opportunity early in life have a
relatively small vocabulary during school years.

Among the children who do not learn to speak are,
unfortunately, some who are deaf or partially deaf. As
mentioned earlier, deafness is extraordinarily difficult to
detect during the first two years of life. Often, failure
to articulate is the first indication that all is not well.
Deafness is a great handicap to development. Some children have been thought to be mentally handicapped and
were later discovered to be deaf. Hearing aids, where
possible, and special help from speech therapists and
special schools are necessary to help the child to develop
with a minimum amount of difficulty.

Expanding family and social relationships

In families in the United Kingdom, children generally
form their first attachments to their mother. As described
earlier, this is quickly followed by the formation of
attachments to other members of the family. Fathers may
take responsibility early for child care, but it is during
the pre-school years that fathers become more actively
involved in the child's life (for a fuller discussion see
Parke, 1981). It is possible at this stage for the child to
have more opportunities to interact with his father. For
example, he can sit with the family at meal times, play
games, or go on outings. Thus, the child learns to seek
attention from both parents, rather than one, and he
quickly perceives differences in his parents' attitudes and
personalities. This can lead to difficulties when the child
tries to play off one parent against the other. The child of
this age can attempt to manipulate the behaviour of his
parents by rejecting one parent's authority in favour of
the other's, e.g. by saying something like 'Mummy lets
me do it' when father has said 'No'. Another ploy is for

the child to express favouritism, e.g. the child may say, 'I want Daddy to bath me, not you, Mummy'. Parents can resist these attempts at manipulation by agreeing and sticking to their preferred methods of child rearing which they intend to use.

Learning to conform

The child's curiosity at this stage is not confined to harmless actions. He tries to suck things which are dirty, he throws things which are breakable, attempts to touch a fire or pull the tail of a cat. Some of his activities could be dangerous, others cannot be allowed because the objects he uses might be damaged. It becomes necessary at times to restrict the child. The parents do this either by physically removing the object, or the child, or by showing their disapproval. To avoid trouble by keeping dangerous objects such as pills, matches or pins out of the child's reach is an obvious act of child care but it is often sadly neglected.

A great deal of success in upbringing depends on the parents' skill in conveying disapproval without making the child feel that he is losing their love. The infant is learning to give up the gratification of some of his wishes in order to avoid losing his parents' approval.

Obedience to the parents' prohibitions is essential to protect the child from dangers and the parents must give commands absolutely clearly, indicating that obedience is expected. Commands and firm prohibition should be given on the rare occasions when obedience can be enforced. If prohibitions occur too often, and when urgency is less compelling, it is easy to become inconsistent. Often it is easier and wiser to divert the child's attention and bring up a new interest rather than forbid the undesirable activity. Awareness of his parents' disapproval is the child's first step towards an appreciation of right and wrong. It can only happen if the child is secure in his parents' love and if his compliance with prohibitions reinforces his feeling of being loved.

Children feel very insecure if a parent threatens to go away, to abandon the child in the street or to send him away if he is naughty. Such threats often fail to produce the desired effect. Instead of learning to behave more in accordance with the parents' wishes the child may learn to distrust them, or may cling excessively. Feeding problems have been found to be associated with anxiety about the parents' withdrawal of warmth and love.

Relationships with siblings
It is during the pre-school years that important relationships with brothers and sisters develop. First-born children may experience the arrival of a baby in the family and later-born children begin to interact with older brothers and sisters. The arrival of a new baby in the family is a disturbing event in the life of the toddler. Having been used to the exclusive attention of his parents, this attention has now to be shared. It may well be that the child may view the new arrival as an intruder, and communicate his distress by innocently suggesting that the baby should be 'sent away'. Emotions are strong at this age and freely expressed.

Love and hate
Many mothers find it difficult to understand how strong a child's emotions can be and how vigorously and promptly these emotions are expressed. A feeling of anger, resentment or hate is quite natural when the child is thwarted and the stronger his love for his mother the deeper the feeling of anger against her when frustration occurs. Feelings of hatred and anger are very frightening, but the child can be helped to learn to manage his emotions

by his mother's understanding and acceptance. When he is aware that his mother still loves him and is still in command of the situation this helps him to gain self-control and to lose the terror of his own temper. If the child is made to feel guilty, wicked, and unloved he cannot learn to control his feelings; instead he learns to hide them. He may become docile and polite, but full emotional development may later become more difficult.

The father's frequent appearance, regular play, friendly interest, help the child to tolerate periods of separation from his mother. It has often been noticed that the child is angry with his mother, but not with his father, after an enforced removal from home.

Younger brothers or sisters may sometimes be the next people to enter the child's world. If the infant is less than 18 months old it is extremely difficult to prepare him for the event. Before the age of 3 years the appearance of a new infant simply means separation from the mother and a feeling of being neglected and unloved because she devotes time to the little brother or sister. However clearly the mother may know that love is infinite and indivisible, the child believes that there must be less love to spare for himself if the new baby receives some of his mother's love. The child's resentment is shown in his behaviour both to his mother and to the newborn baby. At times, hostility to the newborn can entail physical danger and the mother's protective attitude increases the infant's resentment against her. In order to regain her attention, the older child may become more babyish in his behaviour. He may again wet and soil his pants or bed, may suck his thumb, cry or whine and generally behave like the younger child. Extra attention and care may quickly reassure him and help him to enjoy the companionship of his sibling. (This word is used to denote a brother or a sister.)

The emotional turmoil of the first few years of life finds expression in the stories which the child makes up for himself or to which he likes to listen. In his play, too, he gives vent to his feelings. The treatment meted out to a doll often gives an indication of the fate which the child would like his siblings or parents to suffer. He may solve some of his problems of family-living by inventing 'dream companions' with whom he has lively discussions. He can escape from the harsh reality of his real family by creating a fantasy family of his own, which he can order about to his own liking.

Play

In an earlier section, reference was made to the child's need to play. The infant plays with his fingers and toes, arms and legs and thus gets to know about his own body. He plays with every object he handles and learns about the material world in which he lives. As he grows older he uses most of his energy in the active exploration of his environment. He grows in strength and develops neuro-muscular coordination in the process of playing, climbing, jumping, gymnastics of all kinds and all this is essential to his physical development and is thoroughly enjoyable to him.

The nature of play

Piaget's work on cognitive development included an examination of play which suggested that the child de-velops from relatively simple physical play to much more complex methods of play, reflecting the child's developing powers of thought (Piaget, 1962). Play as a concept is difficult to define as is its relationship with work. Western society has valued highly the work ethic, considering play to be of less worth. It is only relatively recently that the value of play for the young developing child has been recognized. In hospitals, for example, recognition of the importance of play to the psychological well-being of sick children can be seen in the change of emphasis on play from the limited provision of the one rocking horse in the corner of a ward in the early 1950s to the playrooms and playleaders of today. Garvey (1977) discusses the attempts which have been made to classify children's play in terms of its content.

As the child plays he meets many new and strange situations. Whenever he feels unsafe or startled he rushes back to his mother, whose love and support provide the security he needs for his explorations. Children who lack love and security play much less vigorously and with less inventiveness and variety. The psychologist Harlow (1961) has shown that the same holds true of monkeys. Only those monkeys who at least had a substitute mother in the form of Turkish towelling played freely. They rushed to the towel-mother and vigorously rubbed against it whenever they were startled by unexpected noises or movements. Monkeys reared without any substitute for their mothers remained apathetic and inactive although surrounded by play material. It is clear that the basic needs are closely related to each other. The need to play, to be active and to satisfy curiosity depends on fulfilment of the need to be secure.

During play the child begins to discover not only the physical characteristics of his environment but also the feelings of the important people in his life. In his play and in his demand for stories he tries to come to grips with emotional difficulties. The stories which he enjoys most at an early age are tales of good and bad characters, fairies and witches, bad people and good children, stories in which his growing ideas of moral values are clearly thought out and good always triumphs. The sameness of the stories, the rituals, the repetitive intonations all contribute to the child's security.

Ritual plays an important part in the child's life. There are fixed rules for almost every activity. Bath, meals, bedtime stories, dressing and undressing, tucking in and good-night kisses must all conform to the daily pattern. The child is learning the rules of life and needs a framework within which to move.

At the same time there is little difference between fantasy and reality. The child's play consists in animating the environment, and surrounding himself with imaginary playmates with whom conversation is sustained. The adult world of material objects is still unknown. So when he calls an upturned chair a car or a boat he is not pretending—this, to him, is absolutely real. Adult models of cars or boats may not even be recognized as such. As the child plays, ordinary objects which surround him, for instance boxes, cups, saucepans, garden tools and tins, provide him with endless material for amusement and learning. Water, sand, plasticine and later paint and clay are essential play materials which permit expression of feeling, creative activity and satisfying sensations.

Companionship in play

Not until towards the end of the third year is companionship with other children needed or appreciated. Before that the toddler tends to play alone or alongside others, but there is little cooperative effort. During the fourth year of life children begin to take more notice of each other, respond to each other's needs, communicate with each other and begin to more obviously enjoy social intercourse.

Although the child's play is still very egocentric, mutual help is often given. Bigger projects can now be undertaken. Large objects can be moved or lifted by joint action and group activities, such as organized party-games, sing-songs and tug-of-war, are now enjoyed. The child is beginning to learn that it is necessary at times to give way to others. When there are several children in the family, early social experiences are provided at home. If there is no opportunity to play with other children at home, as in the case of an only child, and when no suitable playmates can be found in the neighbourhood, much benefit can be obtained from attendance at a nursery school or playgroup.

Day nurseries and nursery schools have come under severe criticism because it was felt that young children needed their mother's continuous presence and should not be separated from her for long periods of the day. By the age of 3 or 4 years, however, the intelligent, active child needs the companionship of other children and thus to be provided with more outlet for his energies than he can be allowed in his home. In recent years, the importance of providing nursery schools has been rediscovered, particularly for those children who lack companionship in the home, for those who, because of housing difficulties, are deprived of adequate space for exploratory play, and for those whose parents are unable to provide the necessary stimulation for constructive play. By attending a nursery school for a new hours a day the child becomes used to being away from his mother for short periods and has the opportunity of using suitable play material which cannot always be provided in the house. He stays at the nursery school for much shorter hours than is necessary when real school starts and he learns social adaptation before the more serious change to school life begins. Teachers in nursery schools function to some extent as mother substitutes. The child's attitude to his nursery school teacher provides a gradual transition to the later approach to school teachers.

Role-playing games

Role-playing games become important. Children take it in turns to play the part of mother, father, baby, doctor, nurse and patient, or, later on, teacher and child. Not only do they learn in this way to cooperate, to understand each other's point of view, to settle quarrels and differences of opinion, to fight and make peace and generally live with each other, but they also begin to appreciate the feelings and experiences of adults. The child's desire for power finds an acceptable outlet; reversal of roles gives practice in learning to accept power in others.

Throughout life we ascribe to people certain roles we wish them to play in life and we have fairly well-defined ideas of the kind of behaviour befitting each role. We may think of policemen as powerful, just, incorruptible and of professors as brilliant, benevolent, absent-minded. Certain characteristics appear to be essential to each role, some are permissible but not essential, others are incompatible with it. Motherhood, for example, entails loving kindness and consideration towards children as an essential part of the role. Neglect, cruelty, disinterest and prolonged absence are incompatible with the role of a mother. In role-playing games children interpret and learn what is expected of a mother and other grown-up people. When they become the mother in the game they behave towards the children in the way in which they think the mother should behave. The children, in the game, are bathed, fed, taken for walks, put to bed. They are also scolded and punished, often very severely. This is not an imitation of mother's behaviour towards them, but an attempt to understand the mother's anger and the punishment she gives. It is at the same time a way of accepting the mother's standards and making them their own, and a method by which the child learns to cope with feelings, to express his own fears and anxieties and to become sensitive to other people's feelings. In the game children are much more exacting, much stricter and more punitive than their parents ever are. The standards they set for each other are infinitely higher than their parents' standards and their wrath much more uncontrolled. In reversing roles they learn how it feels to do things which usually are done to themselves and they change the actions in the game to make responses more and more realistic.

Mother and child games may become very detailed and complicated as the child becomes more and more familiar with the mother's real life: cooking, shopping, housework, concern for the father and for other children, the need for order and cleanliness, preparations for visiting—all these become part of the child's reality and are associated with the mother role. The fascination of dressing up is an important aspect of role-playing games. When the child wears different clothes he feels that he is a different person.

Other people who enter into role-playing games are never as well known as mother and children. Acquaintance with them is restricted to a particular situation; shopkeepers are only known to sell goods. What they do with the rest of their time never becomes known to the child. In much the same way fathers may only have the function of going out and coming back. What they do at work remains a mystery. They may be entitled to special privileges because they work, but their duties and responsibilities cannot be rehearsed in play.

If role-playing games are thought of as a preparation for life it is easy to see that children's preparation for life may remain inadequate. Adulthood in games consists largely of the right to tell other people what to do and not, oneself, having to obey. Work consists of going out and coming back; parenthood largely consists of privileges and only to a small extent of duties. Adults who enter into role-playing games can help considerably in preparing the child for the role he will be expected to play. By adding detail and realism to the part played by the adults one can help to prepare the child for the fact that growing up brings with it increased duties as well as increased scope. Role-playing games continue until well into school age. The parts played by each child become more complex and often more carefully scripted and rehearsed. They continue to take the child a little way ahead and thus prepare him for the next phase.

Before the child goes to school it is advisable to initiate 'school games'. Before admission to hospital each aspect of hospital life could be played out so that the child enters a familiar routine and understands the part each person in hospital has to play. The hospital game may have to be played many times, in different ways, with the child acting as the patient, doctor, nurse, and visitor. Many likely events and attitudes are thoroughly understood and anticipated and the child's fear and anxiety are recognized and conquered. Hospital games may continue for some time after the child's discharge from hospital. He may try, in the game, to convey to his mother his emotional turmoil while ill. He may relive the anxieties he experienced about all the frightening events and the fears he endured of being forgotten by his parents.

At school, role-playing games are used as a means of much factual learning. Games of shopping may involve valuable arithmetic lessons, for example. Knowledge gained in this way about people continues to make acting valuable, whatever other information may be involved. Even as adults, role-playing may be a useful device for preparing for forthcoming ordeals. Examinations become less terrifying as experience in taking them is gained and may well lose much of their terror when the candidate has acted as examiner to others. This is an activity which student nurses would be well advised to carry out. Acting the patient, during practical nursing procedures, is invaluable in learning to anticipate the patients' reactions to the real thing. Playing at applying for jobs, being interviewed, interviewing and selecting others are generally practised techniques in the preparation for administration.

As the child grows older the characteristics of play change. Before children go to school they do not distinguish between work and play. The small girl who dresses her doll, washes dolls' clothes, or helps her mother to bake a cake, puts intense effort and concentration into what is play at the time but will soon become work. The child's absorption in a construction game, or in painting or woodwork is indistinguishable from later attitudes to work. Many lifelong interests have their origin in the enjoyable experiences of childhood play. When the child goes to school, play becomes a relaxation from work, purposive yet subject to fewer external rules and restrictions than work.

Group games

Real group games now become important. At first they are usually games like 'cops and robbers'; a few years later these are replaced by organized games such as football, cricket, hockey. In these games the child learns the rudiments of the rules and standards of the adult world. Piaget has shown that children have some difficulty at first in distinguishing between different types of rules. If they are shown how to play a game (in Piaget's example, a game of marbles) they accept the rules as absolute and become indignant at the suggestion that rules can be changed. Later, when they play team games at school, they can understand that the rules of the game are simply

social agreements, convenient ways of arriving at cooperative effort, and subject to change when all players
agree. They understand the difference between 'social
rules' and 'moral rules' which cannot be changed. Group
games are thought to be valuable in providing an opportunity for learning moral rules. Cheating at games, for
example, is not allowed; 'playing the game' means competing in a friendly way; 'it is not cricket' means it is
unfair. Children learn to lose without being upset, to
admire achievement in others, and to submerge their
own interests in the interest of the team.

Expression in play
When children meet difficulties in their development they
often express this through play. An observant mother
knows from the way her child treats her doll that she
is hurt or upset. Children's moods are often reflected
in their painting. Pictures tend to be all dark and grey
when all is not well at home; they are brilliantly coloured
and full of sunshine when the painter is happy, and
sometimes very red when the child is angry. The fact
that play expresses so well what the child may feel, while
words may not easily come to him, has led to play therapy
as a form of treatment for severely disturbed children.
Observation of a child at play with a doll's house may
help one to diagnose where the problems lie; for example,
in the play the baby doll may be thrown out of the
window or the mother doll may have pins stuck into her.
The child's comments about his painting, or even the
painting itself, may help one to understand the problem.
In the painting, for example, the family may be inside
the house except for the child, who is left outside—an
indication, perhaps, of the child's loneliness and sense of
exclusion from the family.

In play therapy the child is encouraged to play freely

in whatever way he likes provided, of course, that he is safe. The presence of a kind, helpful, accepting adult helps the child to feel safe, and as he acts out his problems he begins to understand them. He learns to act out his emotions freely, yet safely, in the playroom. Instead of hiding his anger about his baby sister he can safely be angry in play and learn how to control his emotion in real life. In the play therapy room he is free to play with material with which he may have wished to play earlier in life but was prevented. Water, dirt or mud may not have been allowed because of his mother's excessive desire for cleanliness. In play therapy these materials are safe and permitted and, however childishly he uses them, he need not fear any ridicule or criticism. Finger painting provides an exciting alternative to mud or dirt. The emotional release which accompanies play and the improvement in the child after he has obtained satisfaction from play show how basic a need is involved.

Personality development

As individuals we are each different from one another. Our general appearances and physical characteristics contribute to the differences, but individuality is also seen in the way in which our behaviour differs from everybody else's behaviour. These differences are based both on differences in life experience and on variations in temperament or emotional patterns.

Evidence has shown that differences in temperament are not acquired through learning, but are there from birth. For example, in a longitudinal study conducted in America, Thomas and Chess (1977) identified three general personality types. The majority of children were characterized as 'easy children'. Easy children had friendly dispositions, regularity of body habits and a positive approach to new situations. A second group, called 'slow-to-warm up', had a low activity level, reluctantly involved themselves in new experiences, but given time would adapt. A much smaller group, difficult children, were irregular in body function, intense, and tended to withdraw from new situations.

Thus, differences in the behaviour which expresses degrees of tension, relaxation, irritability and general responsiveness to internal and external events are present early and, moreover, people tend to retain their behavioural style throughout life. These differences in temperament are likely to have an effect on the child's parents who, in turn, will have their own characteristic ways of coping. How the child begins to regard himself is a product of his own temperament and the expectations others have to him.

The formation of social attachment has been discussed earlier, but little has been said about how the child develops feelings about his world. Erikson (1964) describes the development of attitudes towards the world in terms of developmental tasks. During infancy the child develops 'basic trust', an expectancy that his needs will be met and people are reliable. If the child's needs are unsatisfied, or only met inconsistently, the child will view the world with an attitude of 'mistrust' which may interfere with the formation of healthy relationships later on.

However, as the child develops attachments, he also begins to strive for independence and the emergence of self is seen in his recognition of himself as a person. Most of the time the child does as he is told, but his independence is asserted when he responds persistently to any request with a firm 'no'. Erikson refers to the development of 'autonomy' and, where there is major conflict, the toddler may be over-controlled by his parents and then an attitude of 'doubt' or 'shame' may develop.

As the child begins to gain his independence and can venture forth, he develops 'initiative' in dealing with his world. But, if the child believes himself to be powerful, he may develop a sense of 'guilt' accompanying events of which he is not the cause, but of which he may well imagine himself to be the cause.

It is during the pre-school years that the child begins to develop a concept of self as a male or a female. Boys identify with their fathers and girls with their mothers. In role-play, for example, children take on sex-appropriate roles. Parents often reinforce the sex-appropriate behaviour of their children and discourage its opposite. Of course, there may be differences between familes in what is considered as sex-appropriate behaviour, but many of the traditional stereotypes persist. Boys are encouraged, for example, to play with appropriate toys such as cars and trains, and girls with prams and dolls.

References

Ainsworth, M.D.S. (1979) Attachment as related to infant–mother interaction. In Rosenblatt, J.S., Hinde, R.A., Beet, C. & Busnel, M. (eds) *Advances in the Study of Behaviour*, Vol. 9. New York: Academic Press.

Barber, J.H., Boothman, R. & Stanfield, J.P. (1976) A new visual chart for pre-school developmental screening. *Health Bulletin* **34**, 80–91.

Bower, T.G.R. (1977a) *A Primer of Infant Development*. San Francisco: W.H. Freeman.

Bower, T. (1977b) *The Perceptual World of the Child*. London: Fontana/Open Books.

Bowlby, J. (1969) *Attachment and Loss: 1. Attachment*. Harmondsworth: Penguin

Chomski, N. (1976) On the nature of language. In Harnard, S.R., Steklis, H.D. & Lancaster, J. (eds) *Origins and Evolution of Language and Speech. Annals of the New York Acadamy of Sciences* **280**, 46–55.

Condon, W.S. and Sander, L. (1974) Neonate movement is synchronized with adult speech: interactional participation and language acquisition. *Science* **183**, 99–101.

de Villiers, P.A. & de Villiers, J.D. (1979) *Early Language*. London: Fontana/Open Books.
Donaldson, M. (1978) *Children's Minds*. London: Fontana/Open Books.
Dunn, J. (1977) *Distress and Comfort*. London: Fontana/Open Books.
Erikson, E.H. (1964) *Childhood and Society*. Harmondsworth: Penguin.
Garvey, C. (1977) *Play*. London: Fontana/Open Books.
Garvey, C. (1984) *Children's Talk*. London: Fontana.
Gibson, G.J. & Walk, R.D. (1960) The visual cliff. *Scientific American* **202**, 64-71.
Halliday, M. (1973) *Explorations of the Functions of Language*. London: Arnold.
Harlow, H.F. (1961) The development of affectional patterns in infant monkeys. In Foss, B.M. (ed.) *Determinants of Infant Behaviour*, Vol. 1. London: Methuen.
Klaus, M. & Kennell, J. (1982) *Parent-Infant Bonding*, 2nd edition. St Louis: C.V. Mosby.
MacFarlane, A. (1977) *The Psychology of Childbirth*. London: Fontana/Open Books
Parke, R.D. (1981) *Fathering*. London: Fontana.
Piaget, J. (1962) *Play, Dreams and Imitation in Childhood*. London: Routledge & Kegan Paul.
Rutter, M. (1981) *Maternal Deprivation Reassessed*, 2nd edition. Harmondworth: Penguin.
Schaffer, R. (1977) *Mothering*. London: Fontana
Stern, D. (1977) *The First Relationship: Mother and Infant*. London: Fontana.
Thomas, A. & Chess, S. (1977) *Temperament and Development*. New York: Brunner-Mazel.
Trevarthen, C.B. & Hubly, P.A. (1978) Secondary intersubjectivity: confiding and acts of meaning in the first year. In Rock, A. (ed.) *Action, Gesture and Symbols: The Emergence of Language*. London: Academic Press.
Tucker, S.M. (1982) Deafness in babies: How soon should we start to screen for it? *Modern Medicine* **27**, 9.
Wasz-Höckert, O., Lind, J., Vuorenkoski, V., Partanen, E. & Valenne, E. (1968) *The Infant Cry*. London: Heinemann.

Further reading

Shaffer, D.R. (1989) *Developmental Psychology*. California: Brook/Cole.
Stern, D.W. (1985) *The Interpersonal World of the Infant*. New York: Basic Books.

8 Development in later childhood

THE SCHOOL YEARS

In the United Kingdom the child is thought to be ready for school at about the age of 5 years. In those countries where school begins later, attendance at nursery school is much more common than it is in the United Kingdom. On starting school the child enters another phase of development.

ELABORATING PHYSICAL SKILLS

During middle childhood the smooth perceptual–motor coordination is further refined, when the child practises motor skills. The child becomes better able to jump, hop and skip. Ball games become interesting when accuracy and strength in throwing, catching and kicking, increase with age. Many specific motor skills are elaborated at this time, when children participate in such activities as gymnastics, dancing, ice skating, swimming and so on. Some children, however, seem to perform poorly in motor skills. This may be due to any of a large number of possible factors and not merely to poor perceptual–motor coordination.

COGNITIVE DEVELOPMENT

Small children cannot sit still for long and learn best if they are allowed to be generally active. Reading and writing are learnt more easily if large cards are handled, sentences pinned upon the board, exhibits labelled and words made with blocks and plastic letters, rather than by sitting still at a desk. The more practical use the child finds for the written word the greater the interest. The child's movements are at first big and bold. He can write on the blackboard and only much later can he learn to write on paper. It is also easier to make vertical movements on a board than horizontal ones on paper. This is why walls prove irresistible for early writing practice.

The child's ability to understand and use numbers tends to develop rather later than his understanding of written words. Although many children can count when they start school few have any real concept of numbers. Small children can think of numbers only in sequence. They can count fingers or beads and add one at a time, but they cannot think of numbers as entities or configurations. In a practical way, by using money, giving change, serving in the school shop, counting out bottles of milk or giving out books, the child learns to use numbers without acquiring a fear of arithmetic. Piaget has shown that the number concept is very complex. The idea that number operations are reversible, for instance, is not really grasped until the child is about 7 or 8 years old (e.g. you can add 5 to any number and take it away again to arrive at the original number). The concept of number may entail the idea of size and an understanding of what 'to be bigger' means. The figure 9 does not only come after 8 in counting, it is also bigger. Nine children are more than 8, 9 pennies are more than 8. Nine remains more than 8, whichever way the items are arranged. Small children have difficulty in understanding this. They may believe that 9 pennies laid on the table far apart are more money than 9 pennies in a small pile. The concept of number may involve the idea of classification and of manipulating 'sets'. For example, 3 boys and 4 girls are 7 children. The boys and girls are separate 'sets', children is a 'set' which includes both the other sets.

Small children can count and use the words for numbers, but, at first, the more complex understanding of numbers is beyond them. By about the age of 6 or 7 the child can sometimes carry out an arithmetical operation but at other times he appears completely unable to understand the problem. Piaget calls the phase of sporadic understanding 'intuitive thought'. In the next phase of the child's development he can solve problems in a practical way when he has objects which he can count and arrange. As mentioned earlier, Piaget calls this the stage of 'concrete operational thought'. Only later in the early teenage years can he manipulate ideas as opposed to things as objects. Piaget calls this the level of 'formal operational thought'. These phases of thought development—intuitive, concrete operational and formal operational—with transitional phases in which the child sometimes operates on a concrete and sometimes on a formal level, apply not only to his grasp of number but to all his intellectual activities. Successful schooling is achieved if teaching is adapted to the child's level of development.

Learning and intelligence

Progress during school years depends, among other factors, on the child's intelligence and on his motivation for learning.

The development of intelligence testing
It is well known to teachers that, in spite of all efforts, children learn at different rates. The French psychologist

Binet was one of the first to attempt to determine whether different methods of education could affect the child's progress. He tried to choose questions and tests which were, as far as possible, independent of the educational achievements of the children he tested. He selected tests for the youngest age groups in such a way that a child with normal physique and normal opportunities could not fail to learn the required responses. Such skills as tying up laces, copying a square, cutting paper or stringing beads according to a given pattern were among the test items. For older children there were pictures in which some essential part was missing and questions about the correct thing to do in common circumstances. For very much older children or adults some of the test items required the ability to read, but apart from this, educational achievement was not tested.

Items for the test were finally selected in such a manner that when 50% of the children of any given age successfully completed them they were considered to measure the normal intelligence of that age group. Children who only completed tests for a younger age group were considered to have the 'mental age' of a younger child. Those who succeeded in tests beyond their age had a higher mental than chronological age. The comparison of chronological and mental age, calculated as follows, was called the intelligence quotient.

$$\frac{\text{Mental age}}{\text{Chronological age}} \times 100 = \text{Intelligence quotient (IQ)}$$

When mental age and chronological age are the same the intelligence quotient is 100.

Since Binet's tests were first published many others have appeared—some are easier to administer, some are more suitable for adults or for more intelligent people.

Because mental age as a concept is not useful after the teenage years the final IQ scores are now usually calculated using the notion that intelligence is normally distributed in a population. This calculation is called deviation IQ.

Increasingly, we have become aware of the need for an encouraging, stimulating environment, early in life, to enable the child to make full use of his intellectual abilities. There are some children so deprived of opportunities to develop that they appear to be of very low intelligence. After a change to a more stimulating environment, for example a move from an institution to a foster home, the increase in the score on intelligence tests can be quite dramatic.

Rutter and Madge (1976) discuss the many influences which research has found to have their effect on intellectual performance and scholastic achievement. Many programmes have been designed, first in the USA, and then in the United Kingdom, to remedy the intellectual and scholastic impairment found in children from socially disadvantaged homes, e.g. the American Head Start and the British Educational Priority Areas Projects.

Tests of intelligence

Children with high intelligence are generally more able to profit from teaching and are good at most subjects. Contrary to popular belief, many intelligent children are good at school subjects as well as sports, arts, and practical subjects such as cooking and sewing. They may develop special interests or receive more encouragement in some of their activities than in others, but high intelligence would enable them to be more successful than less intelligent children in whatever subject they chose to study. Intelligence remains fairly constant throughout life.

There are, however, few reliable tests and the administration of tests to small children is so difficult that most people feel doubtful about test results before the age of about 11 years. If the child is unwell, or in a bad mood, results may underestimate the child's intelligence. Children develop very rapidly during the first few school years; there are sometimes sudden bursts of developing insight into the kind of problems which intelligence tests present. Increased interest in the child's progress at home and changes in home environment may increase test scores considerably over a period of one or two years; however, practice or coaching in the use of intelligence tests produces only a very small amount of improvement.

High scores in intelligence tests can almost certainly be accepted as a measurement of high ability. Low scores may underestimate the child. Intelligence is normally distributed in the population. This means that nearly 70% of all people have an intelligence quotient of, or near, 100. Fifteen per cent are more intelligent and 15% less intelligent. The top 5 to 10% are of outstanding ability. The lowest 3 to 5% of all children have such impaired intelligence that they require special care throughout life.

Social learning

Learning facts and skills is only a very small part of the child's new life. By far the most important aspect of school life is the social learning which it provides. For many children this may be the first time they have been obliged to submit to discipline imposed by someone other than their parents or other members of the family. Authority suddenly becomes dissociated from those the child loves most and, often for the first time, the child sees that parents are subjected to the same kind of rules as he is. Many parents may still retain their fear of, and respect for, teachers and readily convey this fact to their children. What the teacher says suddenly becomes much more important than what the mother says. There are times when small children find their dual loyalties to teacher and parents very confusing. Small children cannot understand half measures or compromise. To the child people are either good or bad, right or wrong. It is impossible to believe that the teacher may sometimes be right, the mother at other times. As the child begins to accept the teacher's authority he may become critical, defiant and badly behaved at home.

His account of what a teacher has said is not always accurate; nevertheless, his mother may believe what he says about the teacher, may blame the school for deterioration in the child's behaviour at home and may become resentful of the school. It may be difficult to discuss fully with the teacher what the problems in the home are; parent–teacher contact may be rare and the parents' critical attitude to teachers may in turn result in the teachers' hostility towards parents. When antagonism occurs between school and home it is created by the child who exploits the situation, enjoying the fact that parents and school feel possessive about his person. Yet lack of cooperation and understanding between home and school may leave the child bewildered, unable to settle down to work and may begin an ambivalent attitude to authority which may hamper adjustment throughout life. Parent–teacher associations can help to establish cooperation between home and school if the problems are clearly understood.

Parents, friends, aunts and uncles can help the child in the difficult stage of transition by taking an interest in all that he chooses to tell them about school without prying, criticizing or belittling him. Many of the child's activities at school are never discussed at home. It is important to the child to have, for the first time, a life of his own about which his mother need not know everything. Though he enjoys sharing his experiences with his mother it makes him feel big and important to be able to keep something back.

Culture and language

Numerous reports, e.g. the Plowden Report (DHSS, 1967), have shown correlations between parental social class and both IQ and scholastic attainment. In relation to language, Bernstein has argued that the language of working class boys is characterized by short sentences with little description. He named this type of speech *restricted code* and contrasted it with the longer, more descriptive speech of middle class boys which he labelled *elaborated code* (see, for example, Bernstein, 1971). From this work it was suggested that social groups differ in communication styles and this has an effect on the children's intellectual development. Bernstein's work has stimulated much research and has been criticized by a number of workers. In particular, Labov (1970), in studying the speech of black American children, argued that these children used language which was different from middle American English and in its own way was just as complex. More recently Tizard and Hughes (1984), studying the educational context of home in the lives of young children, found that 'Although there were social class differences in the mothers' conversation and style of interaction, the working class children were clearly growing up in a rich linguistic environment' (p. 8).

Relationships at school

Relationships with other children at school are very different from those of the nursery years. For the first time the child's work and performance are judged on their merits and compared with those of other children. The teacher's approval is related to good work or good behaviour. At home the child is loved simply because he happens to be the child of his parents. Love is not conditional on performance, however much love and approval may be associated with conformity to rules. At home the standards set for the child are not competitive. Allowances are made for age, for feeling unwell, tired or cross. At all times the child at home is in a very special position. At school he is merely one of a large number of children treated as equals by the teacher until they prove to be otherwise. Experience of an independent figure of authority who treats all children in the same way is closely connected with appreciation of justice. Justice means that no exception is made for anyone, not even for onself.

During the first years at school the child learns to form real friendships. Playmates before school age are rarely of the child's own choice. At school it becomes of the utmost importance to make special friends. In the characteristic way of young children, a 'best friend' is found who lasts a few days and then becomes a 'worst enemy'. Friendships at this early age are completely exclusive, guarded with jealousy and bought by special favours. The criterion for the choice of a friend varies rapidly; the best behaved may be chosen one day, the naughtiest the next. Then may come the turn of the one with the nicest books or pencils, or the one who has talked about his home or his dog. Topics of conversation between friends are great secrets and the shared secret becomes the symbol of friendship.

These short-lived friendships form a valuable experience for later, more stable relationships. Because friends invite each other home, meet each other's parents, borrow each other's books or toys, the child's experience of the world expands beyond his own family circle. The other child's possessions may appear to be much more valuable and other children's parents much more exciting than the child's own. Sometimes parents reciprocate this feeling and may tend to think all other children are better behaved and much nicer than theirs. They have little idea how angelic their own offspring can be when away from home. Sometimes, of course, children who are well behaved at home have difficulties in adjusting at school.

By the time children are 11 or 12 years of age, groups have come to assume a greater importance and these groups are usually made up either of boys or girls exclusively. Rubin (1980) draws on research to argue that the nature of a child's friendships contributes to his level of happiness, and may also influence later adult relationships.

During the junior school years the child is becoming more competent in motor, intellectual and social skills. An interest in competition, feelings of competence about acquired skills and ability to cope with new experiences, now arise. Erikson (1965) describes the school years as the time when a sense of 'industry' develops which, in later occupational life, may colour the child's attitude to work. The child will feel that he is able to cope with new experiences where he has succeeded in mastering earlier ones. With repeated failures, however, the child is likely to develop a sense of 'inferiority'.

DISCIPLINE

Most children want to conform. They do not always know what is expected of them and have to be told, or they may know but have forgotten. However, they only need to be reminded and will immediately correct their behaviour. The parents' methods of exercising control are well understood, but the same rules may not necessarily apply at the school and the child has to experiment with the extent to which it will comply with the demands of teachers and peer group.

Sometimes it is great fun for them to be difficult and to see just how far it is possible to go in order to establish a right to be contrary. Most children play this game at some time, and in every class, with every teacher, it must be played at least once. This is a way of getting to know the teacher, leading to a very clear understanding of the teacher's personality. Each teacher acquires a reputation of sternness or leniency, of being just or erratic, of being bad-tempered or placid as the result of the manner in which he deals with those children who try him out. It does not much matter how soon he draws the limits or what methods he uses, his peculiarities will become known and the class will settle down to a particular pattern of accepted behaviour. When the class has settled down, however, bad behaviour must be taken seriously because it may be an indication of more deep-rooted trouble. Persistent bad behaviour may be the only way in which some children succeed in gaining recognition. They may be so discouraged that they no longer try to do good work or to impress by their good behaviour. To be noticed at all they must be bad.

Some children may have failed to establish sufficiently satisfactory relationships with the teacher to want to please. Some may find that they can gain esteem among other children only by being a hero in taking punishment. When a child's behaviour is persistently out of step with the others, punishment cannot really help and one must try to understand the underlying cause. This does not mean that punishment is necessarily wrong.

Good teachers do not need to, and indeed cannot, resort to physical punishment, but their reprimand or other forms of punishment can be more hurtful than corporal punishment.

The child's growing awareness of right and wrong carries with it the belief that a choice can be made between the right and the wrong act. Freedom of choice to behave badly gives the wrongdoer the right to be punished. We punish only when we think the child could have acted in a different way. If we do not think that he could have chosen any other action we absolve him from blame. A child who deliberately chooses to act wrongly may be asking to be punished and it may be necessary to respond to his demand. He may, in fact, feel guilty about something unknown to the teacher and his subsequent naughtiness may be a device for getting punished for two things at once. Or he may be trying to confirm in his own mind his judgement about right or wrong. If, for example, he thinks he is doing the wrong thing by arriving late and yet nobody takes it seriously, he becomes confused about his own standards and he has to try again until eventually he is punished.

Inconsistency by the teacher may lead to bad behaviour which could have been avoided without much punishment. Small children like to conform. They feel secure when there are firm limits to their behaviour. They enjoy the approval of the adult. Later, they accept adult standards as their own and self-discipline can be encouraged. Inconsistency in parents and teachers early in the child's life leads to confusion of standards.

IN HEALTH AND ILLNESS

At birth most children are already within the health care system and are consumers of nursing services. For the first 10 days of life the midwife has a major responsibility for their care in hospital and in the community. In the United Kingdom, responsibility for health promotion and preventive health care for children between the ages of 10 days and 5 years rests with the child health services, and health visitors play a major part. On entry to school the school nurse takes over as one of the professionals in the school health services. Preventive health care for young children involves home visiting, programmes for immunization, developmental assessments and medical physical examinations at intervals throughout childhood.

DEVELOPMENTAL ASSESSMENT

The work of Gesell in the USA mentioned earlier, of Sheridan in Britain, and of others has formed the knowledge base for the development of screening tests for infants and young children. Their close observation and detailed description of normal developmental milestones has made it possible to detect developmental delays and abnormalities. The Court Report (1976) drew attention once again to the importance of early detection of developmental problems, recommending the setting up of developmental assessment clinics and the involvement of specifically trained doctors and health visitors in formal screening procedures. The earlier problems are identified the more amenable they are to corrective/ameliorative intervention.

Health visitors have been involved for many years in developmental assessment, including the assessment of growth. Apart from tools to measure height and weight, health visitors have used rather crude estimates of other development parameters, relying on everyday observation of children's behaviour or parents' reports of their children's achievements. Indeed it has been suggested that psychologists have not given the same attention to constructing tests of development as they have given to devising intelligence tests.

Health care workers require to have standardized tests which can be administered to young children in their own homes as well as in clinic settings, and a recording system which is easy to interpret by both testers and parents. Paediatricians, both in the United Kingdom and in the USA, have devised a number of developmental testing programmes and record forms which are, on the whole, still being researched and standardized.

In the USA, one of the most widely used tests is the Denver developmental screening test. Four principal areas of development have been highlighted: personal–social, fine motor–adaptive, language, and gross motor control. It has been designed for administration by doctors and other health care professionals to children from birth to 6 years of age, and has been modified for use with British children (Bryant, 1980). Tests and programmes have also been developed in the United Kingdom. One which has been designed for administration by health visitors and general practitioners was reported by Professor Barber et al. in 1976 and again after it had been in use for a further four years (Barber, 1982). The four principal areas of development which are tested are gross motor, vision and fine motor, hearing and language, and social adaptation. The recording sheet is described as a 'centile-type step chart' on which developmental progress could be displayed visually, delayed or abnormal development readily demonstrated, and examination timing varied. Development was considered to be delayed if in the first year the child was unable to complete the tests appropriate to his age but could complete at least some of the tests appropriate to the previous step three months earlier. If the child could not complete the previous step tests at all, then developmental abnormality was assumed. For the second year the steps were at six monthly intervals and for the third year and beyond at yearly intervals.

As with any examination of children, their parents (particularly the mother) are usually present and even in routine developmental testing are extremely anxious about their child's progress. This is particularly so when the child is very young. Parents, generally, are less familiar with the timing and nature of early milestones of development than they are with later, more obvious ones such as sitting, walking and the beginnings of speech. Thus pointing out to parents the positive aspects of development—what the baby can do, what a healthy, strong baby he is—can do much to alleviate anxieties and direct the parents' attention to environmental influences which may enrich their child's development.

When it is suspected that a child's development is delayed or abnormal, the nurse requires skill in communication (see Chapter 12) to convey her findings. It may mean that the child requires more detailed examination of some aspect of development such as hearing. Professor Barber reported that when developmental delay was discovered, the health visitors told the child's mother and described to her how the child could be helped to improve that particular aspect of development. On the next testing in all cases improvement had occurred but it was not known whether this was due to the health visitor's intervention or the normal 'catching-up' process (Barber, 1982).

This idea of children's ability to catch up after a delay in growth and development, for example following a severe illness, taken in conjunction with the wide range of ages at which children reach milestones makes it imperative that development is assessed over time using a broad range of techniques. Single, one-off examinations are very unreliable and only useful as a guide for baseline for further assessment.

CHILDREN IN HOSPITAL

In recent years, much attention has been given to the experiences of small children while in hospital. There is a widespread belief that great harm can be done, not only at the time, but in the child's subsequent development, if the child's basic psychological needs are not recognized.

Very small children who have not yet developed any understanding of the world around them have one overriding need: the security of the love and presence of their mother or the person who is a substitute for her. Children cannot bear to be separated from parents for long, least of all when new, unusual and perhaps unpleasant things are happening to them. As the child is constantly learning new things he can cope with the new experience of sickness, even hospitalization, provided his parents are close by.

Drawing on evidence which included observational studies in institutions containing children, Bowlby (1951) argued strongly that disturbances in mental health and personality development resulted from maternal deprivation. Other evidence emanated from cine-recordings filmed in hospitals and nurseries, showing the distress of children when separated from their parents. As a result of this accumulating evidence supporting the thesis of maternal deprivation, the Platt Report on the Welfare of Children in Hospital made its recommendations in 1959. Among these recommendations were: mothers should stay with their children in hospital, there should be un-restricted visiting, and children should not be admitted to hospital if it could possibly be avoided.

However, in recent years it has been recognized that the psychological theory which stressed the importance of the mother–child relationship placed too little em-phasis on other relationships within the family. Moreover, some consider that perhaps damage is not as deep or permanent as the early work of Dr Bowlby, for example, led us to believe. Indeed excessive emphasis on the dangers of separation may lead to guilt feelings in mothers who have to leave their babies in nurseries or hospitals, guilt feelings which may interfere with the mother–child relationship.

Despite these arguments, there is strong evidence that very small children suffer from a sense of loss, mourning and grief when away from their mothers (Robertson, 1970; Hawthorn, 1974). It is as if the children felt that their mothers must have rejected, forgotten or lost them. At first they may be tearful or angry; later there is a stage of resignation, with lack of interest and an apparent inability to accept love or return affection. How much this affects the child's development and his ability to form relationships with other people later on in life, depends to some extent on the nature and duration of the separation from his mother and on the mother–child relationship before separation (Clarke and Clarke, 1976; Hall and Stacey, 1978; Rutter, 1981). Rutter, in particular, argues that the concept 'maternal deprivation' has been used to cover a wide range of different child-hood experiences which have different effects on devel-opment. On admission to hospital children experience many other distressing events, e.g. the fact of being ill, strange medical and surgical procedures, different daily routines, and a variety of unknown people. Too often the emphasis given to the effects of separation has resulted in less attention being paid to other distressing events in hospital.

Nearly always, however, the child's rate of progress both physically and mentally, is affected when there is lengthy separation or repeated separations from his mother. On returning home the child may refuse to recognize his mother and remain detached and unresponsive for some time. Bowel or bladder control achieved earlier, for example, might be lost. There may be excessive clinging, nightmares, or other indications of emotional disturbance.

PREPARATION FOR ADMISSION TO HOSPITAL

It is now commonplace for hospitals to provide booklets explaining to parents what is likely to happen in hospital and offering advice about how best to prepare the child. Similarly, children's books dealing with the topic of being in hospital are readily available for parents to read to young children. Many hospitals encourage parents to visit clinical areas with their children, to view the ward and play area, and to meet the staff who are likely to be most concerned in looking after the child. All this is excellent for the child whose admission to hospital is planned and whose level of understanding allows such preparation. Very young children, those admitted as emergencies, and others who have not had the advantage of careful preparation, are more likely to experience psychological distress on admission to hospital.

IN HOSPITAL WITH MOTHER

Many hospitals now make arrangements for very young babies to be admitted with their mothers. Small children respond better to treatment if their mothers attend to their basic needs. Older children can bear separation from their mothers more easily, but their security is still dependent on the knowledge that their mothers are available, and frequent visiting is important.

When a mother is admitted to hospital with her child she feels relieved to be able to carry out all those care activities she normally provides. It is comforting to both mother and child if the mother can confidently feed and wash her baby, play with him, hug and hold him whenever he is upset, tuck him in at night. The child's routine is not altered and the mother feels useful and appreciates the fact that she is fully in touch with the child's progress.

Any setbacks of course are most upsetting to the mother and she may become very anxious if she sees her child suffer. She would, however, feel equally worried about him were she at home, unable to get adequate information. If the mother is in hospital the doctor and nursing staff can help her to express her worries, to feel secure in the knowledge that the child is having good nursing care. Her contact with other mothers, too, and the fact of being useful to the hospital are of great help.

VISITING CHILDREN IN HOSPITAL

If it is impossible for the mother to be admitted to hospital, unrestricted visiting is the next best thing. The more frequently the mother comes, the less disturbing her departure becomes. Her repeated absences and reappearances come to be taken for granted. Most hospitals which have tried to allow unrestricted visiting have not found that the mother's presence interferes with the work. On the contrary, the help mothers can give, especially at meal-times and bedtime, gives more time for the nursing of those children who are very ill or who are not visited.

Small children who are admitted to hospital may need the comfort of some tangible reminder of home. A teddy-bear or a favourite piece of ribbon or cloth taken to bed with him may establish a link with his previous experience during his mother's absence. His own personal baby language and signs for toilet should be used by the hospital staff. Information about details of the child's life should be available.

THE NURSE AS MOTHER-SUBSTITUTE

If it is impossible for the mother to be present the nurse must attempt, as far as possible, to replace her. Ideally, one nurse should look after the child throughout his stay, but, as this is obviously impossible, the fewest possible number of nurses should share in his care. It is very bewildering for the child to have a large number of strangers handling him, each giving a small part of the total care. However kind the nurses are the child cannot establish emotional attachments with too many people. He needs one person who is his special or primary nurse. Fear of showing favouritism sometimes deters nurses from singling out a particular child for attention. There is no danger of favouritism for small children unless one child was everybody's favourite, which is as impersonal a relationship as being no one's favourite. Each small child must feel he belongs to someone.

Hospitals are sometimes afraid of the adverse effect on the child when his favourite nurse has to leave. This is, of course, a bad thing, but better than if no favourite nurse had ever existed. It is easier for a child to form a new relationship if his previous experiences have been satisfying, just as it is easier for the child to form a satis-factory relationship with the nurse if he is secure in his relationship with his mother. If nurses are assigned to the care of individual children they are in a much better position to notice signs of distress early and to respond to the child's need for comfort and companionship. If too many nurses are sharing the care of the child each may believe, from the fleeting glimpse she has, that the child has settled and is happy.

There is inevitably some disturbance when visitors leave and fear of children's tears has, in the past, led to restrictions on visiting by parents. It seems, though, as if tears and a show of emotion are much to be preferred to the restrained, detached behaviour of those children who appear to have settled down in hospital.

One of the greatest difficulties of the small child is his inability to understand the concept of time. He cannot measure the interval between his mother's visits and so he needs to be kept informed about her actions throughout the day. The nurse can give a running commentary to the child of what his mother is probably doing. 'She is cooking the dinner now for your brother; she is doing the ironing; she has gone out to do the shopping.' These remarks help the child to realize that life has not changed much at home. The future is measured in all the activities the child will carry out before his mother's return; for example, 'you will have your lunch, then you'll have a sleep, then the doctor will come, then we shall play, then your mummy will arrive.' Some of the hospital events can be rehearsed in play before the child's admission or before a specific treatment is carried out (Rodin, 1983).

The period in hospital is not the time for a child to give up well-established habits, however deplorable the nurse may think they are. Some children suck dummies when they are upset, some are fussy about food, some make a noise when they are being washed. There is no point at all in nurses being critical of the child's upbringing and in trying to change behaviour of which the mother does not disapprove. When this is attempted, the child may conform to the nurses's request during his mother's absence. When she comes, however, the conflict between nurse and parent results in more pronounced disturbance in the child and an increasingly critical attitude between parents and nurses (Cleary, 1977; Hall, 1978).

OLDER CHILDREN IN HOSPITAL

Older children, once they have recovered from the most acute phase of the illness, enjoy the companionship in the ward. They may benefit from the independence from parental control, from the fact that nurses represent an impartial authority. Freedom from the pressures of the educational system and being the centre of attention owing to illness may contribute to a constructive use of hospital experience during development. Some children derive great benefit from the individual attention a school teacher is able to give, and return to school later with enhanced prestige of having been in hospital and increased attainment. Children who do not like school benefit particularly from individual tuition.

It is important that children's routine in hospital should resemble normal life as far as possible. In order to achieve this nurses should know enough about the stages of child development to recognize whether a child's speech, play, interests and general behaviour are normal for his age or not. During illness a certain amount of regression may well occur, as it does with all patients. The fact that the child behaves in a manner more appropriate to a younger age needs to be recognized, but the child needs encouragement and help to return to more mature behaviour. He should not be penalized, for example, for wetting the bed, or for whimpering or for resorting to baby talk. But he should not be insulted by being given play material which he has outgrown, or by being placed in a cot when he is already used to a bed, or by being given a spoon to eat with when he already uses a knife and fork. A child's day normally follows a very well-established routine. There is, in the child's opinion, a right time for play, for stories, for bath and for rest. There is a time for attention from mother and a time for watching television and a time for quiet occupation. Older children have a regular time set aside for school work and they use for play any spare time they can find. In hospital the routine tends to be upset. Children have more time to play, sometimes more things to play with, but they may find it difficult to become interested in play when they are in strange surroundings and when play becomes the main occupation rather than the change from other events. Children's conversation is concerned with the events of daily life. They comment on all they see and do and their talk makes them more interested in what they do. If children in hospital do not have enough to do they cannot find much to talk about, and if they have no one to talk to about their play this becomes boring.

To the small child in hospital play may be of additional significance because, unlike an adult, he may be unable to explains his needs or express his feelings in words. In play he may be able to express frustration by projecting feelings on to dolls, to play out the drama of his own life in the dolls' house or to control his emotions through aggressive play. In his choice of play material he can demonstrate his level of maturity and his temporary state of regression. Such play can have therapeutic value only if it is planned and progressive. This means that the child needs time set aside regularly and a person who can devote her entire attention to him, who can enter his world and share with him the experiences of life in the ward and the memory of play that has gone before. Nurses can learn to use play therapeutically, but they are often too busy to accord play the priority it deserves. For this reason some hospitals employ 'play leaders' who are trained to help the child and interpret his play. Communication between 'play leaders' and nurses can be of great benefit and allows the play needs of the child to be fully incorporated in the nursing care plan. Other schemes have been devised to minimize the distress of admission to hospital, e.g. ward granny schemes (Jolly, 1974).

DISCHARGE FROM HOSPITAL

One of the dangers of long illness in childhood lies in the fact that the child may have difficulty in settling down at home. A few months in the life of a small child is a very long time. A child's development is closely linked with people and things in his environment. While in hospital he is learning about things which are not of great use to him outside. Social conventions, language, routine, are totally different from the child's family culture. Meanwhile people at home change, develop new interests, start on ventures of which the child remains ignorant. When he gets back home he may return to an unfamiliar world, to an environment in which he is a stranger. He has not learnt any of the relationships he should have developed with members of his family. During his illness he is the focus of all attention. Whenever he sees his family they are all concerned with his welfare. On his return home he finds people concerned with each other, interested in the welfare of others rather than in himself. Once he is well there are no special favours; no allowance is made for bad behaviour. He is expected to fit in with a way of life which is quite unfamiliar to him. It is important to remember that he needs extra love, care and attention on returning home.

It is a difficult task to help a child to use his period of sickness constructively. He must be helped to realize that there is a greater advantage in being well than in being sick. It is easy for a child to learn how to use sickness as a means of tyrannizing over others and of gaining attention and affection. It takes firmness and much love and patience to give affection without waiting for the child to demand it and to treat sickness in the detached manner which makes it not worth while. Small children do not understand the meaning of sickness very clearly. They cannot understand cause and effect, symptoms and treatment. They may appear to blame the nurse or the doctor for their pain. It may be necessary to separate the functions of the nurses so that the nurse who gives the child his daily care is never associated with causing him pain. Some children appear to associate the nurse's uniform with the unpleasant experience of sickness and pain.

The child's early experiences with sickness, pain, hospitalization, separation from his mother and being cared for by nurses may influence attitudes to sickness later in life.

References

Barber, J.H. (1982) Preschool developmental screening—the results of a four year period. *Health Bulletin* **40**, 170–178.

Barber, J.H., Boothman, R. & Stanfield, J.P. (1976) A new visual chart for preschool development screening. *Health Bulletin* **34**, 80–91.

Bernstein, B. (1971) *Class, Code and Control*, Vol. 1. London: Routledge & Kegan Paul.

Bowlby, J. (1951) *Maternal Care and Mental Health*. Geneva: WHO.

Bryant, G.M. (1980) Use of Denver developmental screening test by health visitors. *Health Visitor* **53**, 2–5.

Clarke, A.M. & Clarke, A.D.B. (1976) *Early Experience: Myth and Evidence*. London: Open Books.

Cleary, J. (1977) The distribution of nursing attention in a children's ward. *Nursing Times, Occasional Papers* **73**, 93–96.

Court Report (1976) *Report of the Committee on Child Health Services: Fit for the Future*, Vol. 1. Chairman: Emeritus Professor S.D.M. Court. London: HMSO.

DHSS and Department of Education and Science (1967) *Children and Their Primary Schools*, Vols. 2. Advisory Council for Education (England) (Plowden Report). London: HMSO.

Erikson, E.H. (1965) *Childhood and Society*. Harmondsworth: Penguin.

Hall, D.J. (1978) Bedside blues: the impact of social research on the hospital treatment of sick children. *Journal of Advanced Nursing* **3**, 25–36.

Hall, D.J. & Stacey, M. (1978) *Beyond Separation: Further Studies of Children in Hospital*. London: Routledge & Kegan Paul.

Hawthorn, P.J. (1974) *Nurse—I Want My Mummy*. London: Royal College of Nursing.

Jolly, J.D. (1974) The ward granny scheme. *Nursing Times* **70**, 573–574.

Labov, W. (1970) The logical non-standard English. In Williams, F. (ed.) *Language and Poverty: Perspectives on a Theme*. Chicago: University Institute for Research on Poverty, Monograph Series.

Platt Report (1959) *The Welfare of Children in Hospital*, Ministry of Health. London: HMSO.

Robertson, J. (1970) *Young Children in Hospital*. London: Tavistock.

Rodin, J. (1983) *Will This Hurt?* London: Royal College of Nursing.

Rubin, Z. (1980) *Children's Friendships*. London: Fontana.

Rutter, M. (1981) *Maternal Deprivation Reassessed*, 2nd Edition. Harmondsworth: Penguin.

Rutter, M. & Madge, N. (1976) *Cycles of Disadvantage*. London: Heinemann.

Tizard, B. & Hughes, M. (1984) *Young Children Learning*. London: Fontana.

Further reading

Mayall, B. & Foster, M. (1989) *Child Health Care*. Oxford: Heinemann.

Muller, D.J., Harris, P.J. & Wattley, L.A. (1986) *Nursing Children: Psychology, Research and Practice*. London: Harper & Row.

9 Development in adolescence and adulthood

There is no precise definition of adolescence. Adults refer to adolescence as the age in which young people are no longer children but are not yet grown up. Children, looking to the future, do not contemplate adolescence, only adulthood. Adolescents may not recognize themselves as such, preferring to be known by some other term, such as 'teenager'. Growing up is a gradual process involving physical, intellectual, emotional and social growth. Development in these various ways does not always occur smoothly. Around the age of 14, intelligence reaches its maximum and physical development may be very advanced or very much retarded. Emotional and social development are incomplete.

Physical development is particularly erratic in adolescence. Sexual maturity may occur as early as 11 or 12 years and as late as 16 to 17 years of age. Physical growth occurs suddenly and unevenly. The proportion of feet and hands to limbs, or limbs to trunk, may change rapidly; facial growth may radically alter the appearance. The result is often seen in a physical awkwardness which makes life almost intolerably miserable. Unthinking adults may aggravate the situation by commenting on the adolescent's clumsiness, gawkiness or ungainly appearance. To a certain extent, participation in sports can help to overcome physical awkwardness.

INTELLECTUAL DEVELOPMENT

When large numbers of individuals are repeatedly tested over many years, it is found that overall intellectual ability increases rapidly during childhood and adolescence and then slows down during adulthood. Such tests also demonstrate that the adolescent years are very important, for it is during this period that our capacity to acquire and utilize knowledge reaches its peak.

It is around the age of 12 years (although there is marked individual variation) that children reach what Piaget describes as the period of formal operational thinking. The kinds of thought processes which are involved in formal operations are fairly complex and abstract, and, it is thought, form the basis of scientific reasoning. The concepts which the adolescent attains include, for example, proportions, probability and concepts which go beyond immediate observable experience (e.g. energy). In other words, in childhood the emphasis is on *what is*, but the adolescent is able to consider *what might be*. However, a number of researchers (e.g. Wason and Johnson-Laird, 1977) questioned the idea that everyone reaches the stage of formal operational thinking and Piaget, in his later writings (Piaget, 1972) acknowledges that not all intelligent adults operate at the level of formal operations. Indeed many adults find it difficult to solve logical problems in a formal manner. When the same type of logical problems are presented in real everyday contexts, solving them becomes much easier. It has been suggested that it is because of the adolescent's new found ability to consider what might be that leads to his taste for theorizing and criticizing.

The young person may find this period one of special difficulty, but there are many people whose secure early environment enables them to pass through adolescence without difficulty. The rapid development of intelligence may create conflict between parent and child. The adolescent, who is conscious of his intellectual superiority, may, at the same time, become aware of the occasional faulty judgement of his elders. He has not yet gained the necessary experience of life to apply his intelligence well, nor the maturity to make allowances for the older generation. He suddenly realizes that his knowledge and power of reasoning are equal or superior to his parents' and becomes aware that parents, who hitherto had been thought of as paragons, can be fallible. The adolescent is still sufficiently childish to believe that if parents are wrong in one thing they must always be wrong and that if he himself is right in one thing he is always right. This attitude of absolute self-confidence in his own judgement is sometimes irritating to older people. When parents are in fact of lower intelligence than their children, or less well educated, they may strongly resent the intellectual superiority and the cocksure manner of their children and they may feel that their children are beyond their control. Adolescents delight in catching older people out and can be quite merciless to teachers or other adults once they have lost confidence in their judgement. On the other hand, they unreservedly admire those superior qualities which they most desire for themselves. Hero-worship is a characteristic of the adolescent stage.

IDENTITY SEEKING

Children begin early in childhood to play out different roles, but it is during adolescence that identity seeking becomes evident. Erikson (1968) says that the young person becomes concerned with how he appears in other people's eyes. He typically identifies with, or imitates, a number of different key people in his life. Thus he makes a number of identifications, which may be inconsistent and contradictory, and possible identity confusion may arise. However, Coleman (1980) in reviewing the research stimulated by Erikson's notion of a 'crisis of identity' argues that although identity problems do exist there is no evidence to suggest that the majority of adolescents experience a serious crisis of identity.

Because of this search for identity the young person may be seen to have many affectations, but he is trying out identities, and mockery by adults will certainly not help. Clothes become extremely important in making the adolescent feel comfortable. There is no greater humiliation than clothes which have become too tight or too short, or look too childish or too dowdy. Many adolescents, especially girls, feel so strongly about clothes that they prefer to leave school as soon as they can rather than wear school uniform, which they believe accentuates their physical disadvantages. The fact that adolescents feel unsure about their physical appearance often causes them to spend a considerable amount of time in front of the mirror in order to get used to their altered body image. Girls experiment with hair-styles and make-up, for example, and often worry a good deal about their figures. If their breasts have not yet developed they feel childish and conspicuous, yet when they do develop they worry about them becoming too big. They often worry about weight increase and experiment with slimming diets. This may well lead to eating problems, severe enough to require treatment. Boys take some time to get used to their new voice when it has broken. They may feel ambivalent about their growth of beard and about the necessity to shave.

During adolescence, detachment from family ties nears completion and independence is established. In the most favourable circumstances detachment from the home is gradual while interests widen, friendships are formed among people of the same age and adult models are found outside the family circle. Sometimes, however, the period of detachment from home is stormy and disturbed.

Adolescents, who are still in the habit of making wild generalizations, of seeing issues in black and white, of wholehearted acceptance or rejection, may suddenly experience a most powerful rejection of all that their family stands for. They may go to opposite extremes from parental values in their views about religion, morals, or their future careers. They may fight their battles with parents on these important issues or they may do so on relatively unimportant matters, such as clothes, tastes in interior decoration, methods of spending their leisure time or opinions about music. However, there is little evidence to suggest that major conflict with parents is experienced by most adolescents.

Some adolescents find in religion the support they require. The search for absolute values, trust in God, and the understanding of metaphysical concepts may be of immense value to them during this period of emotional insecurity. The ultimately accepted religious beliefs and ethical codes may not be those of the parents but rather those arrived at by the adolescent's own struggle for truth.

Adolescent friendships

Most adolescents gain support in their newly found independence from others of their own age. The approval and admiration of members of their own age group becomes much more important than the approval of adults. Adolescents need to form groups and to belong wholeheartedly to them. At school there is evidence of gang formation and complete conformity to the standards of the gang is essential. The word 'gang' may not denote undesirable group formation, but expresses the peculiar adolescent way of forming rival units distinctive in dress, in speech or in some other outward sign in such a way that members of the gang can recognize each other instantly and also members of rival groups. Each member of the group accepts and adopts unquestioningly the mannerisms, opinions and habits of the other members. Unless conformity is absolute there is no way of indicating loyalty to the group. Fashions in hair-styles, in clothes, in popular songs and in spare-time activities are created in this way by adolescents. The ethics of the gang are in marked contrast to the self-centred thinking of the small child. Whether the fashions are socially acceptable or not depends partly on the leadership and opportunities of the group, partly on the extent to which adults create antagonism in the adolescent. Even membership of a delinquent group is, from the point of view of the mental health of the adolescent, better than going through adolescence as an isolated individual or remaining too closely attached to the family group. Rutter (1978) has suggested that difficulties in making relationships with other children is one of the most reliable indicators of current or subsequent mental disorder or delinquency.

Crazes about ballet, concerts and visits to art galleries are as much the manifestation of adolescent gregariousness as are discothèques and street-corner gatherings. The latter tend to evoke more criticism from adults and thereby may become more obviously antisocial. Youth clubs may sometimes satisfy adolescent needs for recognition. Some social organizations, the scout movement for example, deliberately attempt to satisfy the need for uniform and instant recognition of members. Badges, rituals and sign language all make it easier to identify members of the group. Very often, however, young people feel dissatisfied with the organizations of the scout kind because they are too formal. They like youth clubs organized by themselves, not for them. At the time of their greatest antagonism to adults they cannot tolerate adult patronage.

In late adolescence the urge to conform to peer groups diminishes. Adolescents then begin to see the advantages to be gained from independence.

The adolescent in society

The adolescent's position in society is very ill defined. Parents and teachers expect adult behaviour and attitudes, yet they are unwilling to treat the adolescent as an equal. He resents being treated as a child, yet he finds comfort at times in behaving like one. If the adolescent is still at school he feels inferior to those who, until recently, were his equals but who have entered the adult world of work and are earning money. Those who start working find that they are not really accepted as adults by the world in general. Youth, inexperience and lack of knowledge are held against them. In some primitive societies transition from childhood to adulthood is marked by definite, prescribed 'initiation rites'. In our social structure adolescents belong to neither the adult nor childhood fraternity and the path to adulthood has to be found by trial and error. This may be the reason that special units for adolescents are to be found in many hospitals.

It is difficult for children to have any clear conception of adulthood. The fact that adults have duties and obligations as well as rights is quite unknown even to adolescents. Their choice of work or careers may be based on completely unrealistic ideas and their first experiences of adult life are very disappointing. Adults

are not only expected to accept responsibility willingly
for their own actions, but sometimes, indeed, for the
actions of others—a fact for which adolescents are often
ill prepared.

It is sometimes difficult for the young person to deal
with the change in status which accompanies changing
roles in family, school and work. Within the family the
child's status may increase as he begins to contribute
financially and as he becomes independent. Outside the
family the senior pupils of a school enjoy relatively
high status in relation to the other pupils and even the
teachers treat them with a certain amount of respect.
To assume a position of low status at the place of work
or in the junior ranks of an institute of higher education
may be very painful to the adolescent's self-esteem.

Emotional as well as social development may reach
an unstable point in adolescence. Children experience
rapidly-changing, strong emotions and are able and
allowed to express these freely and immediately in
words or actions. Adults can control the expression
of emotions and experience lasting rather than rapidly
changing ones. Children react rapidly to people and
things, showing strong liking or disliking of people,
and sometimes anger at objects which happen to be in
their way. Adults differentiate in their emotional reaction to people—they love some very deeply but are
emotionally unaffected by others. They may devote
deep feeling to ideas such as patriotism, pacificism,
justice. Children need to be loved and adults need to
give love. The adolescent's emotions lie somewhere
between those of childhood and adulthood. He feels
deeply but often indiscriminately. He may not yet be
able to control the expression of feelings but, in trying
to do so, he may give the impression of being cold and
hard. He is beginning to feel strongly about ideas but

covers his feeling with bumptiousness or the appearance of being opinionated. He still needs to be loved but cannot accept it without feeling self-conscious. He is beginning to give love, not yet for the satisfaction of other people's needs, but rather because he obtains emotional satisfaction from giving. At this particular moment of emotional turmoil the adolescent may become aware, perhaps for the first time, of sexual urges and desires. He may be unsure of the way to deal with his sexual feelings and feels unable to discuss them. In the next pages we shall refer again to sexual development and to the help which may be needed in the form of sex education. Sexual feelings are mentioned here only as yet another difficulty in the adolescent's experience of life.

Problems of adolescence

Some young people indulge, for a time, in behaviour which adults regard as 'delinquent'. There may be a number of reasons for this. Some behaviour, for example, which a few years earlier would merely have been regarded as naughty, becomes delinquent in adolescents mainly because adolescents, by virtue of their greater strength and size, can be so much more destructive. Throwing stones, for example, is an innocent pastime with some nuisance value when a child is small, but it becomes vandalism in adolescence. Fights among small boys are relatively harmless, among adolescents there can be serious injury.

Some delinquent behaviour occurs almost accidentally because of the young people's tendency to form gangs. Some adolescents live in such cramped, uninteresting, surroundings that almost any activity results in annoyance to someone near by. The provision of sports centres and playing fields and facilities for getting into the country, to the mountains or the sea, may help young people who find themselves frustrated by lack of space. Some housing estates are particularly unsuited to the interests of adolescents. Having been originally built for young couples with small children, they have failed to develop a real community feeling. In the absence of meeting places, discothèques, cinemas or any other community centres, young people are obliged to meet in the street or in cafés and often find insufficient outlet for their energies. One of the additional problems of housing estates arises from the fact that the age distribution of the population is quite unlike that of older communities. Having been, in the first instance, provided for young couples and small children they are now populated by middle-aged adults and adolescents. There are few old people, few young adults and few small children. The young people, who are now adolescent, have grown up without any models of older children to copy and without their guidance into adolescence.

While it is true that delinquency occurs chiefly among adolescents it is not true to say that most adolescents are delinquent. It is only when adolescents are antisocial, even in relation to their own peers, or when they have grown to distrust all people and to hate all authority, that their actions give cause for concern. Some young people have the desire to enlarge their experience by experimenting with drugs. While sensational newspaper articles have possibly exaggerated the problem, there is justifiable cause for alarm. it is particularly worrying that adolescents are easy prey for drug pushers, who earn their living by introducing new customers to the use of drugs and who, by bringing young drug takers into contact with the underworld, can easily lead them on to other serious forms of delinquency. Many young people have sufficient stability and common sense to give up drugs after experimentation, having realized that it is simply not worth it. Others need education and information about the dangers of the first steps on the road to drug addiction and they need protection from those who try to involve them in this kind of behaviour.

With so many problems reaching their climax in adolescence, it is surprising how successfully most children pass on to adulthood. Recognition by adults of all that is good and positive in young people contributes perhaps more than anything else to the self-confidence necessary in adolescence.

SEXUAL DEVELOPMENT

During adolescence, physical development reaches its maturity. Changes in endocrine function, in physique, voice and facial appearance, may increase the adolescent's self-consciousness and emotional turmoil. With the awareness of bodily readiness the adolescent may experience sexual urges and emotional changes which may be frightening and profoundly disturbing. The climax of sexual development is reached later, in adulthood, when bodily maturation is accompanied by the ability to love and to choose a partner with whom a permanent relationship of marriage and the foundation of family life are wholly satisfactory. Adult sexuality consists not only of the unique relationship between one man and one woman which makes intercourse a profoundly satisfying experience to both, but of being able to love the partner to the exclusion of all other potential partners. To enter into a permanently binding relationship entails a complete reorientation of attitudes, interest and social adjustment—changes which make it possible later to enter into parenthood and to give children the love and affection they need. Physical relationship without an accompanying emotional development cannot be considered complete. Sexual urges and sexual behaviour do not suddenly manifest themselves in adolescents, but adolescent and adult sexual behaviour are stages of a gradual development which begins at birth.

For a long period during the early school years the child is engaged in social learning. Not until he reaches early adolescence is his interest in his body reawakened. The young adolescent has sufficient factual knowledge to associate his genital organs with sex; he is aware of his bodily tensions and recognizes them as being sexual. One method of relieving sexual tension is masturbation. Nearly everyone masturbates at some time in their lives. Kinsey and colleagues in their investigations with volunteer subjects in the USA, put the incidence as high as 92% for men and nearly 60% for women (Kinsey *et al.*, 1948, 1953). It is the belief in some religions that masturbation is sinful and many young people feel intensely guilty about their indulgence. For this reason they keep their practice strictly secret. They believe that they alone are guilty of such practices and their guilt feeling increases correspondingly. Some people also believe, erroneously, that masturbation is harmful. The conviction in medical quarters is that masturbation is not the cause of any psychotic disorders. Most people abandon the practice for other sexual activity when a suitable sexual partner is available. The adolescent does not always, however, have this information available. His parents may still disapprove of the practice, or condemn it, or the adolescent may think they do and he may refrain from confiding in them. He may have developed sufficient inhibitions to make it difficult for him to obtain sexual information from his parents or to discuss sexual problems with them.

Quite suddenly the adolescent may become interested in the opposite sex. For a long period boys and girls consider each other to be stupid and friendships, therefore, are made almost entirely with their own sex. At that stage there is little concern for appearance. Those, for instance, who are interested in clothes or cosmetics are ridiculed. Suddenly interest in the other sex is aroused, or rather the adolescent seeks to awaken the interest of the opposite sex. Emotionally the need is still to be loved and noticed rather than to give love. Girls begin to take care of their clothes, hair and personal hygiene, become interested in fashion and seek advice about beauty in women's magazines. Boys smarten up in appearance and both sexes give up childhood games and interests. This phase strikes adults as being the awakening of sexual urges. In fact it should be seen to be only one phase, though at times it may be a particularly stormy one.

The adolescent is still groping for standards of beauty and moral behaviour. He is conscious of his looks but does not know if his looks appeal to the opposite sex. Attempts at choosing clothes, using cosmetics, selecting jewellery often meet with derision from adults instead of evoking encouragement and offers of help. The result often is that parental standards are deliberately rejected. Adolescents find each other attractive because of the obvious effort each makes, despite the fact that there may be little that could be called aesthetic success.

Boys sometimes find the transition to manhood easier than girls find transition to womanhood. Girls, who are less free to experiment with methods of self-expression and self-display, may not find their feminine role easily identifiable. Adjustment to work, on the other hand, is more easily accomplished by girls than by boys.

General interest in the opposite sex usually gives way to a specific interest in one person of the opposite sex. While there is general interest, mixed social gatherings in discothèques or clubs are attended and enjoyed. Couple formation disrupts social gatherings. The two people concerned are interested only in each other, so they usually leave the group and find enjoyment where they can be alone. Most youth clubs suffer constant depletion from among their senior and more reliable members and, because of this, come to rely on adult leadership. There may be many rapid changes in the attraction felt towards a person of the opposite sex. Dating and flirtations are necessary experiences before the right person for marriage can be found. At this stage the adolescent is learning to give love as well as to receive it. It may be given profusely and guishingly and often may be unacceptable to the other. The emotion of love often overflows and embraces society as a whole; there is an overwhelming desire to do good, to be of service, to care for others.

By the time a sexually mature relationship is possible, love is given to satisfy the needs of others rather than purely selfish needs. Interests become adapted to those of others, opinions change in accordance with others and activities cease to be self-centred.

Adult sexual and emotional relationships can be completely satisfying. Some people believe that this is so to such an extent that there is little energy left for activities of social usefulness. They believe that wholehearted devotion to the arts, or science or business, or the care of other people's children is possible only as a substitute for sexual satisfaction. The term 'sublimation' is used to describe this feeling for some cause which is entirely satisfying and not consciously connected with sexual satisfaction. Many people, however, if they fail to find sexual satisfaction, retain a longing which they are unable to admit even to themselves and which leaves them angry and dissatisfied.

In order to lead a full, normal life, each stage of development must give rise to satisfaction. This does not mean that people should be encouraged to give way to all sexual urges and impulses. It means that in the early stages the child's need for love and food must be satisfied. Later he must learn to recognize his feelings and deal with them consciously. If guilt feelings are associated with sexual thoughts this makes it impossible to talk about and control difficulties.

Education about sexual development is essential in order to avoid the confusion in standards. Most parents believe that the best way of teaching their children about sex is simply to answer all questions frankly and simply when they arise. It must be remembered, however, that children's questions may not fully reflect their misconceptions and they may ask questions so badly that the parents' answer becomes irrelevant. Even simple answers can be very bewildering. Children may, for example, know that babies grow inside the mother's abdomen. What they are puzzled about may be how the 'seed' got in or how the baby comes out. Some children feel sure that the 'seed' must be eaten to get in and, because they often think they too could have babies if they tried, they may develop food fads or abnormal preoccupations about food in the fear of becoming pregnant. Children may believe that kissing is the way to start a baby and may, for a time, become reluctant to kiss anyone. The umbilicus is sometimes thought to be the place through which babies are born and fears of the abdomen splitting open occur. Other children believe that bowel or bladder functions are associated with childbirth.

Some of the irrational beliefs of young children still exist in adolescents or are reactivated. Many young people reach adolescence without full knowledge of biological facts, or are secretly afraid that they are not fully informed. Many moral problems may trouble the adolescent and he needs an opportunity for full and free discussion of sexual matters.

Parents inevitably have anxious moments and thoughts about the sexual problems of their children. The solution of this dilemma does not consist of warnings against possible dangers before the true significance of sex is understood, but in building up over the years a relationship of confidence, trust and understanding. Frankness is essential but tact and understanding are also necessary. Sometimes it is better for a person outside the family to advise the adolescent on matters of sex. Emotional reactions may be quite strong, even in families which pride themselves on their open frankness on most topics.

Any discussion of sexuality must take account of the changing values and attitudes in Western society, as reflected in a growing emphasis on 'self-discovery and self-expression' among young people (Conger, 1979). Young people are now more open about sexual matters compared with young people of say 30 years age. Adolescents freely discuss among themselves such sexual matters as, for example, masturbation, homosexuality and contraception—giving added weight to their need for information. Surveys in which young people were asked about their sexual behaviour present methodological problems which may to some extent distort the findings (Coleman, 1980). Reviewing the research in the USA and Europe, Coleman suggests that promiscuity is not increasing to any great extent among young people.

Thus the fear of most adults that sexual freedom inevitably leads to more and more promiscuity is unsupported by the available evidence. In times of changing values, inconsistencies of standards are widespread, leading to confusion and difficulties for the adolescent in coming to terms with questions related to sexual matters.

THE ADULT

Maturity

Children and adolescents look forward to adulthood. Yet when this is reached it may still be felt that something is lacking. The sense of satisfaction, of completeness, which for so long has been anticipated, is not experienced and people still feel that there must be some way in which the purpose of maturity can be more adequately fulfilled. 'Maturity' is spoken of as being the highest aim. Because most people aim higher than their current achievement, maturity is elusive, always to be aimed at, never to be reached. The more mature an individual's behaviour is the more it is likely that he is aware of those qualities within himself which are still undeveloped and doubt is often expressed as to whether anyone can ever be said to be mature, or whether any definition is entirely adequate.

The idea that psychological development is a life-long process is relatively recent. Earlier psychologists thought that all significant development occurred in childhood and viewed adulthood as psychologically unimportant. The way we have presented development reflects a view that it is possible to describe life as a cycle with the individual passing through various stages or milestones. The Rapoports (e.g. Rapoport and Rapoport, 1980) describe adulthood in terms of three major 'phases'—

young adulthood, the establishment phase, and the later years. They view leisure, work and family as three interacting aspects of life each of which has its own sequence and forms what they call 'careers'. Careers are viewed within a 'spiral' framework, since each new phase is influenced by what has happened in earlier phases. On the other hand, Bromley (1974) describes the adult phase of life in terms of seven consecutive stages following late adolescence (Table 3).

Bromley emphasizes the importance of biological factors in ageing. He argues that 'all or most of the psychological and social consequences of ageing arise directly or indirectly from an accumulation of defects and failures in the biological foundations of behaviour' (Bromley, 1977).

Emotional development

Since it is difficult to describe a mature person, it may be helpful to consider trends in development which lead towards desirable stages of adulthood and to examine the ideals which should be kept in mind when maturity is sought. The most important changes taking place

Table 3. Stages of adult development.

Age (years)	Stage	
Early twenties	1.	Full engagement in social, economic and industrial systems of the community
25–40	2.	Adulthood proper—consolidation of occupational, domestic and other social roles
40–55 or 60	3.	Late adulthood or middle-age—continuance of occupational, domestic and other social roles
55 or 60–65	4.	Pre-retirement period
60 or 65–70	5.	Retirement
70 and over	6.	Old age
	7.	Terminal stage leading to death

during development lie in the range of emotional experiences and the manner in which emotions find expression. Children react to a very small number of stimuli; adults to a very large number. Children have a very limited selection of emotional responses; adults have a large range of emotions. Children react with immediate response; adults can delay and control emotional expression. In childhood, emotion is aroused equally by objects, people and events. As the individual gets older emotional response is increasingly evoked by abstract concepts and ideas. Infants and small children react irresponsibly; adults take responsibility not only for their own actions but also for those of their subordinates.

Emotional maturity, then, entails the ability to withhold or delay emotional responses and to display and express emotion in a socially accepted manner. Temper tantrums, for example, are disapproved of in most societies, but grief or pleasure may be freely displayed in some cultures. British people, by reason of training, show a minimum of emotional display. It is, however, necessary to retain the ability to feel emotions deeply, strongly and lastingly. To do this people must learn to recognize their emotions and not to deny that they exist. While it is wise to help children to control their behaviour it is dangerous to make them feel guilty about their feelings. If the strength of a child's emotion becomes too frightening he grows up as if he had never had the emotional experience and emotion becomes unconscious and inaccessible. Many adults are motivated in their behaviour by emotions which properly belong to childhood, but which have never been adequately dealt with because they were too rapidly pushed into unconsciousness. It is a part of maturity to recognize that actions are not always entirely rational. A large area of personality is unconscious and much of what appears to be well-reasoned behaviour results from unconscious emotional motivation.

The objects of emotion change during the maturing process. Inanimate things no longer arouse feelings; instead the individual feels strongly about people. In childhood, the mother, later the father, and then relatives and friends matter a great deal. There is a great need to be loved. All emotion is self-centred. All new knowledge is evaluated according to the child's own feelings about it. People are seen as good or bad according to the way they impinge on his emotions.

The adolescent is still preoccupied with his own feelings and is critical of others because they do not sufficiently satisfy his emotional needs. However, he experiences a change from the need to be loved by his parents to a need for acceptance by a community of peers. The feeling of belonging to a group becomes most important and with this he develops the ability to assess how others feel, what others expect, what pleases them and to assess, to some extent, how others will react to his own behaviour.

During adolescence there is increasing need to give rather than to receive. At first this is all-embracing. The adolescent feels strongly for all the members of his group. He obtains satisfaction from giving and searches for people on whom he can bestow his love. Children, animals, helpless people, become the objects of his emotional bounty. Soon he becomes more selective and seeks reciprocity for his emotion until, in a monogamous relationship, there is the potential for complete satisfaction in the love given to and received from his partner.

Parenthood entails a change in emotion towards an entirely altruistic attitude of giving love. Possessive mothers love their children because they need to be loved in return and because they derive satisfaction from being able to give. Completely mature motherhood would make it possible to give all the love the child needs without taking anything in return and for the child's sake entirely, not for the mother's own satisfaction. It is difficult to say whether this completely unselfish love is ever possible. Whenever the question arises whether an unloved or orphaned child should be adopted or placed in a foster home one must try to find out how far the prospective mother is able to satisfy a child's needs and to what extent her desire to take in a child's is a result of her own need to be loved by a child. There is a great danger that children who were deprived of love early in life may take a long time before they can respond to mothering. If the motive for taking in the child is not entirely altruistic the mother, disappointed by a lack of response from the child, may reject him, regret her decision and blame the child for the failure.

In the middle years it is possible to widen the scope for emotion and feel strongly about ideas and causes as well as about people. The psychologist McDougall (1912) called this 'sentiment' and spoke, for example, of the sentiment of patriotism or of pacifism. A sentiment comprises all the emotions which may be felt in relation to a particular idea. Patriotism, for example, evokes pleasurable feelings when the country does well in competition, fear if it is threatened and anger if it is attacked. Perhaps the most mature people have the greatest number of sentiments and the widest range of interest. They have formed sentiments attached to more abstract ideas. This concern for events beyond the individual's own experience might be called a philosophy of life. The ability to become interested in people and ideas far removed from daily experience is closely related to one other aspect of maturity, namely integration in society.

Social development

In our particular society adults have formed a fairly characteristic pattern of social grouping around themselves. They have a very close emotional bond with one other person—a bond different from any other relationship in its intensity and in the extent to which it is reciprocated. The relationship between husband and wife, or between mother and baby, are examples. A little further removed but still very close is a circle of a few people very important to one another, e.g. the rest of the family and a set of close friends where the relationships are reciprocated. Any disaster occurring to any person in the circle would greatly affect every other person in it. This circle is formed during childhood, adolescence and early adulthood and does not change much after that. As people grow older it becomes progressively more difficult to admit new people into this very close relationship and, of course, the loneliness of old age is a result of the gradual thinning out of this circle. Within it, emotional bonds are so strong that they survive differences of opinion and separation in space and time.

A little further distant is a more populated circle of good friends, workmates and well-liked relations. These are people about whose welfare the individual still cares very much but whose disappearance causes him less concern. They have friends who are not included in one's own circle of friends. Behaviour towards this group of people is governed by social convention and learnt with difficulty during childhood. We can all think of examples of children's failure to distinguish the appropriate behaviour towards friends of their parents or even towards total strangers.

Apart from these closer relationships there are many people with whom the individual has some kind of social contact in a more and more distant way: the people with whom correspondence is maintained, people with whom Christmas cards are exchanged, people met on the way to work, tradesmen and bus conductors. Adults know how to behave towards all these people but think about them only during actual social contact. There is not reciprocity in relationship. The relationship between customer and salesman, for example, is totally different for each of the two people involved.

Maturity can, to some extent, be measured by the extent to which a person cares about the people in the distant circles of his social field and by finding out how far his social field extends. Children do not care about anyone they do not know personally. Adults begin to care about people in their street, or village, or club, even if they do not know them personally. An accident, or a case of cruelty to children, or poverty, matters if it has happened to a friend. As maturity is reached such occurrences matter even if they happen in some other part of the country or in a foreign land. The sense of personal involvement in all that happens to human beings anywhere is again an expression of a philosophy of life.

Mature attitude to work

One other aspect of maturity will receive only brief mention in this chapter as it is more fully dealt with later. This is the mature person's attitude to work.

Late in adolescence or early in adulthood, a decision is made about work or choice of career. The way people decide on the work they wish to do is usually complex. Family influence, teachers' opinions, the glamour of propaganda, all enter into the choice of work but rarely succeed in the long run in deciding what is to be the individual's working life. Most people find it difficult to state what caused them to make their choice. The truth is that many factors enter into it, most of them unconscious.

Work is a contribution towards the well-being of society. Most people find it necessary to work because only in that way can they justify their existence. Many people say they work only for money, but, in fact, to be out of work even if there is no shortage of money is extremely demoralizing. Disabled people, old people, and those without work during slumps have expressed their feeling of uselessness and their loss of self-respect during periods of idleness. Some people gain satisfaction from being useful to their family rather than from a contribution to society in general. Women may gain sufficient satisfaction from their usefulness to husband and children. This, however, is increasingly not the case and many young mothers feel frustrated by their inability to go out to work.

The extent to which the work is seen to be useful gives it a certain amount of prestige. Many people gain satisfaction from their work because of the status it confers upon them. People who feel that their work lacks prestige must either change jobs or convince others of its importance.

The mature person may be one who has found satisfaction in his work and whose personal plans and ambitions have either found fulfilment or have been submerged in a concern for the general well-being of the community. He is looking forwards and backwards at the same time; plans for the future are related to past achievements.

Plans for the future are realistic and the ambitions and ideas of others are taken into account.

OLD AGE

Just as it is difficult to define adolescence and maturity, so also old age defies definition. To children, parents in their thirties appear old; grandparents seem ancient. As the years advance old age recedes and some people of 70 and 80 years do not consider themselves old at all. Therefore it is important to view old age in the context of the elderly person's whole lifespan. Fundamental to understanding an old person's needs and aspirations is an appreciation that he is an individual with a life history behind him.

Most people feel that they are getting old when they are physically unable to do all the things they still feel inclined to do, although physical ageing occurs at different rates in different people. With advancing years breathlessness supervenes more easily; tiredness may be felt in the middle of the day. The older woman finds increasing difficulty in carrying out the chores at home in a reasonable time. This is often upsetting to her husband who may have retired but finds the house less relaxing than he had anticipated. Damage to the brain tissue, owing to lack of oxygen, brain injury or infection may cause premature and exaggerated manifestations of ageing which are in no way characteristic of the ageing process of normal people.

Gradually eyesight and possibly hearing become less acute. It is easier to become aware of failing eyesight. Often the onset of deafness is not perceived and many old people complain of other people's lack of consideration in not speaking clearly, not realizing that the fault lies in their own deafness. It is even possible for them to become suspicious when people are laughing and to create hostility in others by their inability to hear. The suggestion that hearing aids might be used is often vigorously rejected, partly because the realization of a disability is too painful, partly because old people are embarrassed by wearing these aids and also, after trying to use one, are bothered by the very strange noises they experience. When we hear well we succeed in picking out voices and speech from the general background noise and ignore the rest. As deafness advances more and more noises become inaudible. Hearing aids magnify all sounds and after a period of silence the irrelevant noises may become unbearable.

With increasing age the daily activities of washing, combing hair, pulling on stockings, become more and more strenuous. These activities, which during adult life are habitual and therefore accomplished without thought, become important activities occupying conscious thought.

It may become more difficult to remember what is happening, although gross memory defect for recent events occurs only in the dementia of old age. However, the elderly person finds it more difficult to attend to many things at the same time and consequently fails to take in some information which may later be required, appearing then to have forgotten the information, but in reality never having grasped it. It happens often, on the other hand, that the apparent forgetfulness of the aged in fact represents refusal to accept information, especially if it is not in accordance with their accepted ideas. Contrary to the belief often held by old people themselves, learning new material is perfectly possible in old age, though it may take a little longer. In normal senescence intelligence does not decline very markedly. Vocabulary remains at a high level, but, in intelligence tests the ability to solve certain problems in a given time diminishes. Incidental learning diminishes. The older a person is the more he only learns what he sets out to learn and the less does he pick up incidental information which he interprets as unrelated. The range of performance can be increased if the old person does not resist.

Some old people tend to think of everyone younger than themselves as children, just as children consider everyone else to be old. This attitude of old people leads to a certain amount of selfishness, condescension and what may appear to be interference in the life of young people. In homes where grandparents, parents and children live together relations are sometimes strained by the fact that the grandparents treat the parents as if they were children.

On the other hand, old people and young children usually get on extremely well as their relationship is quite natural, uncritical and accepting. Parents often feel that grandparents spoil small children, but there is no reason to believe that the genuine love and understanding which passes between alternate generations is in any way harmful.

Old people's habits are fairly well fixed—an asset when conscious efforts become difficult. Interference by younger people is quite understandably resented. The problems which must be resolved by the aged are related to their increasing loneliness as their contemporaries die, one by one, to the realization that they must retire from work and accept the fact that they are no longer needed, and to the need to think about death and to come to terms with this thought.

We live in an adult-centred society which thinks most highly of the productive section of the community. According to our society the purpose of childhood is to get over it as fast as possible, and we talk of the 'problem of old age' as if old people served no purpose and were merely a burden. This is not the case in all societies. There are people who consider that childhood is of supreme value and that the function of adults is primarily to support the young. In some eastern societies old age is the period of life most cherished and esteemed and the time looked forward to throughout life.

If we are to solve our problem of old age we must try to stop looking at people as valuable only as long as they can work, and put greater value on the fund of knowledge and experience old people have to offer.

The personal loneliness of the very old cannot be avoided, but the feelings of isolation can be overcome by widening as early as possible the circle of friends and acquaintances and by developing a sense of responsibility for the welfare of others. There is ample scope in voluntary work, in local government or other local organizations for those who are still interested in others and free from personal obligations.

Retirement

Retirement can be very traumatic, especially if too many years have been spent in the same job and too much interest has been given to work to the exclusion of outside interests. The problem of when to retire is often discussed. Some people believe that work should be continued as long as possible. This may, however, lead to many difficulties, including the uncomfortable awareness of blocking promotion for younger, perhaps abler people. Old people's methods cannot be readily changed and although their own work may still reach a very high standard, their rigidity may have adverse effects on the efficiency and morale of the people with whom they are working. If retirement is left entirely to the decision of the individual he may reach a stage at which he is no longer capable of recognizing his limitations. Most damaging, however, is the fact that late retirement makes it impossible to take up new interests and there is a good deal to be said for early compulsory retirement when the individual is still young enough to start making new friends and taking up new interests.

Once retirement has occurred it involves the elderly persons in reorganizing their lives. At first it may well feel like being on holiday but as time passes the retired person begins to notice the loss of the relationships associated with the job—colleagues, clients, and all the people normally encountered in the course of getting to and being at work. This loss can lead to feelings of apathy and depression. Even if new work is found it is usually of low status and pay compared to pre-retirement work and some elderly people might find it difficult to make the psychological adjustment.

In preparing for old age it seems wise to have so many interests and friends that life is still full even when some activities have to be given up. Much is being done by education authorities and much more could be done to encourage hobby activities for older people. Too many are restricted to gardening and knitting for their hobbies. Sewing, craft and cookery classes are held for older people in some areas. Townswomen's Guilds and social clubs for the aged often provide valuable meeting places and interesting activities, but encouragement and participation by younger people is necessary to ensure success. Some recent housing developments make it possible for the aged to live near their families. Frequent visits from the 'extended family', i.e. grandchildren, nieces and nephews, sons-in-law and daughters-in-law, help to keep the aged interested in the events of the day.

Theory of disengagement

The means of psychological adjustment to ageing is sometimes referred to as 'disengagement' (Cumming and Henry, 1961). It is argued that the ageing person disengages himself by reducing the number of inter-actions he has with others and by reducing the number of roles he plays in society. He also does so by restrict-ing his horizons. Long journeys, which he might have enjoyed earlier in life, are no longer contemplated. He no longer feels he can visit relatives or friends who live a long way away and he shops only in his immediate neighbourhood.

Old people may also disengage themselves emotion-ally. They may no longer feel as intensely about events as they did during maturity and this may allow them to develop an attitude of detached tolerance where they might formerly have become angry or hurt. This emo-tional disengagement may earn the old person a repu-tation of broadmindedness which often surprises those who were acquainted with them during an earlier period of strong emotional expression. Cumming and Henry believed that this withdrawal was a healthy adjustment as emotional disengagement allows the elderly to accept the death of contemporaries with equanimity. However, other theorists take a different view. Havighurst (1963), for example, suggests that elderly people may give up some pre-retirement activities but generally replace them with new ones. Predictions from this theory would suggest that only those who have been able to find new interests to replace former ones will make healthy ad-justments in old age.

Old age is the time when there is an increasing tend-ency to look backwards and to be aware that the future is short. Planning ahead is normally the most exciting and most stimulating part of life. Planning a holiday, work, a visit to friends are important considerations to most people. When we are very young plans for the future are vague and unrealistic because the future appears infinitely long. Later in adulthood, planning is realistic and down to earth. There are short-term and long-term plans, plans concerning the individual's own future, plans for others or for the development of the daily sphere of action. Only on rare occasions in adult life may one suddenly realize that these plans may not come to fruition. When a young friend dies at the height of his powers of when a dangerous venture is about to be undertaken,for example an operation or a flight, the healthy adult suddenly thinks of death. But this is momentary and does not interfere with any long-term plans.

Old people are aware that they may die before plans can be fulfilled. Consequently less thought is given to the future and there is a great tendency to live only in the present and in the past. Life becomes somewhat disorganized if there is too much concentration on the present. Houses are not redecorated or gardens re-planted, new clothes are not bought or holidays arranged by those who believe they may not live to enjoy the results. The house, garden and clothes become shabby and the old person becomes more and more de-tached and isolated from others and finally loses any sense of purpose of self-respect. It is the duty of the younger people to include the older generation in their plans. Talking of the future, though not of the very distant future, is a great help. It may be useful to help the old person to realize how much there is still to be done, how much to be enjoyed and that it should all be done soon.

If the younger people show by their attitude that they

are confident of the older person's future, active old age becomes possible. Inevitably, however, the time must come when the older person thinks of death and must accept the fact that the future is limited—at any rate on this earth. To many people the thought of unlimited life after death and their general religious beliefs are of an importance which cannot be overstressed.

The thought of dying is often more uncomfortable to the young than the old; often, therefore, the old person's attempt to discuss death is pushed aside, even ridiculed. It is not helpful to deny the possibility of death or to deprive the old person of the opportunity of talking of it. Old people die more contentedly if all is in order; if a will has been made, if they can be certain that their property will be well disposed of, that their family is provided for, that all arrangements are made for the burial. To discuss these matters freely and openly need not imply that death is imminent or that the younger one wishes the old person dead. On the contrary, guilt feelings about these wishes often prevent younger people from discussing death.

By the time old age has arrived the prospect of completing life is not usually terrifying. It is made easier if the younger people succeed in conveying to the old their admiration of their past achievement and a determination to carry on where they have left off.

References

Bromley, D.B. (1974) *The Psychology of Human Ageing*, 2nd edition. Harmondsworth: Penguin.

Bromley, D.B. (1977) Adulthood and ageing. In Coleman, J.C. (ed.) *Introductory Psychology*. London: Routledge & Kegan Paul.

Coleman, J.C. (1980) *The Nature of Adolescence*. London: Methuen.

Conger, J. (1979) *Adolescence: Generation under Pressure*. London: Harper & Row.

Cumming, E.M. & Henry, W. (1961) *Growing Old*. New York: Basic Books.

Erikson, E.H. (1968) *Identity, Youth and Crisis*. New York: Norton.

Havighurst, R.J. (1963) Successful ageing. In Williams, R.H., Tibbits, C. & Donahue, W. (eds) *Processes of Ageing*. Vol 1. New York: Atherton Press.

Kinsey, A.C., Pomeroy, W.B. & Martin, C.E. (1948) *Sexual Behavior in the Human Male*. Philadelphia: W.B. Saunders.

Kinsey, A.C., Pomeroy, W.B. & Martin, C.E. (1953) *Sexual Behavior in the Human Female*. Philadelphia: W.B. Saunders.

McDougall, W. (1912) *Introduction to Social Psychology*, 5th edition. London: Methuen.

Piaget, J. (1972) Intellectual evolution from adolescence to adulthood. In Wason, P.C. & Johnson-Laird, P.N. (1977) *Thinking: Readings in Cognitive Science*. Cambridge. Cambridge University Press.

Rapoport, R. & Rapoport, R. (1980) *Growing Through Life*. London: Harper & Row.

Rutter, M. (1978) Early sources of security and competence. In Bruner, J.S. & Garton, A. (eds) *Human Growth and Development*. Oxford: Oxford University Press.

Wason, P.C. & Johnson-Laird, P.N. (1977) *Thinking: Readings in Cognitive Science*. Cambridge: Cambridge University Press.

Further reading

Bee, H.L. & Mitchell, S.K. (1984) *The Developing Person*. New York: Harper & Row.

Fiske, M. (1979) *Middle Age: The Prime of Life?* London: Harper & Row.

Hyland, M.E. & Donaldson, M.L. (1989) *Psychological Care in Nursing Practice*. London: Scutari Press.

10 Some psychodynamic theories of development

In the preceding chapters we trace development from infancy to old age. At times a possible connection between early development and later personality characteristics was pointed out and in discussing motivation it was suggested that unconscious mechanisms may be at work. The fact that we are at times unaware of the motives of our actions, that there is an unconscious part of human personality, and that early childhood influences are of importance is undisputed, though there is some controversy about the precise nature of the causal relationships between childhood experience and adult personality.

In this chapter, a brief outline of the main points of psychodynamic and related psychological theories will be given.

SIGMUND FREUD

Sigmund Freud, an Austrian physician, died in England in 1939. His main interest during and on completion of his medical studies lay in the investigation of the structure and function of the nervous system and he had done some valuable work in neurophysiology and neurological disorders before he became interested in those apparently neurological disorders in which no organic lesion could be found. He spent some time in France studying hypnosis and he observed the phenomenon of post-hypnotic suggestion. Although the process of inducing a hypnotic state was not clearly understood, the hypnotist was able to demonstrate that his subject would carry out later, at a specified time after waking, any act suggested to her.

It is, for example, possible to tell a hypnotized subject that at 3 o'clock in the afternoon she will interrupt her work, leave the room, pick up an umbrella in the hall, open it, replace it and return to her former occupation. The subject is then roused from the hypnotic state and remembers nothing of what has been said to her. At precisely 3 o'clock she becomes restless and eventually carries out the activities mentioned above and returns to her previous occupation. When questioned, she cannot explain her actions and becomes uneasy, but, if one insists, she finds a perfectly reasonable explanation; for example, 'I thought it was getting worn out and wanted to see if I needed to buy a new one soon'. This is rationalization but appears to the subject to be the true reason. The suggestion made to her during hypnosis is not accessible to her conscious thoughts. It is 'unconscious' but nevertheless motivates the behaviour described. It is possible under hypnosis to suggest the loss of power of a limb, to tell the subject that he will not be able to see or to suggest that he will fail to recognize a particular familiar person or object. On waking from the hypnotic state the subject suffers from the symptom suggested to him. He cannot explain how he developed the symptom but is strangely indifferent to it. Under subsequent hypnotic influence the symptoms are easily removed.

The purpose of the demonstrations was to study the phenomenon of hypnosis itself. Freud, however, was struck by the significance of the fact that the subjects were unconscious of the causation of their behaviour and by the similarity between some of the symptoms which could be produced and those displayed by his patients. The most important points of Freudian theory arise from these observations—namely, the discovery of the dynamic nature of the unconscious. Freud became interested in methods of bringing some of the unconscious material back into consciousness. Under hypnosis it is possible for the subject to remember more and more of his past life. In fact it is possible to relive incidents of childhood which appeared to be completely forgotten and to experience emotions as deeply as was done originally.

Psychoanalytic theory

Freud decided not to use hypnosis and instead developed the method of 'free association' to delve into the unconscious. If the individual feels completely relaxed and allows his ideas to wander freely, without anyone imposing any criticism or restraint, and without any selection of what appears relevant, more and more memories return to consciousness.

Psychoanalysis is the term used to describe this method. Because many people feel frightened at the thought of revealing some of their most closely guarded secrets, of which even they themselves are unaware, the analyst must help the subject to relax. A friendly, non-judgemental, persuasive attitude is necessary with complete acceptance of anything that is said. The atmosphere is unhurried. Freud felt it was an advantage for the patient to lie down on a couch for complete relaxation, and to arrange the furniture so that the facial expression of the analyst could not be observed. By using this method Freud was able to discover more and more about unconscious mental mechanisms. Because he analysed people suffering from neurotic illness he first believed that some of the events recalled from the unconscious by his patients were responsible for their illness. However, analysis of normal people and discoveries about his own unconscious convinced Freud that at least some of his findings were true of all people.

During the process of free association many unpleasant, often extremely painful, events are recalled. Freud believed that these had become unconscious because they had been too painful to be dealt with consciously. He used the term 'repression' to describe the process of forgetting unpleasant, painful material. Repression is not deliberate. It is an active but unconscious way of forgetting and serves the purpose of leaving the person emotionally undisturbed. At times, however, repression is incomplete. Events are forgotten but the emotion attached to them remains and interferes in daily life. Quite inappropriate emotional reactions can occur and can be sufficiently distressing to amount to neurotic symptoms. Irrational fears, excessive nostility, a general attitude of aggression and excessive submissiveness may have their origins in repressed childhood experiences. Repression occurs in everybody. The first few years of life, which are full of important and highly significant events, are almost completely forgotten by all people. Only isolated events can be recalled without the help of psychoanalysis. During analysis the subject can recall much of his first few years without any direction or suggestion from the analyst. Recalled material is usually believed to belong as far back as the second year of life.

Freud at first believed that the recollections of his patients were accurate and factual and he was very perturbed to find that so often experiences of a sensual nature were recalled. However, he later realized that some of the recollections were not based on reality but on fantasy, although they were none the less important to the individual. Children are unable to measure time with any degree of accuracy, consequently recollections of events are not always accurately timed. There is also a lack of vocabulary during childhood to describe events and experiences clearly. People talk of their early feelings as if they were related to the state of tension in their body. In recollection, adult language is used to describe events to which such language did not at the time apply and for which it may be inappropriate, with the result that reference is often made to sexual experiences in childhood. Emotions are accurately recalled and are clearly recognized, but often the event to which the emotion originally referred is described in more adult form than is justified.

The Ego and the Id
Freud believed that everything that is unconscious has been repressed. We repress those things which are painful and unacceptable and consequently there must be in each of us a mechanism capable of selecting what ought to be repressed. Freud tried to present his idea in the form of a model, using words which could easily be understood but did not refer to anything else. The Latin personal pronoun Ego is used to refer to that part of the personality of which the individual is usually aware, the part referred to as the 'self'. This Ego has developed, Freud said, from the Id. Id, the third person neuter of the pronoun *it*, indicates that there is something disowned and not consciously recognized as the self.

Originally, Freud said, the infant is entirely Id, entirely motivated by impulses and urges which seek pleasure in an unrestrained, sensual way. The infant seeks immediate gratification of its most primitive, instinctive needs. Very soon, restrictions are imposed on him. He cannot always obtain food or comfort as soon as he wishes. Reality impinges on the Id and restrains it. Gratification must also be postponed at times because the child's mother wishes it. Her approval may depend on some curb on the gratification of instinctive desires. The child values approval and soon begins to accept as his own those standards which are first demanded by his mother. More and more the standards of behaviour of people whose approval is valued are accepted by the child. He forms a conscience which Freud called Super-Ego.

Healthy adjustment means that the Ego is well developed and strong, not easily threatened by the forces of the Id or by the excessive demands of the Super-Ego. Whenever there is a danger to the defences of the Ego we respond with anxiety.

The defence mechanisms, or in some people their neurotic symptoms, may be used to deal with strong forces from the Id or with a Super-Ego which is too severe.

Stages of personality development
Freud did not explain why some people have more difficulties than others in establishing a satisfactory balance between the various aspects of personality, but he did attempt to trace certain adult personality traits back to childhood experiences. In particular he maintained that there is continuity from infancy to maturity in the way in which people derive sensual and emotional satisfaction. At each stage satisfaction must be obtained before it is possible to progress to the next phase of development. Failure at any one stage to gain satisfaction results in arrested development which Freud called 'fixation', or even a return to an earlier method of gaining satisfaction, 'regression'.

Adults obtain physical, sensual satisfaction in sexual relationship and orgasm. Freud believed that this special form of satisfaction can be traced back to childhood. Relaxation and satisfaction in infancy is gained during feeding by sucking. This is the *oral* stage of development.

Later, elimination is a profoundly satisfying activity in the *anal* phase of development. Later still, stimulation of the genital organs by masturbation has the same effect. The next stage of sexual satisfaction is the *phallic* stage. This term refers to the male sex organ, the penis, but is used for both women and men. Freud did not say that sucking and elimination are sexual activities but that the satisfaction obtained from these activities is similar to the satisfaction obtained by adults during the sexual act. These activities are remembered during analysis with the kind of feeling which in adulthood accompanies sexual ideas. He also said that the earlier phases must necessarily be passed through during the development towards adult sexuality. After the phallic stage Freud describes a *latency* period before more mature sexual interest arises.

The mouth continues through life to have erotic significance, for example in kissing. Psychoanalysts consider that an interest in food, sucking of sweets or pipes or smoking sometimes represent a substitute for sexual gratification. The connection between elimination and sexual development is less clear in healthy people, but the amount of secrecy, shame and guilt which often accompanies thought or talk of elimination may strongly support the connection with sex. Freud drew attention to the fact that the faecal material is the first product of the infant. He presents the faeces to the mother as a gift. Withholding faeces is a way of depriving mother of the gift; it is the child's most certain way of causing anxiety and anger in the mother, the first opportunity for asserting himself and winning a victory.

Fixation at this level of development, Freud said, not only concerns sexual development but also the adult's tendency to orderliness, his attitude to money, parsimony, or even avarice in adulthood and the way in which aggression is expressed; for example obstinacy and vindictiveness are, according to Freud, related to fixation at the *anal* level of development.

Not only does adult physical satisfaction have its origin in childhood, but also emotional development. Mature adults are capable of special, warm, emotional relationships with members of the family, e.g. husband or wife and children. The particular feeling for a person of the opposite sex and the protective, altruistic relationship with children, are characteristics of healthy adult adjustment. Some people would go so far as to say that the fulfilment of heterosexual love in procreation represents every person's greatest desire. There are, of course, some people who cannot, through force of circumstances, find fulfilment in marriage and some who choose to devote their lives to the arts, to creative work or to public service. Some of the world's greatest creations have been produced by people who gained more satisfaction from their work than from their own personal relationships. This may be considered as a higher form of development, but Freud believed that this is 'sublimation' of the emotions which should normally be experienced in love.

Adult love is, according to Freud, a goal which is reached by going through a series of emotional experiences in childhood. The most important of these is the experience of being loved by the mother, or by a mother substitute, quite early in infancy. All children need love and protection. The idea of an 'ideal mother' is universal. A sense of deprivation is felt when mother love is absent, or if separation from the mother occurs. However, even the best and most loving mother inevitably falls short of the child's image of the ideal mother. Every mother must at times cause frustration to the child. She may fail to pick him up when he wishes it, may interrupt feeding before the child is satisfied or fail in some other way to respond to his needs. Frustration creates anger and hate in the child, directed against the very person whom he most loves and needs. The problem of love and dealing with it, of experiencing hate and dealing with it without overwhelming feelings of guilt, and the ambivalence of feelings to the same person, all have to be worked through in childhood before adult adjustment is reached.

Some people believe that children should be spared the unpleasant experience of meeting frustrations. They believe that Freud, having drawn attention to the child's feeling of ambivalence of aggression, advocated that children should never be thwarted in any way. There is no justification for such a belief. On the contrary, the child gains security from the knowledge that an adult, not he himself, is in command. But he does experience strong emotions in response to frustration and may learn to deal more adequately with these emotions if he is allowed to recognize and control them, than if he is made to repress them in order to avoid guilt feelings.

The Oedipus complex

Adult attitudes to women, particularly to older and maternal women, may depend on the way in which feelings towards the mother are dealt with. Early in infancy the presence of the father may be felt as a threat and may often be resented because he seems to distract the mother's attention from the child. The relationship between mother, father and child provides the first opportunity for feelings of jealousy. This situation is referred to as the 'Oedipus' situation by Freud, who draws an analogy between this and the Greek story of Oedipus who, in accordance with the oracle and in spite of all precautions taken against its fulfilment, kills his father and marries his mother in ignorance of their incestuous relationship. Themes similar to that of the Oedipus saga occur in the stories of many cultures and Freud saw in this an indication of the universality of incestuous wishes in human beings. Normally, Freud thought, the Oedipus situation is resolved by identification with the parent of the child's own sex—one becoming like his father to retain his mother's love, another like her mother in order to share in the love of her father. The successful solution of the Oedipus situation results in a healthy attitude to men and women. Fixation at this stage of development may mean that excessive dependence on the mother or on a mother figure and a resentment of men is carried into adulthood—a form of maladjustment termed the 'Oedipus complex'.

In many families the father represents authority. Adult attitudes to people in authority or to those who are potentially in authority are largely patterned on attitude towards the father, though this may differ with the position fathers hold in varying cultures. Love and respect for the father may lead to an acceptance of reasonable authority and, in turn, to the use of authority in a similar manner. Resentment of the father, or the belief that the father is excessively restrictive, may lead to fear and rebellion in the face of authority and to an authoritarian attitude when the occasion arises.

Other children in the family provide an opportunity for competition, rivalry and cooperation. Freud does not say much about the effect of sibling rivalry on social development. This is discussed much more fully by Adler (1929), one of Freud's early collaborators. The arrival of a new baby undoubtedly creates jealousy and a feeling of insecurity which need to be resolved during childhood in order to develop independence.

When school begins, relationships with people outside the family become important. Teachers, for the time being, replace parents in the position of authority. They substitute impartial, detached authority for the personal one of the parents. It becomes possible for the child to see that he is equal to others, to develop a sense of justice and to dispense with an authoritarian father figure.

Some people, however, continue to feel the need for absolute authority. When they begin to doubt the absolute wisdom of their parents they obtain support from their belief in God or in the absolute truths of scientific values.

Freud has shown that these few basic attitudes to the mother, father and siblings form the pattern for later relationships. People tend to repeat over and over again the reactions they have learnt to adopt in childhood. It almost seems as if nothing can be done to change people. The emotional tie with the mother determines later reactions to other people who play a maternal role in the life of the individual, e.g. a nurse. Later it affects the kind of mother one turns out to be. Absence of love in childhood may well make it difficult for a person to accept love from people who are very willing to give it and may also make it difficult for her, as a parent, to give love and security to her own child.

Resentment of the father's authority in childhood tends to be repeated when one meets any person in authority and leads to the wielding of authority in a manner resented by others. We repeat the attitudes we have learnt in childhood throughout life without being aware of their origin and often without recognizing that our attitude depends more on our own personality structure than on other people's behaviour. We describe others as authoritarian or hostile, fussy or over-solicitous without becoming aware that our own attitude to them makes us see them in that light and elicits from them the very behaviour to which we refer.

Transference

This repetition of childhood attitudes to people we meet in adult life is sometimes referred to as 'transference'. Freud first used the term to describe how his patients used him as if he were the wonderful father, the loving mother or the hated authority to which they referred. They transferred on to him emotions which properly belonged to others. A positive transference, i.e. the feeling of love and trust which the patient temporarily places in the analyst, is helpful during stressful phases of analysis and acts as a strong motivation to continue the analysis. Negative transference, that is hate, anger and resentment towards the analyst, can be utilized to make the patient aware of feelings of which he may have been unconscious and to help him accept characteristics hitherto repressed. Later in analysis it becomes clear to the patient that his feelings were misplaced. His judgement of the analyst becomes free from the distortion of transferred emotions and the analysis can come to an end when the patient feels he no longer needs the analyst as a target for his feelings.

In analysis, transference is part of the planned process of bringing unconscious material into consciousness. In everyday life, however, transference frequently takes place. Patients in hospital sometimes behave as if they were in love with nurses when, in fact, they may be investing in the nurse the love which they feel for their mother. Relatives may be afraid to ask doctors for their opinion and may treat doctors with the deference which might have been appropriate for their own fathers. Parents often transfer to their children's teachers the mixture of fear and respect they formerly had for their own headmaster. Nurses may find that their attitude toward the sister or nursing officer is irrational and represents a transference of feelings from their own family experience.

Transference is often very useful. In new situations and when meeting new people it is helpful to be able to use well-tried patterns of behaviour and to proceed on the assumption that the old approach will be found useful again. It helps the patient trust each nurse as if she were his mother. Order in society is more easily maintained if people respect authority automatically just as they used to do in childhood. Transference is a hindrance, however, either if the original attitudes are in themselves abnormal or if they are maladaptive to the present situation. Excessive resentfulness of authority or an excessive need for love may prevent the formation of satisfactory adult relationships. Transference also interferes with getting to know people as they really are, because the individual may go on treating them as if they possessed the characteristics which he has projected onto them.

Freud's apparently fatalistic outlook in pointing out that we cannot help behaving as we do because we merely repeat what we have learnt has, in reality, led to the awareness that change is possible, provided that people recognize the unconscious mechanisms at work in themselves as well as in other people. In psychoanalysis the analyst helps the patient to re-examine his own attitudes and, in being traced back to childhood, they automatically change. This process of re-examining attitudes can be carried out—though perhaps less thoroughly and less systematically—by anyone who is interested in human relationships. Nurses may find their attitudes changing considerably the moment they begin to ask why the patients, their colleagues or they themselves behave in the way they do.

Reports written about a patient, for example, often reveal more about the nurse's attitude than about the patient's condition. The nurse may find a particular patient irritating and trying. When she begins to investigate either what part she herself plays in provoking the patient, or what it is about herself which makes her react to this particular patient with irritation, the feeling is often recognized as transference and it then becomes possible to give the patient the care he needs without emotional interference.

Dreams

Freud found that during the process of free association people began to talk of their dreams and that dreams became more frequent as analysis progressed. He began to investigate dreams and came to the conclusion that some unconscious forces are expressed in dreams. He referred to the story which is remembered as the 'manifest' content. Behind this is the 'latent' dream content; the meaning of the dream is expressed symbolically in the manifest dream content. During the dream the dreamer understands the symbolism and often wakes feeling happy and elated. When the sleeper awakes the dream appears meaningless and he wonders how the absurd dream content could ever have been thought of. Freud said the 'censor' keeps the latent dream content unconscious and even during sleep only allows disguised symbolic expression of the unconscious wishes. To understand a dream it is necessary to see what association each of the items brings forth. The symbolism used by each person is private and individual, but certain characteristics can be observed in the dreams of many people. Sometimes concrete objects represent figures of speech. We talk, for example, of feeling fenced in or of reaching rock bottom. In the dream, fences or rocks may appear to represent these feelings. Often several separate parts of the dream produce the same association; this is called 'over-determination'; at other times one thing in the dream stands for a number of different ideas, referred to as 'condensation'. Some dream symbols are thought to have a sexual meaning and some occur so frequently that it is almost possible to guess at their meaning instead of inviting the dreamer to produce his own associations in order to interpret the dream. However, another person's dream cannot be accurately interpreted this way.

Freud believed that all dreams express the fulfilment of an unconscious wish. Other psychologists do not entirely agree with this statement, but they do consider that dreams can be important and significant expressions of the unconscious

Psychoanalysis is both a method of investigating personality development and a theory of personality structure. The method used by Freud has resulted in a far-reaching extension of our knowledge of human personality. It continues to be a valuable method of investigation and represents a useful preparation for those who need to know themselves better in order to learn how to understand their patients. As a method of treatment it has undergone many modifications. Some of these make treatment more acceptable to the patients and some are reputed to speed treatment. Occasionally a psychoanalytic method without modification is used in the treatment of some form of mental disorder, but this is usually too long and costly to be of practical value. Many people doubt whether, in fact, it is possible to cure mental illness by this method.

The psychoanalytic theory as developed by Freud has aroused a great deal of anger and criticism. Freudians say that the degree of 'irrational' emotion with which criticism is expressed indicates how accurate the theory is. One is profoundly uncomfortable when one is told that one is not entirely aware of one's own personality and when one's unconscious tendencies are brought out in the open. Everybody dislikes the thought of his own irrational motivation and tends to react by rejecting and denying it.

At present, more objective criticism is being made by those psychologists who attempt to carry out scientifically conducted experiments to test the separate facets of the theory. There appears to be no doubt that some of the prolific hypotheses put forward by Freud may be confirmed but in general Freud's theories are difficult to test. Much of the original criticism of Freud's theories is connected with his use of the concept of sex. Many people find it unacceptable to associate sexual concepts with child development and Freud's description of infantile sexuality has offended some people. Some of Freud's disciples have now re-examined and modified much of his theory. Less emphasis is placed on the in-stinctual explanations of behaviour and much more on the influence of culture.

Many people also doubt some of Freud's theories because the method he used is unscientific. Usually it is only possible for anyone to practise psychoanalysis after he has himself had a personal analysis—a procedure which leads to bias by those who are analysts and excludes from discussion all those who are not.

One of the difficulties in using the psychoanalytic theory lies in the fact that it does not explain adequately how the differences in personality development occur. Freud at first believed that the traumatic events which his patients uncovered in analysis accounted for their neurotic symptoms. Later, however, he showed that even normal people recalled the same kind of childhood events. It may be that his theory reveals more of the universal patterns of development than of the causation of psychological disorder. Those who criticize Freudian theory also argue that many examples can be found where the same event causes diametrically opposed behaviour. The restrictions which parents impose on the child may, for example, cause hostility in later life or may result in reaction formation, leaving the child too submissive and passive.

There has been some anxiety about the effect of Freud's 'deterministic' theory on the moral standards of people. If it is true that adult behaviour is caused by what happened in childhood then people cannot be held responsible for their actions. This fatalistic outlook is potentially harmful and, it is thought, could have detrimental effects on standards of behaviour. However, one's understanding of other people is helped if it is assumed that they cannot always be held responsible for their actions and opinions. Interest replaces irritation and anger. Very often it pays the student to examine his own preconceptions and prejudices and to try to bring into consciousness hidden parts of his own personality. People appear incapable of guiding their own behaviour. However, they have to believe in their free will and the power to control their own actions, even when they make allowances for other people's behaviour.

The main findings of Freud are unchallenged by his collaborators and disciples. However, some deviations from his theory and elaborations of parts of the theory have occurred during the last 60 years.

In this chapter some of the main points of difference between Freud and other psychologists of the schools of *depth psychology* will be outlined. If only a few names are mentioned and less space is devoted to them than to Freud it is not because these theories are less important but because they also are based on his psychodynamic theory.

ALFRED ADLER

Alfred Adler, an early collaborator of Freud and one of his compatriots, later became interested, not so much in the causation and determination of behaviour, but rather in its purpose. Though he agreed with much of what Freud said about the early influence of the environment Adler was primarily interested in the possibility of change. Environment and heredity, he agreed, are important, but it would be an error to believe that adult personality was entirely determined by early environment and heredity. On the contrary, we shape our experiences in the environment in which we live as a result of our own potentiality. His emphasis on the wholeness of the human organism is one of the most important contributions to current psychological thinking, though his is not the only influence in this direction.

Adler's psychology can be termed 'teleological' or purposive psychology. Our main purpose in life, he said, was the effort to become powerful. We are all born helpless and in the process of growing up we aim to become strong and independent. How we do this depends partly on our view and understanding of our own inferiority, partly on the method we use to establish our strength.

The 'striving for power' arising from our 'inferiority complex' is the foundation stone on which Adlerian theory is built. Adler succeeded in explaining almost every kind of behaviour on the basis of this. Some people feel that this is an over-simplified concept of development.

The task of the child is to explore his environment, to organize his experience into a meaningful whole. Very soon everything the child sees, hears and feels and his every experience is utilized in the light of the 'scheme' which the child has already formed. He approaches new experiences with certain expectations and in the first few years develops a 'style of life' which makes his behaviour characteristic of him. Adler assumed—without examining his assumption in any critical way—that a certain style of life is good and desirable, others maladjusted and unhealthy. He believed that people ought to develop 'cooperation' and 'independence' and that it is wrong to make use of others by being helpless or excessively aggressive.

Child guidance

Adler was particularly interested in education and was a pioneer of child guidance. The function of the teacher or the doctor, who tries to help the child and his family, is to discover the child's particular style of life and to make the family conscious of it. The style of life can be changed by a cooperative effort of the family or the school and the child.

One of the causes of the child's original feeling of inferiority is to be found not only in his total helplessness, but in specific organic debilities. Most people are born with some organs more developed than others: they may have defective sight or hearing, a limb may be weak, speech may be impaired, ugliness, variations from the normal in height or weight may be experienced as signs of inferiority, so may sexual differences, a point on which Adler agreed with Freud. While Freud, however, talked of 'castration fears', the anxiety of the body that he may lose his male organ and of the girl that she may have lost something she ought to have, Adler talked of the 'masculine protest'—a type of behaviour which leads to increasing competition for power.

The inferior organ is used in an attempt to become

powerful. Some people compensate by greater practice and determination to develop the inferior organ. Others develop different skills and make up for deficiencies. Yet others use their deficiency to gain power over others by a show of helplessness. Organs 'speak' before real speech is developed and 'organ language' should be learnt by those who want to influence the child's development. One source of the feeling of inferiority is found in the way in which a child reacts to his position in the family. The eldest child, for example, suffers 'dethronement' when the next child is born. He feels less important, less well loved than the younger child. His way of becoming powerful may well consist in developing into a trust-worthy, authoritarian type of person, adopting for himself the role of parent substitute.

The eldest child, Adler believed, often has great respect for tradition. His outlook tends to be pessimistic and he looks on the past with regret. The second child may become ambitious, optimistic, forward looking. He may be preoccupied with the need to compete and to catch up with the older child. If he cannot hope to beat the eldest in direct competition he may strike out into new fields. The youngest child, who is often petted by the parents, may reach his unique position by particular graciousness. He may dream of being the best, the most useful, the hero of the family and, if he is unable to make dreams come true by using any outstanding ability, he may do so by becoming the favourite as a result of his endearing behaviour.

The only child may develop a style of life characterized by timidity. He does not develop in competition with contemporaries. Instead, the standards of adults and their ambitions for him make the world seem to be a dangerous place. He dare not disappoint by striving and failing. If he makes no attempts to strive forwards he guards against failure and retains the protection of the adult. The position in the family, in Adler's view, is a very important factor in developing a style of life, but this alone does not determine development. If there is a marked difference in ability between children, competition may be abandoned quite early. The child who appears to lack interest and initiative may well be one who has been discouraged in competition. The child who comes from a family in which disharmony exists between parents may become concerned with maintaining his relations with his parents rather than with the other children. Those who experience neglect may think the world is hostile and may permanently fight imaginary enemies or guard themselves against imaginary dangers.

In investigating the style of life, Adler observed the behaviour of the members of the family towards each other. While other workers in the child guidance field tried mainly to understand the child's point of view Adler saw the whole family and discussed problems openly with parents and child simultaneously.

Adler, like Freud, was interested in the paucity of recollections of the earliest time of life, but he investigated not what was forgotten but what was remembered. The earliest recollections often give an indication of the style of life. The fact that a particular incident was recalled shows what appeared important to the child at the time. The part the child himself played in the remembered incident, whether he recalls himself as being active or passive, strong or weak, successful or a failure, is an indication of his outlook on life.

Adler paid particular attention to the pattern of behaviour which makes use of helplessness. The most powerful weapon of all is for the individual to demonstrate weakness. The weak succeed in holding back others, gaining attention, impressing everyone with the immense difficulty of their tasks. Weakness provides people with excuses for possible failure and at the same time magnifies success should it occur.

Adler's own method consisted of showing the child how successful his manoeuvres were. By making the child conscious of his effect on his parents when, for example, he is sick in the morning before going to school, the behaviour can be maintained only deliberately instead of unconsciously. He is more likely to develop a new style of life if he can be shown that power and success are to be gained by more cooperative methods. There is no danger, Adler said, in interpreting to the child what the purpose of his behaviour appears to be. If the interpretation is wrong it is rejected; if it is right it clearly strikes home whether admitted or not.

Adler's general ethical and practical outlook, his determination that all our life's activities could be classified as 'communal living, work and sex' and his discussion on the meaningfulness of life made his psychology important at the time.

THE NEO-FREUDIANS

Many psychologists who base their work on the theories of Freud have, in their own work, placed greater emphasis on social and cultural factors than on biological ones.

The work of some anthropologists consisted in testing psychoanalytical hypotheses in the very different and more simple cultural environments of primitive societies. An advantage of the anthropological approach lies in the fact that the culture patterns are relatively fixed, social pressures are uniform on all individuals and can more easily be taken into account because of their fairly stable pattern.

Malinowski, Kardiner and Mead, working in the 1920s and 1930s, have confirmed some of the findings of psychoanalysts. On the other hand, they have shown that some assumptions which we are inclined to make about the universality of human behaviour all ill-founded. There are, for example, societies in which the men manifest what we would consider feminine behaviour and vice versa. Methods of child rearing, breast feeding, weaning and toilet training vary considerably and it is not possible to be as dogmatic as formerly about the long-term influence on personality development of each method.

In the USA psychoanalytically-orientated psychologists have investigated whether Freud's theory, which was developed in central Europe, applies in American culture. It would appear that in the less paternalistic society authority is less associated with the father figure than Freud believed. Maladjustment and neurotic personality traits appear to the American to be more related to the individual's position in society than to his instinctive drives.

The psychologists who have tried to develop psychoanalytic theory further are called 'Neo-Freudians'.

Horney (1951), for example, classified people into those who move 'with', 'away from', or 'against' society. Fromm (1941) has examined the concept of freedom and independence as the goal of personality development. Sullivan (1947) has stressed the importance of interpersonal relationships in personality development.

In the United Kingdom, psychoanalysts have devoted more time to the study of social groups. Psychoanalytic theory and technique have been applied to the study of industrial problems and of social behaviour in school and work. Relationships among hospital staff, and between staff and patients, are being studied by psychologists at the Tavistock Institute of Human Relations.

Psychoanalytic theory has been taken a step further by Klein (1932) working in the UK, who has developed techniques of psychoanalysis to be applied to young children. Her findings about fantasies and emotional development in the first few months of life make it possible to compare these with the behaviour of patients suffering from psychotic disorders (e.g. depression and schizophrenia) which had not previously been studied by analysts.

ERIK ERIKSON

Mention has already been made of Erikson, a later psychoanalyst, whose contribution to the understanding of children and of adult personality has been considerable. Erikson (1964) describes the stages of development as a progression of psychosocial events, the outcome of which is determined by the manner in which the person solves the special problems created by his state of maturation. Erikson lists eight stages of development. The first four of these coincide chronologically with Freud's stages of psychosexual development of the child, but Erikson emphasizes the personality characteristics which result from the favourable or unfavourable outcome of the child's management of its developmental task. In the first years of life the child's task is to cope with dependency and to develop trust. Mistrust becomes an enduring personality characteristic if the task is not mastered.

In the second year, as the child becomes capable of independent action, success results in the development of autonomy; failure results in the development of shame and doubt.

In the third year of life when the child's fantasy life is most active and when distinction between fantasy and reality has to be mastered, the child's task is to develop initiative, but repeated failure will lead to tremendous feelings of guilt.

The child enjoys the awareness of being the cause of events but can easily feel overwhelmed if he believes himself to have caused disasters for which, in reality, he may be in no way responsible. The break-up of the family for example, through a parent's death or the fact that one parent leaves the home and a divorce takes place, may result in the child blaming himself and developing guilt feelings of immense proportions.

The period which Freud describes as the 'latency period' is in Erikson's terminology, the time when the child develops 'industry' or, failing that, begins to suffer from a sense of 'inferiority'.

Freud pays relatively little attention to the development of personality after early childhood. Erikson, however, explores in far greater depth the critical experiences of adolescence and adulthood. He agrees with Freud that little boys and little girls have developed an idea of their own sex during the early phase of the oedipal situation. Adolescence is, however, the period in which 'identification' occurs with the sexual role one is later to play in life (see Chapter 9). The young boy is no longer concerned with what is expected of him as a male child; he has to learn what to expect of himself as a man, a husband, a bread-winner, a father. Similarly, the girl learns to identify with her role as a woman, a wife or a mother. Erikson shows how difficulties in the adolescent's behaviour in sexual matters, in education, in the choice of career and in adaptation to social standards can be seen as manifestations of an 'identity crisis'. The successful outcome at this stage of development is 'devotion and fidelity'.

Adults, according to Erikson, go through three more

stages in which they cope in turn with problems of intimacy and solidarity to develop 'affiliation and love' with 'generativity versus self-absorption', to develop the ability to care and, lastly, with what may appear to be the essential significance of human existence, the 'purpose of being'.

At this stage the adult has developed 'integrity and wisdom'. He copes with the idea of no longer being and if successful achieves 'renunciation', if unsuccessful gives way to 'despair.'

Erikson's interpretation of the tasks of adulthood rests on his discussion of the changing radius of significant human relationships and it has much in common with the theories of disengagement we met in the discussion of old age and with Maslow's view on motivation.

CARL JUNG

Carl Jung, a Swiss psychologist, was also an early collaborator of Freud. His theory soon deviated from Freud's and in his later writings he was mainly concerned with the mythological and religious aspects of human thought. His most important contributions to psychology concern his theory of the collective unconscious and of personality types.

He, like Freud, realized that much of the personality is unconscious and that repression takes place to protect the conscious Ego from unacceptable emotions and ideas. However, Jung believed that only some, not all, of the unconscious consists of repressed material. Jung distinguished between a 'personal' unconscious, i.e. our own repressed material, and a 'collective unconscious' which we have in common with all other human beings. From the collective unconscious, ideas emerge into consciousness resulting in the highly individual personality pattern of each person.

Jung's procedure of reaching the unconscious is not unlike the method followed by Freud. Jung, however, went more deeply into the analysis of fantasy and dreams and found symbols of universal meaning which he called 'archetypes'.

Individuation is the process of developing a conscious Ego. Only certain aspects of personality become important and well-established by this process. The whole personality consists of all aspects: those which are well developed and also those of an exactly opposite nature which remain unconscious. The total personality is one which is balanced, in which there are present at the same time characteristics of opposing nature. During the early part of life the dominant personality characteristics emerge and it is possible to classify people accordingly. The most important classification, into extroverts and introverts, is widely accepted. As has been discussed earlier, extroverts are people who, in the extreme form, are easily influenced by other people's opinions of them. They are aware of the effect they have on others and are sensitive to other people's expectations. Introverts, on the other hand, are self-contained, relatively unaffected by other people and unresponsive to their environment. Most people are neither extreme extroverts nor extreme introverts. One or other is more fully developed in the early part of life. The opposite is present in the unconscious, capable of developing later in life. Other personality characteristics which appear in the conscious Ego also have their unconscious counterparts. Masculine characteristics, which Jung called 'animus' have an unconscious feminine counterpart, 'anima'. It is also possible to distinguish characteristic reaction types; for example, feeling–thinking, sensation–intuition; one of each pair is dominantly conscious with their opposites in the unconscious. Jung believed it was the task of the second half of life to develop those aspects of personality which had remained unconscious and to endeavour to achieve a well-integrated personality by one's own efforts.

Treatment of mental disorder by Jung's method does not end with analysis. Throughout treatment the analyst interprets and helps in resynthesis and integration. Jung believed that individuation and integration represent a process which can be achieved by deliberate effort and this makes his psychological outlook less deterministic than that of Freud.

The psychologists mentioned in this chapter are all concerned with the development of the person over time. They trace personality back into childhood and predict how, in the future, this personality will affect people and events. They see people as agents whose actions affect the environment in which they function. Their psychological theories can be described as 'dynamic schools of psychology'.

Jung's classification into personality types forms a link between the dynamic psychologists and those who study personality by other methods.

References

Adler, A. (1929) *The Science of Living*. London: Allen & Unwin.

Erikson, E. (1964) *Childhood and Society*, revised edition. Harmondsworth: Penguin.

Horney, K. (1951) *Neurosis and Human Growth*. London: Routledge & Kegan Paul.

Fromm, E. (1941) *Escape From Freedom*. New York: Farrer & Reinhart.

Klein, M. (1932) *The Psychoanalysis of Children* (authorised translation by Strachey, A.). International Psycho-Analytic Library, Vol. 2, 1975.

Sullivan, H.S. (1947) *Conceptions of Modern Psychiatry*. Washington: William Alanson White Psychiatric Foundation.

Further reading

Badcock, C. (1988) *Essential Freud*. Oxford: Blackwell.

Brown, J.A.C. (1961) *Freud and the Post-Freudians*. Harmondsworth: Penguin. This book describes and discusses the theories of the neo-Freudians and post-Freudians.

Freud, A. (1966) *The Ego and the Mechanisms of Defence*. London: Hogarth Press. The various defence mechanisms are well explained by Freud's daughter.

Fromm, E. (1960) *Fear of Freedom*. London: Routledge & Kegan Paul.

Kline, P. (1972) *Fact and Fantasy in Freudian Theory*. London: Methuen.

Stafford-Clark, D. (1967) *What Freud Really Said*. Harmondsworth: Penguin.

11 The Concept of Attitude

One of the key concepts when studying social behaviour is that of attitude and as such it has long been a central concern of social psychological theory. Our attitudes reflect part of who we are, our needs, desires and values. They also reflect the needs and demands of the society and environment in which we live. Thus, our attitudes will influence the way we see and act upon the world— our lifestyles, choice of friends, careers and such things as political opinions and social conscience. Similarly, our lifestyles, friends, careers, etc. will influence our attitudes. Attitudes are not immutable but we see them as relatively enduring states of being that not only give a consistency and structure to our personalities, but make us and others, to a large extent, predictable. Tajfel and Fraser (1978) describe attitudes as:

> . . . an individual's summing up, in various ways, of his experience. Were it not for this summing up, we would have to start from scratch in deciding what to do about each new event or individual confronting us.

It might be of use to take a closer look at the terms values and attitudes and discuss how they can be distinguished from each other. Compared with our attitudes, it is argued that our values occupy a far more central part of our personality structure. Attitudes are seen as arising from personal value systems. An example might be valuing honesty as an ultimately desirable goal and standard for behaviour. That being the case, then it would follow that positive attitudes would be held towards those who express or exhibit aspects of honesty and perhaps very negative attitudes held towards any distortion or deviation from truth. In this way values can be seen as reflecting enduring and general beliefs from which specific attitudes may arise. Indeed, values are considered far harder to alter than the attitudes that may stem from them.

Smith *et al.* (1978) put forward three main ways in which our attitudes equip us to deal with the world. Firstly, they allow us to make speedy assessments of our environment. Secondly, attitudes facilitate and maintain relationships, allowing us both to identify with and differentiate ourselves from others. The third function identified is of a more subtle nature whereby it is suggested that unresolvable inner tensions can be alleviated by externalizing and liberating such tension in the form of an equally intense attitude towards an external object, event, or issue.

Before looking at how attitudes are acquired, it is well to remember that the attitudes someone holds at any one time may well conflict, perhaps violently, with those of others. Indeed, severe attitudinal disagreement has been the cause not only of local disputes, but also of historical devastation. The root of all argument and debate is a difference of attitudes and the attempt to persuade others that there is only one that is right. However, in the society in which we live, we profess to value individual freedom of thought and, within certain socially determined parameters, we respect alternative viewpoints such that a degree of dissent is tolerated and often recognized as a key to achieving change. As Voltaire (1694–1778) is reputed to have said:

> I disapprove of what you say, but I will defend to the death your right to say it.

Streufort and Streufort (1978) accounted for different degrees of tolerance by what they called a general incongruity adaptation level (GIAL) but recognized that GIAL may itself be dependent on both the personality and the particular situation—for example, a flippant light-hearted manner quite acceptable at a party is not so well tolerated at a serious business meeting the next day.

ACQUISITION OF ATTITUDES

As may well have been anticipated, there are many ways in which attitudes can be acquired. Psychologists, influenced by their own particular attitudinal set and theoretical penchant, have emphasized different aspects of attitude acquisition. Some have focused directly on personality factors. Others, recognizing that personality is in itself dependent on the environment, have looked at interpersonal interaction, especially between adult and child during the formative years. A similar interaction takes place whenever one person is held in high esteem or seen as powerful and influential by the other. Studies have also been made of group membership and attitude formation. More generally, social and economic factors, the role of government, and the mass media, have been widely studied for their effects on the attitudes of both individuals and the communities to which they belong.

Psychologists such as Eysenck who stress a physiological basis for personality describe individuals as inherently introverts or extroverts. He argues that as introverts are far easier to condition than extroverts, they will adopt values and attitudes much more readily

(Eysenck, 1970). Another approach that stresses the influence of personality on attitude formation is that of Adorno *et al.* (1950). He conceptualized the 'authoritarian personality' and by various sophisticated and sensitive tests demonstrated the world view held by such a personality type. It is an extreme example of dispositional effect on attitude formation. However, it is always difficult to discern the effect of personality *per se* without taking into account the environmental factors. Freud recognized this and his theory of personality suggests that our first attitudes acquired as children are gained by identification with our parents as an ideal of how our values, attitudes and behaviour should be. However, Freud realized only too well that as the child moves from home and meets the many external societal influences, initial values are modified and replaced by those of other significant people and by those of the social group to which the child belongs.

The process by which an individual acquires the values, attitudes and role experiences of the group and society to which he belongs is known as socialization. There is a tendency to confine this process to childhood, but although this is where the process starts and where, arguably, the enduring foundations are laid down, it is a process that continues throughout life via successive interpersonal relationships, group membership and societal demands. In other words, it is how an individual becomes and is maintained as a member of society. It is not mere moulding of the individual, but an interactive process whereby, as indicated, personality factors influence the quality of the socialization process. Learning theory and social learning theory explain most aspects of socialization, the latter stressing that reinforcing behaviour was not the only means by which learning was achieved. Bandura *et al.* (1963), in a study of social learning, were able to show that the mere observation of behaviour and seeing its intrinsic value (real or imaginary) led to the observer initiating and displaying the same behaviour at a later date. Hence in Bandura's experimental work the small child, watching an adult aggressively hit an inflatable clown, was far more likely to exhibit the same behaviour to the clown, either when frustrated in some way or when the aggressive behaviour was seen to be rewarded. Bandura argues that by mere observation the child was able to establish guidelines and attitudes to govern future experience.

The family obviously plays a crucial role in establishing the foundations of our attitudes and behaviour. As the individual grows and enters many other social groups new expectations are placed on him which may well conflict in part with formerly held attitudes, such that feelings of increasing pressure and discomfort can be created. Attitudes may be constantly subjected to change. By adulthood the individual has developed a relatively enduring value system and attitudinal set; a result of the interaction of all the factors considered: personality, socialization, group membership and environmental experience. However, attitudes can continue to change throughout our lives.

So far nursing has not been discussed directly, although many nursing examples could be drawn from what has already been said. To address nursing and nurses directly, it could be argued that one of the most critical changes that occurs is on first entering the world of nursing when the necessary occupational socialization is experienced. The new social group presents the neophyte nurse with a new set of norms and values. The role to be adopted casts certain expectations on her thinking and behaviour. However committed the individual might be to becoming a nurse, entering the new social group may not always be easy. Fundamental attitudes and values may be shaken. The norms and values of nursing may not necessarily sit happily with those already attained. Melia (1983) shows just how difficult the transition from lay to professional person can be. She highlights, from a sociological and ethical perspective, the potential for conflict between the personal values and attitudes of the individual and those of the profession of nursing. It may take time for the new nurse to accommodate to her new social group and feel that her personal equilibrium has been restored. On many occasions it may well be that the nurse's behaviour complies with the demands of her new reference group, but that her underlying attitudes are still in conflict.

THE COMPONENTS OF ATTITUDE

We have to accept that attitudes expressed may have little to do with actual behaviour. Conversely, behaviour we observe cannot necessarily be assumed to reflect underlying attitudes. The fact is we cannot see attitudes; we can only infer them from behaviour observed which may well be misleading. Attitudes can be seen as consisting of three different components (Rosenberg *et al.*, 1960), the affective component, the cognitive component and the conative* (behavioural) component. The affective component relates to the way the person feels, the cognitive component relates to the knowledge and beliefs the person may have, and the conative component is the tendency to act in a certain way. By knowing the way a person feels and thinks and professes to act in relation to an event, person or issue, allows others some degree of prediction as to how he or she is likely to behave.

---

* Conative, from conatus (Latin)—effort, will, desire, tendency.

However, in the real world, many other forces may make us behave counter to attitudes. Bendall (1975) noted, sadly but astutely, that knowledge, beliefs and attitudes, expressed in nurses' written examinations, were poor predictors for actual nursing behaviour in the clinical arena.

CHANGING ATTITUDES

Despite the problems stated, a great deal of research has been carried out looking at the attitudes held by individuals and groups as a means of predicting behaviour. Experimental work was able to show, however, that it is not an unidirectional matter. Individuals will alter attitudes held in order to agree with certain decisions they have made about behaviour. Many may identify with the dieter, who after several weeks of making a conscious behavioural effort to comply with the dietary advice given and avoid chocolate, eat fresh vegetables, fruit and wholemeal bread, finds that he actually rather likes raw carrots and has completely lost his desire for chocolate. However, the question becomes has the individual really changed his attitude so that it sits more comfortably with his behaviour, or is there some external force—the threat of ill-health due to overweight or the reward of good health, the praise of others and clothes that fit—that is directing his behaviour and no permanent attitude change has really occurred, despite the lip service. Here we enter the areas of psychological research that looks at such issues as the compliance, described above, conformity, identification, internalization and, of great importance, the concept of cognitive dissonance.

It is quite possible that we greatly underestimate the

degree of compliance that occurs in the real world and that our behaviour is easily influenced by others, even when it runs counter to our established attitudes. It would seem we have a compelling desire to be like others and for others to be like ourselves. Research by Asch (1958) showed that under experimental conditions, individuals would discount what they saw with their own eyes, if everyone else was prepared to say to the contrary. Milgram (1965) demonstrated, somewhat disconcertingly, how experimental subjects could be persuaded to inflict pain on others, especially if directed by a person of prestige and influence and if the 'victim' was unknown and also physically separated from the subject. It was argued and extrapolated to the real world that under such conditions the individual experiences minimal responsibility for his behaviour. His negative attitudes towards inflicting pain have not altered and in other settings, where personal involvement and responsibility were at a premium, such behaviour could not have been induced. In nursing, compliance can be seen working for both good and ill in terms of patient well-being, but in any event it is an unsatisfactory state. Compliance embraces the commonly-heard comment from the student nurse:

> I don't like it, but that's the way it's always done and
> I can't do anything about it.

The rights and wrongs of the actual behaviour she may be referring to are not so much the issue here. It is, rather, that it demonstrates how easily we behave counter to our attitudes and feel no discomfort because we perceive in ourselves no power or control over situations.

It may be that the term compliance is used rather loosely in everyday language and that when we talk about compliance—especially in terms of health behaviour—we usually are looking for conformity. Conformity, in psychological terms, implies not just a change in behaviour, but also an attitudinal change as well. No external force, positive or negative, is required to ensure the behavioural change. It is often difficult, by mere observation alone, to be sure which process is occurring. Often it is recognized only in retrospect. Compliance, unlike conformity, has the potential for eventual rebellion. However, it is important to recognize that compliance may be a necessary step on the way to conformity. To return to the dieter, the aim is that he should genuinely adopt the appropriate attitudes to a healthy diet, but initial compliance may actually play an important part in influencing attitude change. Conformity is often enhanced by the desire to identify with the group. A strong identification with the reference group may potentiate not only the internalization of the desired attitudes, but also alter the more centrally-held value systems. Such a process can be recognized in nursing education. Ultimately the nurse teacher may wish the learner to modify her attitudes towards such things as mental illness, the care of children or the principle of asepsis. However, initially it might be that the student nurses behave as prescribed out of respect for authority and knowledge of the teacher and a wish to be identifiable with other nurses. However, over time, the ideal is that the actual knowledge and beliefs that form the attitudinal basis to their behaviour become internalized and the nurses' behaviour is in accordance with their own appropriately acquired attitudes and values.

It has been argued that under external pressure of either reward or punishment an individual may well act in a way contrary to his underlying beliefs and attitudes. However, if an individual behaves contrary to his beliefs and attitudes in a situation of *free will*, he is likely to feel most uncomfortable. Melia (1983) suggests this discomfort when she describes a learner, given the task of feeding a patient, who feels obliged to hurry a patient through a meal in order to satisfy the expectations that meals should be dispatched as quickly as possible, when her own personal 'instincts' are to take it very slowly and sympathetically. The personal discomfort experienced by the nurse, who perhaps feels she does have a degree of choice in her behaviour, is described as cognitive dissonance. Festinger (1957) was the first to describe this phenomenon, but it is one with which we can all identify—perhaps especially so as nurses. Dissonance is another word for inconsistency and cognitive dissonance implies that it is known to the person. The discomfort experienced has been explained in terms of our self-perception (Bem, 1967). We all have views of who we are and what we value. If our own behaviour runs counter to this, it can be seen as undermining our personal equilibrium. The classic example is that of smoking. Nurses know that smoking impairs health and indeed hold very positive attitudes towards a healthy lifestyle and how it may be achieved. If, however, at the same time, a nurse freely takes up smoking, the behaviour is in total discord with the beliefs and attitudes that constitute so much of her personal identity. How such cognitive dissonance is resolved has been the subject of much research by Festinger and his advocates. Many strategies may be adopted. The individual may decide to alter her attitude to smoking. This in itself must involve a change in both knowledge and feelings about smoking that would lead to a tendency to act accordingly in a state of equilibrium if not optimal health! To achieve this the individual might distort or deliberately avoid reading any information against smoking and, at the same time, might seek out or be alert for any informational source that suggests that any links between smoking and ill-health are tenuous. Equally she may seek evidence of those who lived into their nineties smoking heavily all their lives. Other strategies to avoid dissonance may involve stressing the seemingly positive side of smoking, suggesting it 'calms the nerves' or gives them social confidence. However erroneous the knowledge and feelings pursued may be, it brings the attitude held into harmony with the behaviour. It takes only a small cerebral leap to appreciate how those involved in health education aim to change smoking behaviour. By giving the appropriate information about smoking, it is possible to create a dissonance that can be resolved by altering the behaviour to accord with the newly acquired attitude. Success, of course, must depend very much on a sensitive person-centred approach. This will be discussed in more detail later.

Another way of resolving dissonance has already been addressed. This is when failure to act according to one's expressed attitudes is attributed to some external force that denies personal responsibility for behaviour. When an external force is *real*, dissonance is minimal. When a nurse gives rushed and incomplete care to a needy elderly patient, she may well feel badly and ill at ease with her conscience. No one forced her to give inadequate care. In order to feel better about it all, she may spend the evening with friends justifying her behaviour by blaming external factors: too little time, too few nurses, too many patients. In this way she hopes, perhaps, the conflict can be resolved for her. In this situation dissonance has occurred and the nurse is looking for a *real* external force to justify behaviour and reduce the dissonance.

Changing people's attitudes is not easy. It demands

that individuals be willing to alter an integral part of their identity. The perceived power and influence of others and the desire to be like others in our social group can, indeed, be most effective in changing attitudes. However, many of our attitudes may be long established, enduring and seemingly reinforced by successive reference groups. When such an attitude is held about an identifiable group, it is often regarded as a stereotype. This expression was introduced in the 1930s whereby certain characteristics were ascribed in a generalized way to the whole group. Such oversimplifications are often made about racial or religious groups, but also about social and professional groups. Such stereotypes may help us to cope with the complexities of human personality by allowing new acquaintances to be placed provisionally into a category of people about whom we already have information. In this way interaction may be facilitated. How often do we begin a conversation at a social occasion by asking a new acquaintance 'What do you do?' One hopes that in due course the stereotype is modified appropriately but very often, when acquaintance with a particular group remains limited, this is not the case. Stereotypes tend to be very resistant to change and often far outlive the reality. Nursing, as a profession, works very hard to dispel the somewhat romantic and naive image it may have. However, it has to be recognized that, for many patients, the idealized stereotype of how nurses will be serves to help them cope and gain confidence at a time when they need to trust the hospital. However, stereotypes may have both positive and negative aspects. The negative stereotyping of nurses sees them as hyper-efficient, hard-hearted, disciplinarians. If the description sounds bizarre, it only demonstrates what a firm hold stereotypes may have on an individual, however inaccurate. The stereotype a patient may adopt about nurses is dependent both on his own past experience (or lack of experience) and the exposure to attitudes expressed by significant others. We are all subject to the stereotyping of others. Nurses may have stereotypical images, not only about how they as nurses should be, but also about patients and other health professional groups. Such stereotyping may serve only to interfere with both personal and professional growth. Some psychologists have highlighted individual tendencies to form stereotypes. Adorno *et al.* (1950) saw the forming of fixed stereotypes as very much part of the make-up of the authoritarian personality. When the stereotype consists of many unfavourable characteristics, it is often thought of as prejudice. Prejudice literally means prejudgment, a preconceived attitude or opinion made without any relevant information. Characteristically prejudices are notoriously difficult to alter, even in the light of disconfirming information. It is common to associate prejudice with negative attitudes but prejudgments can also be positive.

Closely allied to the concept of stereotyping and prejudice is that of 'labelling'. As with stereotyping, a label attached to a person allows others to approach him in a predetermined way so that behaviour can be, in part, anticipated and attitudes inferred. Problems arise, however, when a label assigns a person incorrectly, for example, labelling a patient as 'difficult' when, with further and more sensitive assessment, the validity of such a statement becomes highly questionable.

ATTITUDES TO ILLNESS

Clearly the understanding of attitudes plays a significant part in the care patients receive from health professionals, be it in hospital or at home. The particular acquisition of values and attitudes of every individual will colour, not just his/her view of illness and disorder, but also his/her view of their treatment and care. To most people, illness comes as an unwelcome intrusion into their lives. Potentially it denies them their preferred pursuits and it may involve pain, discomfort and heartache. Despite this, there are those who regard illness as a challenge. Their efforts to overcome illness and debility may lead to greater achievements than would otherwise have been possible. The term 'compensation' is sometimes used to indicate the mechanism whereby a perceived disability is overcome. Some people, on recognizing permanent impairment of their lower limbs, may compensate by engaging in sports and activities where the use of their arms is at a premium, for example archery. Others may use a time of illness as an opportunity to develop new interests or pursue educational courses. Suffering helps many people find a new faith in religion or discover a new purpose in life. In this way illness can be viewed positively, even leading to great personal fulfilment.

In our modern age, there is a tendency to idealize health and illness which can provoke ambivalent feelings. Of course compassion is felt and a desire to help those who are sick but, even in our enlightened times, attitudes to sickness can include rejection, fear and embarrassment. Parsons (1951) identified what he described as the 'sick role' whereby those who were sick were given sanction to be excused certain obligations that may have been part of the accepted responsibility of an adult, such as earning a living and supporting the family. In return, the sick individual gives up certain rights of independence in order to become the 'good patient'. He accepts medical supervision and behaves accordingly. In this way he plays his part in the restoration of optimal health.

Some illnesses, however, still bear a stigma, despite the efforts of health education and attitude change. The fact that people suffering from such things as mental illness, epilepsy and venereal diseases may still occasionally be treated as outcasts, demonstrates just how hard it can be to alter attitudes. In some cultures, ill health is regarded as shameful and wicked. Children, in particular, may regard illness as some form of punishment and it is not uncommon for people to adopt an attitude of guilt and shame towards their own pain and suffering*, so much so that they find it impossible to discuss the illness, even with a doctor or nurse. Anyone who thinks badly of himself tends to believe that others must share this view. This may be referred to as 'projection'. Certain illnesses are more frequently hidden than others and are often associated with a sense of guilt or fear of moral reprobation. One of the great tasks of all health professionals is to grasp any opportunity to modify such harmful attitudes. Behaviour resulting from such attitudes not only militates against reaching an early diagnosis of the disorder, but may severely and unnecessarily disadvantage the sufferer by delaying the medical and nursing intervention.

When a nurse assesses a patient, she needs to remember that the patient brings with him a wide repertoire of beliefs and attitudes which will influence his receptivity to nursing and medical care. The patient brings into the situation his attitudes to home, family and work, his self-knowledge and his self-esteem. He also brings with

---

* It is interesting to remember that our word 'pain' probably comes from the Greek—poine—which means penalty.

him such things as his attitudes to politics, to the health services, to hospitals and to comfort and deprivation. His attitude to noise and silence, to competition and cooperation, to giving and receiving, to sharing and to personal possessions may well influence the way he may experience a period in hospital. His attitudes to his own and the opposite sex, to youth, adulthood and old age will all have a bearing on his relationship with staff and fellow patients. If time is taken to appreciate fully the patient's perspectives, then his care can be planned with a much greater sensitivity. It will be individualized care.

The discerning nurse also realizes that she brings to the assessment process her own complex network of attitudes. When she describes a patient she may try to keep herself out of the picture, but in many ways it is impossible. Whenever we interact with another person, our behaviour is influenced by the kind of person we think he is and how he will behave towards us. The other person behaves similarly. Both parties in any interaction are constrained by the extent to which they attribute to the other abilities, intentions, attitudes, power and responsibility. This has been referred to as 'attribution analysis' (Jones et al., 1971) and concerns the degree to which we attribute the causes of behaviour to the individual's personality as opposed to attributing the causes of behaviour to situational factors—circumstances. The observation of a repeatedly aggressive manner in a patient should not automatically be assumed to reflect an aggressive and discontented personality. The overwhelming stress of hospitalization, loss of independence and pain may play a far larger part in his aggressive behaviour. The former is described as making an internal attribution, the latter an external attribution.

HEALTH EDUCATION, PATIENT TEACHING AND ATTITUDE CHANGE

If, as has been suggested, we value health so highly, why is it that our behaviour so often contradicts our professed values? Do we live in a constant state of dissonance? Those involved in any aspect of health education and patient teaching recognize that valuing health may have to compete with many other values and attitudes. A young sportsman may have very positive attitudes towards health and physical fitness. However, he may also value a life of challenge, excitement and risk-taking in whatever sport he may have chosen, which in itself may threaten his much-valued health. In many cases, health may be highly valued but the strength of will to change behaviour may not accompany the value—especially when the behaviour to be changed may have become addictive.

Health education follows the premise that people have a basic right to health knowledge, in the same way as they have the right to vote and to have the protection of the law (World Health Organization, 1978). The giving of knowledge and information in order to achieve and maintain health is a fundamental part of health education. Similarly, patient teaching helps the individual cope with disorder such that they are enabled to experience an optimal health state. To participate in both health education and patient teaching is not necessarily an easy venture and very often involves means whereby attitudes counter-productive to health and well-being might have to be altered. However, if any education is to be effective, it must meet the needs expressed by the individuals themselves. Paternalism by the educator/teacher may achieve temporary compliance, but for the internalization of the attitudes associated with the change in behaviour required, there must be a sensitive combination of the information believed to be necessary and the informational, emotional and behavioural needs as perceived from the perspective of the individual. As has been suggested, the initial step by the health educator may be to eradicate negative attitudes that the person may hold towards himself, his illness and his future life. For example, a patient who cannot bear even to look at a newly formed stoma and is full of fear and rejection has set up a barrier to coping, understanding, or allowing himself to see anything positive in his future. The knowledge health professionals have gained from research into attitude formation, assessment and change has contributed greatly in the sensitive field of health education and patient teaching. In many ways knowledge must be the key. If the cognitive component of an attitude is altered then the emotional component may alter concomitantly. This is especially so if the knowledge is given in the context of emotional support.

Personal interaction obviously plays a crucial part in attitude change, but the persuasive power of the mass media must not be ignored. However, Budd and McCron (1981) argue that the mass media is more successful at reinforcing and building upon existing beliefs and attitudes, rather than successfully *changing* attitudes and behaviour. The media may often be responsible for using fear-arousing messages in order to achieve a change of attitude. The explicit use of fear may be considered more acceptable from an impersonal media source, as opposed to face-to-face interaction. It has been suggested that the initial media campaigns to alert the public to the problem of AIDS exploited fear as a motivator for behavioural change. Early research by Hovland, Janis and Kelley (1953) led to the general agreement that fear-arousing messages could indeed be effective in changing attitudes and behaviour. However, modification of the initial research suggested that if the fear became too intense, it might prove counter-productive, triggering a defence mechanism whereby the individual 'shut off', rejecting both the message and the messanger. Current research still debates this issue. Sutton (1982) contends that higher levels of fear consistently lead to greater behavioural change. In the real world we have to recognize both individual fear thresholds and ethical considerations.

ATTITUDE MEASUREMENTS

If we wish to understand the attitudes people hold, how they are acquired, how effectively they are changed or modified and how they compare with observed behaviour, there must be some means of measuring attitudes. If attitudes themselves cannot be measured directly, an indirect approach has to be adopted. Either behaviour is observed and attitudes inferred, or expressed attitudes are correlated with observed behaviour. Often an individual's attitudes are elicited in such a subtle way that the individual is unaware that he is expressing his attitudes at all. Social psychologists have attempted to measure attitudes for many years and many creative strategies have been used with varying degrees of success. The measure most widely used is that of an attitude scale, which broadly constitutes a set of statements or items to which the person gives his approval or disapproval and from which an attitude profile can be created. Such attitude scales differ in construction and, although all have potential pitfalls in the hands of the less than competent, validity and reliability checks have established such scales as useful research instruments. Indeed, attitude scales have gained a wide currency and have been profitably used in the field of nursing. Their contribution to our understanding of the real world of nursing must not be underestimated.

References

Adorno, T.W., Frenkel-Brunswick, E., Levinson, D.J. & Sandford, R.N. (1950) *The Authoritarian Personality*. New York: Harper & Row.

Asch, S.E. (1958) Effects of group pressure upon modification and distortion of judgements. In Maccoby, E.E., Newcomb, T.M. and Hartley, E.L. (eds) *Readings in Social Psychology*. New York: Holt, Rinehart and Winston.

Bandura, A., Ross, D. & Ross, S.A. (1963) Vicarious reinforcement and initiative learning. *Journal of Abnormal and Social Psychology* **67**, 601–607.

Bem, D.J. (1967) Self perception: an alternative interpretation of cognitive dissonance phenomena. *Psychological Review* **74**, 183–200.

Bendall, E. (1975) *So you've Passed, Nurse*. London: Royal College of Nursing.

Budd, J. & McCron, R. (1981) Health education and the mass media, past, present and potential. In Leather, D.G., Hastings, G.B. and Davies, J.K. (eds) *Health Education and the Media*. London: Pergamon Press.

Eysenck, H.J. (1970) *Psychology is About People*. London: Allan Lane.

Festinger, L. (1957) *A Theory of Cognitive Dissonance*. Stanford: Stanford University Press.

Hovland, C.I., Janis, I.L. & Kelley, H.H. (1953) *Communication and Persuasion: Psychological Studies of Opinion Change*. New Haven, Connecticut: Yale University Press.

Jones, E.E., Kanouse, D.G., Kelley, H.H., Nisbett, R.E., Valley, S. & Weiner, B. (1971) Attribution: *Perceiving the Causes of Behaviour*. Morristown, New Jersey: General Learning Press.

Melia, K.M. (1983) Becoming and being a nurse. In Thompson, I.E., Melia, K.M. and Boyd, K.M. *Nursing Ethics*. Edinburgh: Churchill Livingstone.

Milgram, S. (1965) Some conditions of obedience and disobedience, *Human Relations* **18**, 57–76.

Parsons, T. (1951) *The Social System*. Glencoe, Illinois: The Free Press.

Rosenberg, M.J., Hovland, C.I., McGuire, W.J. Abebon, R. & Brehm,

J.W. (1960) *Attitude Organization and Change*. New Haven, Connecticut: Yale University Press.

Smith, M.B., Bruner, J.S. & White, R.W. (1978) The adjustive function of opinion. In Brown, H. and Stevens, R. (eds) *Social Behaviour and Experience*. Sevenoaks: Open University Press/Hodder and Stoughton.

Streufort, S. & Streufort, S.C. (1978) *Behaviour in the Complex Environment*. Washington DC: Winston.

Sutton, S.R. (1982) Fear-arousing communications: a critical examination of theory and research. In Eiser, J.R. (ed.) *Social Psychology and Behavioural Medicine*. Chichester: John Wiley.

Tajfel, H. & Fraser, L. (eds) (1978) *Introducing Social Psychology*. Harmondsworth: Penguin.

World Health Organization (1978) *Report of the Primary Health Care Conference*. Geneva: Alma-Ata.

12   Communication

Communication is the basis of life, from birth to death
and in all circumstances.

(Hockey, 1984)

Communication has to be the heart of the caring process
of nursing, but despite this research, evidence reveals
how dissatisfied patients are with this aspect of their care
(Cartwright, 1964; Ley, 1977). Perhaps in response to
the increasing demand by patients for better communication, nurses have professed to value communication
and to want more of their nursing time to be devoted to
this. For whatever reason, the desire is not necessarily
translated into action. Faulkner (1980) and Stockwell
(1972) showed that even with more time nurses did not
measurably change their behaviour and spend this time
with their patients. Altschul (1972) was not alone in
noting that nurses spent less than 16% of their nursing
time in actual one-to-one contact with their patients.

To communicate effectively does not necessarily come
naturally. It is a highly complex process that must be
understood in psychological terms before one can understand fully either why it sometimes fails so badly, or how
such skills can be acquired and enhanced. One of the
most positive aspects of research in this area is the recognition that communication skills constitute behaviour
patterns that can be learned, practised and improved
(Bandura, 1977; Argyle, 1978). Equally encouraging is
that the implication of this for nursing education has
been fully appreciated.

Any definition of communication must reflect that it is not merely the transferring of information but that this transfer is dynamic and assumes shared meanings achieved by following a common set of rules, be they general linguistic rules or idiosyncracies of custom (Cherry, 1966). To appreciate the dynamic nature of this social interaction, the transactional aspect must be recognized. By transactional it is meant that the process is two-way: both participants affect and are affected by each other.

THE COMMUNICATION PROCESS

To understand the complexities of communication and see it as a concept that means more than talking, conversation or information giving, researchers have sought to develop various models. These models have proved of great assistance in representing a complex process in as coherent and as simple a way as possible. However, it must be remembered that representative models are never totally perfect. Most communication models resemble that developed by Shannon and Weaver (1949). Influenced by their interest in telecommunications, this model includes an information source, a transmitter, a channel, a receiver and a destination. The information to be communicated is encoded into a message, transmitted along a channel, received and decoded by the receiver who can then act upon it. In addition, this model included the feature they called 'noise' that can act as interference with the message transmission. More recent models have stressed the important transactional and feedback elements that Shannon and Weaver did not address. All models include the use of various technical terms in order to make the concept clear.

Firstly there is the information source, the sender.

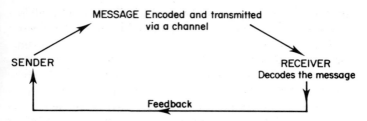

Figure 12. The process of communication.

This refers to the person who wishes to communicate and must embrace all his knowledge, skills and attitudes from which the message will be formulated. The message clearly refers to that which is being communicated, for example, information about a patient's well-being. Coding refers to how the message is transmitted. This may be by words or diagrams or even by such things as flags—as on the high seas. Decoding refers to the activity the receiver of the message engages in order to make sense of code and is obviously dependent on the receiver understanding the code used by the sender. Feedback refers to the process by which the receiver sends a message back to ensure the message has been received correctly or to modify subsequent behaviour of, or message from, the sender. Feedback can be both positive and negative and demonstrates that communication is a two-way process. Figure 12 shows the process of communication in a diagrammatic way.

Influencing this process are both environmental factors that Shannon and Weaver called 'noise' and individual variations. Sources of error in communication can occur for many reasons, at any stage in the process, and will be a greater risk if messages are passed via several people to the ultimate destination. The likelihood of distortion of the original message is humourously captured in the following: 'Send reinforcements, I'm going to advance' becoming 'Send three and fourpence, I'm going to a dance'.

Before pursuing the problems that can arise in our communication, it should be recognized that we, as human beings, have two systems of communication: verbal and non-verbal. In our day-to-day lives we are very aware that communication is far more than verbal or written messages. It involves a wide range of non-verbal messages, perhaps more subtle, subconscious and potentially more ambiguous, but a powerful and arguably equally complex source of communication. Nurses are very aware that many of their patients are unable to communicate verbally, either due to a particular disorder or the necessary management of a disorder. In such situations patients can only communicate by non-verbal means and have to rely on the nurses' skill at interpreting the non-verbal messages. Human communication relies very heavily on language and although the non-verbal support to language is very important, we can feel totally bereft should our ability to speak be lost.

VERBAL COMMUNICATION

The understanding of verbal communication owes much to the science of psycholinguistics and the understanding of how language is acquired. Before a child learns to speak, he can communicate by non-verbal means, however noisy that might be! His first attempts at language may achieve little in the way of verbal communication and have meaning only for himself. However, in a relatively short period of time the child has developed socialized speech whereby he acknowledges the listener and adapts his language to conform to the linguistic rules and regularities that allow mutual understanding of the messages. The style, dialect and code of language that the child will learn to use are very dependent on the linguistic environment in which he lives. Bernstein (1971) demonstrated marked differences in language patterns and skills from different home backgrounds and group memberships. He argued that a closely knit isolated group can quickly develop its own code and verbal shorthand that only group members understand. This may restrict their ability to communicate outside the group or it may serve to exclude outsiders. Bernstein referred to this as a restricted code of language. By contrast, he described an elaborated code which incorporates a wide and varied vocabulary and allows the communication of ideas and events to be achieved in articulate, subtle and complex ways. The two codes are not necessarily mutually exclusive, but Bernstein suggested that a whole social class may be disadvantaged by having only a restricted code of language. For others, the elaborated or restricted code may be adapted according to circumstances and in this way communication can be modified. Patients often feel excluded from a conversation round the hospital bed because the medical and nursing staff use a restricted language of technical terms and jargon he cannot understand. The patient's own linguistic ability may help overcome this problem, but, equally, if the patient's linguistic background is totally alien to those of his carers, the problem of communication may only be compounded. However, if by using and responding to feedback, language is modified and the supporting non-verbal communication is enhanced, it is possible to achieve sensitive and meaningful communication, but this is a delicate skill that does not necessarily come naturally.

It has been suggested that, in the United Kingdom, as

many as 6 million people are literally 'lost for words' and great strides are being made to enable such people to improve their linguistic communication skills. However, language serves many purposes over and above the conveying of information and ideas. Indeed, personality, educational and social background, attitudes, status and mood can be inferred from the way we speak. How we use our speech, independent of the actual verbal content, can determine the quality of the interaction. The non-verbal aspects of speech are known as paralinguistics and are just one part of what is called non-verbal communication.

NON-VERBAL COMMUNICATION

It has been established that social interaction is far more than language alone. It is dependent also on body movement cues, the use of space and touch as well as the non-verbal aspects of speech. We recognize language as an immensely complex, flexible and productive system, but non-verbal communication may be equally so. In many ways a great deal more communication takes place without words than in words and, as indicated earlier, when we use speech we add a wide range of non-verbal behaviour to enhance meaning. At times, for certain individuals and in certain cultures, gestures accompanying speech are often more expressive than the words. It is possible, however, for the verbal and non-verbal messages to be in contradiction such that the receiver gets two opposing messages. This has been referred to as the 'double bind' (Ruesch and Bateson, 1951). This can be exemplified by the nurse, whose words to the patient are those of reassurance, but where facial expression reveals that she is worried and fearful for the patient. Similarly, a nurse may make gentle remarks to a patient while handling him roughly. In both cases the verbal content of her communication is contradicted by the non-verbal content. This has been described as 'leakage' (Ekman and Frieson, 1969) and may reflect that, in emotional terms, we have better control over our words than over our non-verbal behaviour.

The study of non-verbal communication has contributed greatly to the understanding of social interaction and owes much to the work of Argyle, who used a variety of research approaches to explore both the complexities and functions of non-verbal behaviour (Argyle, 1972). In social psychological terms, non-verbal communication can be used to manage the social situation by transmitting aspects of behaviour that denote attitude, status and emotions; to support verbal communication and at times, to replace verbal communication, either by design or of necessity. Patients who experience aphasia as a result of a left-sided cerebrovascular accident, or children who are deaf and dumb, may learn to communicate almost entirely by non-verbal means. Szasz (1961) contended that many symptoms of neuroses may be a form of non-verbal communication replacing language.

One of the problems with non-verbal behaviour is the uncertainty as to how much is just random unintentional behaviour and how much is deliberately being sent as a message. There are cultural regularities that allow for a degree of certainty, but ambiguities can occur. The work of Argyle and others have provided us with the opportunity to understand the significance of a wealth of non-verbal behaviour: facial expression, posture and body movements, paralinguistics, eye contact and gaze, appearance and dress, and the use of personal space and social distance. There are certain conventions that are adhered to in relation to non-verbal behaviour because of what they might or might not communicate and, to a large extent, these are culturally determined. An example could well be the degree of touch we engage in or the distance we maintain from people during discourse. Problems in communication with patients may arise from the fact that nurses may have to break with convention in the process of nursing, having, on occasions, to be too close to a patient for successful communication. On the other hand, a patient is rarely offered a space small enough for intimacy between patient and visitor, or between patient and doctor or nurse. To deny a patient the appropriate amount of space can be a non-verbal signal of what communication is encouraged or discouraged. People also convey significant messages about their thoughts and feelings by such things as posture and dress, and these conventions may also be disrupted for a patient. Take, for example, the situations where the patient has to lie flat while the doctor or nurse stands; where the patient is in night attire and the doctor and nurse are in uniform. Such alterations in conventions not only potentially impair optimal communication, but also would seem to put the patient at a disadvantage.

The regulation of social interaction by non-verbal behaviour requires that the signals of verbal and non-verbal communication are closely entwined. Eye contact itself is vital for successful communication, both in terms of initiating the process, determining who holds the floor and deciding the point at which the communication ends. Without eye contact, verbal communication may be totally unsuccessful. The receiver may fail to appreciate when the sender is initiating or completing a message and the sender may fail to ascertain whether the receiver is attending. The averting of eyes may be used deliberately either to avoid verbal communication or to terminate it unilaterally. The importance of eye contact highlights the special communication needs of patients with severe visual impairment, those who are not fully conscious or whose eyes are bandaged. In such situations, the sensitive use of touch can replace eye contact.

When social interaction is agreeable and relaxed, various aspects of non-verbal behaviour have been noted. The response sequences of the participants show an unconscious imitation such that they appear to mirror each other (Rosenfeld, 1967). Head nods and smiles serve to reinforce the conversation and posture is relaxed and open. An equilibrium is maintained by skilled coordination and turn taking and the communication ends by an apparently mutual decision to withdraw.

Human communication can be seen to work on two levels: that of content and of relationship (Watzlawick et al., 1967). They are, of course, inextricably bound together. Wilmot (1979) showed that where relationships were easy and healthy, as in the description above, then the participants could focus on the content of the message. However, if the relationships were troubled or uneasy, the tendency was for the content to be poorly attended to or misinterpreted. Such findings could support the view that patient dissatisfaction with the information they receive may be, in part, a function of an uneasy relationship with the giver of information.

NURSES AND COMMUNICATION

At the outset of this chapter it was suggested that nurses put a high value on communication. If nurses are to improve their communication skills they must be aware of firstly, the complexities of the process; secondly, the particular needs of their patients and clients; and thirdly, the many variables that may affect the quality of communication. Furnished with the appropriate knowledge, the necessary skills can be developed and enhanced.

Many of the failings in communication between patients and nurses have been explained in terms of the nature and structure of the nursing system. Menzies (1960) argued that nurses avoided too much contact with their patients as a means of coping with the high levels of stress experienced in caring. In addition, Menzies noted that relationships could never be well established with patients when nurses were constantly being moved from ward to ward. On an interpersonal level, Anderson (1973) and Kerrigan (1957) suggested that nurses just simply did not know how to talk to patients or how to listen. Shea (1984), using the Shannon and Weaver model of communication, looked at the problems encountered when the nursing care plan was considered as a channel of communication. Following Weaver (1966), Shea identified three types of problems: technical, semantic and influential. Technical problems related to the accuracy of the message; was the correct message sent or was so much jargon or abbreviations used that the message was indecipherable? Semantic problems related to the meaning attached to the message. The sender must assume shared meanings, but this may not always be the case, especially if the knowledge possessed by the receiver is not that of the sender. In such a situation, misinterpretations are very possible or even total lack of understanding. The third problem identified was the influential problem and this related to the perceived status and influence of the participants. Not only will this affect how much credence and weight is put on the message, but also the degree to which the receiver feels able to respond effectively via the feedback mechanism. It would be useful at this point to draw attention to problems with effective feedback that can occur if the receiver feels unable, for whatever reason, to admit that the message has been imperfectly understood. One of the greatest skills in good communication in nusing lies in creating an atmosphere in which both patients and staff feel safe enough to risk exposure without loss of prestige.

Shea was looking specifically at the nursing care plan, but it can be seen from the above that the problems identified could equally apply to many other forms of communication. It would appear that patients could be at risk of experiencing all three of the problems identified by Weaver. If the nurse or doctor—or other health professional—uses technical jargon and abbreviations, forgets that the patient knows little about the very things they may consider 'routine' (how quickly nurses can forget their first nervous hours on the ward) and, efficiently uniformed, looms over the patient in a seemingly authoritative manner, it is not too surprising that communication is less than optimal. Add to that such environmental factors as noise and distracting activity and such individual factors as fear, anxiety, pain and perhaps auditory and visual impairment, and it becomes quite patent that successful communication is unlikely. This reinforces the assertion that to achieve 'good' communication requires a high level of skill.

By increasingly recognizing the communication needs of patients, an educational awareness of the particular skill nurses require has developed. Not every individual needs every form of communication. Ashworth (1979), looking at the needs of patients in intensive care settings, identified six vital areas of communication. Rubin (1963) looked at the positive effects of the use of touch in situations where patients were experiencing intense personal stress, and Hayward (1975), Boore (1978) and Wilson-Barnett (1979) have showed virtually indisputably the importance of information and explanation on the overall well-being of patients. The needs of nurses have not been forgotten if they are successfully to meet those of their patients and acquire the appropriate skills. Chapman (1976) gave constructive ideas as to how experiential learning methods can be used to develop such skills as empathy, kindness, the ability to listen, how to question and how to give information. Equally such experiential methods can be used to enable nurses to avoid the common communication maladies that serve to disconfirm or devalue a patient. Davies (1981) believes that the acquisition of these skills allows for the personal development and growth of the nurse herself, facilitating a necessary assertiveness and enabling her to manage stressful situations (cf. Menzies, 1960). The acquisition of communication skills means that nurses can be effective, not just on a technical level, but on an interpersonal level, and that the latter is no longer left to chance. Davies (1981) suggests the ideal could be that of a therapeutic environment in which the nurse feels able to give and receive information in an open manner, engage in problem-solving activity and provide true emotional support for patients.

References

Altschul, A. (1972) *Patient Nurse Interaction*. Edinburgh: Churchill Livingstone.

Argyle, M. (1972) Non-verbal communication in human social interaction. In Hinde, R. (ed.) *Non-verbal Communication*. Cambridge: Cambridge University Press.

Argyle, M. (1978) *The Psychology of Interpersonal Behavior*, 3rd edition. Harmondsworth: Penguin.

Anderson, E.R. (1973) *The Role of the Nurse*, London: Royal College of Nursing.

Ashworth, P. (1979) Sensory deprivation—the acutely ill. *Nursing Times* **75** (7), 290–294.

Bandura, A. (1977) *Social Learning Theory*. Englewood Cliffs: Prentice Hall.

Bernstein, B. (1971) *Class Codes and Control*, Vol. 1. London: Routledge & Kegan Paul.

Boore, J.R.P. (1978) *Prescription for Recovery*. London: Royal College of Nursing.

Cartwright, A. (1964) *Human Relations and Hospital Care*. London: Routledge & Kegan Paul.

Chapman, C.M. (1976) Nursing—rhyme or reason. *Nursing Times* **72** (Suppl.), 109–112.

Cherry, C. (1966) *On Human Communication*. Cambridge, Massachusetts: MIT Press.

Davies, B. (1981) Social skills in nursing. In Argyle, M. (ed.) *Social Skills and Health*. London: Methuen.

Ekman, P. & Frieson, W. (1969) Non-verbal leakage and cues to deception. *Psychiatry* **32**, 88–105.

Faulkner, A. (1980) Communication and the nurse. *Nursing Times*, *Occasional Papers* **76** (21), 93–95.

Hayward, J.C. (1975) *Information: A Prescription against Pain*. London: Royal College of Nursing.

Hockey, L. (1984) Conclusions (p. 167). In Faulkner, A. (ed.) *Communication*. Edinburgh: Churchill Livingstone.

Kerrigan, M.R. (1957) Analysis of conversations between selected students and their assigned patients. *Nursing Research* **6**, 43–45.

Ley, P. (1977) Communicating with the patient. In Coleman, J.C. (ed.) *Introductory Psychology*. London: Routledge and Kegan Paul.

Menzies, I.E.P. (1960) A case study in the functioning of social systems as a defence against anxiety. *Human Relations* **13** (2), 95–121.

Ruesch, J. & Bateson, G. (1951) *Communication*. New York: Norton.

Rosenfeld, H.M. (1967) Non-verbal reciprocation of approval: an experimental analysis. *Journal of Experimental Social Psychology* **3**, 102–111.

Rubin, R. (1963) Maternal touch. *Nursing Outlook* **11**, 828.

Shannon, C. & Weaver, W. (1949) *The Mathematical Theory of Communication*. Urbana, Illinois: University of Illinois Press.

Shea, H.L. (1984) Communication among nurses: the nursing care plan. In Faulkner, A. (ed.) *Communication*. Edinburgh: Churchill Livingstone.

Stockwell, F. (1972) *The Unpopular Patient*. London: Royal College of Nursing.

Szasz, T. (1961) *The Myth of Mental Illness*. London: Secher and Warburg.

Watzlawick, P., Beavin, J. & Jackson, D.D. (1967) *Pragmatics of Human Communication*. New York: Norton.

Weaver, W. (1966) The mathematics of communication. In Smith, A.G. (ed.) *Communication and Culture*. New York: Holt, Rinehart and Winston.

Wilmot, W.W. (1979) *Dyadic Communication: A Transactional Perspective*, Reading, Massachusetts: Addison-Wesley.

Wilson-Barnett, J. (1979) *Stress in Hospital*. Edinburgh: Churchill Livingstone.

Further reading

Argyle, M. (1988) *Bodily Communication*, 2nd edition. London: Methuen.

Kagan, C.M. (ed.) (1985) *Interpersonal Skills in Nursing*. London: Chapman and Hall.

Wright, B. (1986) *Caring in Crisis: A Handbook of Intervention Skills for Nurses*. Edinburgh: Churchill Livingstone.

13 Working with other people

Very few activities in nursing are carried out in isolation. Most of her working life the nurse works with others or at least in the presence of other people. There is a great deal of research evidence that demonstrates how behaviour changes in the presence of other people. The term *group dynamics* has been used to explain the effect of the group on the individuals who compose it.

A group, in psychological terms consists of a number of people who have a common interest, goal or purpose and who form some kind of association with each other because of their common business.

CROWDS

If a number of people happen to find themselves at the same place without the bond of common purpose this constitutes a *crowd*. The people travelling in the underground train at the same time, or queuing for tickets for a cricket match, or present at the scene at the time of a road accident have similar interests or aims, but they have not assembled for the purpose of interacting with each other; they form crowds. In a crowd an individual may behave in a markedly different way from his usual standards. Examples have been given of the mass excitement of crowds during political unrest, student demonstrations or at 'pop' concerts. The individuals concerned would not, singly, have behaved in this way; in fact, often they felt ashamed of their actions. In a crowd they appeared to be less conscious of the controlling influence of their own moral standards and seemed to lose the sense of responsibility for their own actions. Similarly, as one of a crowd, the individual can get more excited and exhilarated by such events as peace celebrations, parades, elections, revivalist meetings. Even the enjoyment of a good concert can be heightened by the presence of an excited audience (Milgram and Toch, 1968). Crowd behaviour does not concern us directly when we consider the work of the nurse but the effect of a group on the functioning of the nurse and on the behaviour of patients is, however, very important.

GROUPS

The first group in human life is the family group and we have already shown how experiences in that setting may affect attitudes later in life.

Adults may belong to a large number of groups simultaneously and some of these could be described as *face to face* or primary groups. These groups form when a small number of people meet for the purpose of discussing a problem or carrying out jointly some work-project or to enjoy a game, a meal or some conversation. In a face to face group people are affected by the physical presence of others.

An individual may belong to many groups without actually meeting their other members. In hospitals the nursing staff forms one group of whom only a few ever meet face to face at any one time. The nursing staff forms a separate group from the medical staff or the domestic staff or the maintenance staff, who have their own groups. The hospital staff as a whole, however, also forms a group with interests and activities concerning all.

Nurses may, at the same time, belong to a professional organization such as the Royal College of Nursing or Student Nurses' Association. They may also be members of their church, of a political party, perhaps a trade union. These larger groups are referred to as 'secondary' or official groups. In each group, different demands may be made upon the nurse; sometimes these are conflicting and create anxiety until the difficulties are resolved (see Chapter 11).

A sense of belonging appears to be very important to all human beings. More satisfaction may be derived from membership of some groups than from others. In some groups there is a secure feeling of attachment, although a member may sometimes have difficulty in belonging wholeheartedly and may then feel that she is only a 'fringe' member. Sometimes it becomes necessary for a nurse to deal with people to whom she may not feel drawn at all and to whom she may even feel hostile. There may exist a sensation that certain groups of people exclude a would-be member from close membership. Psychologists speak of *ingroups* to describe the nucleus of people most closely concerned with membership and of *outgroups* to describe those who fail to be integrated into the group or against whom a group appears to operate.

Each group develops its own standards of values, its own rules about behaviour, its own attitudes to which members are expected to conform. When individuals fail to conform, the group as a whole exerts pressure to bring the members' behaviour within the range of acceptable behaviour, or else takes action to expel the offender from membership. Groups differ in the degree of variation from the norm that they are able to tolerate and also in the type of sanctions they use against offenders.

Anyone seeking membership in a group is usually

attracted by at least part of the group's programme. One person joins a sports club, for example, because he likes its range of sports activities or its facilities, its geographical location, or some of the people in it. Another joins a political party because he agrees with its overall outlook. A third joins a particular hospital because he believes it provides good medical and nursing care. Once a person has become a group member he discovers aspects of which he was not previously aware and which may not be entirely acceptable. The sports club, for example, may have some members whose political opinions the new member does not share; the political party may consist of some individuals whose views on health matters are contrary to what has been expected; the hospital may have developed staff social activities which do not appeal. In order to remain a member of the group the individual must make some compromise and behave in such a way that he does not offend the existing members.

Groups appear to have some kind of independent life of their own. They evolve in an almost predictable manner. During their existence they may go through phases of development, maturity and decline until the group no longer exists. This description refers to the function of the group as a whole, not to the characteristics of any of its individual members. Group standards are formed by the interaction of the members. Once standards are formed individual members are affected by them. Some interesting experiments have thrown light on some details of group interaction.

A classic experiment is that of Sherif (1936). If a small ray of light shines on to a screen in a completely dark room everybody who watches the screen has the impression that the point of light moves. This is a universal optical illusion. If people are asked to say how far they think the light has moved they are willing to give an approximate measure. Some people say they saw it move several centimetres, others saw it move a few metres. When, after individual judgement, people discuss their impressions they change their view and gradually come to an agreement which appears to be a compromise between the different impressions. When the experiment is later repeated, each individual's judgement is much nearer the mean than their original estimate. This very simple experiment may appear irrelevant to nursing judgements, but it has served as a standard for other experimental work and it is clear that many judgements are formed by groups of people in the same sort of way. If people are asked to judge the beauty of paintings, or the literary value of poetry, agreement is reached in a similar way.

Decisions about group actions or about group acceptance or rejection of particular points of view are made by a similar process. Some people in the group appear to have greater influence than others in determining the outcome of discussion. People with great influence are said to have a high prestige in the group. The merits of an individual member's remarks are not always examined critically or logically. The higher the prestige of a member the less careful is the examination of his views before they are accepted or incorporated in group decisions. If any particular person's membership is valued by the others he will find his views are more influential than if his continued membership were of no concern to the group. Group attitudes and group standards are, therefore, much more likely to be changed from within than by any attempt to modify them from outside.

Within a group there can be vigorous argument and violent disagreement without damage to group feeling. The purpose of this is to effect change. If a group is criticized or attacked by an outsider it reacts as a rule by closing its ranks and protecting itself. No modification of views is likely to occur as a result of outside pressure; on the contrary, opinions tend to harden and the group tends to become more rigid in its standards when it is attacked. This process can be seen in action in political parties where vigorous disagreement can occur between people of the same persuasion. The party, however, tends to show a united front to its opponents.

In hospitals if the morale is good, there can be very outspoken criticism from within, while all group members have the same purpose of improving existing practices. As soon as an outsider criticizes, all the staff are united in their defence. In joint consultation staff and management always meet each other after their disagreements have been settled from within and when they can present a unanimous decision to each other.

It has been shown that groups can be more efficient in solving problems than are the individual members (Hoffman and Clark, 1976). Small groups have been experimentally engaged in solving puzzles or mathematical problems. It was shown that, while within a given time no single person solved the problems, groups were successful in providing the correct answer. This, of course, happened only when every member of the group concentrated on the problems and was actively trying to cooperate. The hope that committees might be more competent than individuals in solving the complex problems of a hospital is based on the assumption that they are all motivated by the same aim.

When a group is engaged in solving a common problem the more active and also the more silent members are serving a useful function. Often the silent members are the ones who are able to assess all the contributions of the more vocal members. when, perhaps in the end, the silent member speaks his contribution may be of the utmost importance. During the discussion he may show approval or disapproval, look interested or bored, smile encouragingly or frown in disbelief. The non-verbal participation of a silent group member may make a great deal of difference to the success of a group. In discussion groups or committees it is of interest to see how important are the contributions of each member. Sometimes personal feelings between some of the members enter into the outcome of the discussion. There may be a tendency for one person always to contradict another or for the group always to accept or veto the suggestions of certain people.

When a decision has been made by a whole group the members feel much more bound by the decision than if it had been imposed on the group by one person. This was shown, for example, when a group of women, after discussion, decide to give some practical help in a volunteer programme to hospitals. When they themselves had made the decision after discussion they acted on it. When they had been persuaded to do so they had said yes, but had done nothing. In the 1940s, when great efforts were being made to improve the health of the nation, pioneer work by Lewin was able to show that success in changing the way young mothers fed their infants was achieved to a far greater extent when group sessions were used and group persuasion operated as opposed to formal instruction and advice by a health professional (Lewin, 1947). Similarly decisions about nursing care are more likely to be carried out if they are made by the ward staff.

In every group, individual people develop friendships with each other, find that they like some members better than others, benefit more from their association with some, less with others. Individual relationships within the group have an effect on group morale as a whole. The psychologist Moreno (1960) developed a technique of measuring social distance between people which he calls the *sociometric* technique. Either by observing people's interaction with each other or by asking questions about it he formed a picture of the choices people make within the group. Someone can be asked who is his best friend; if everyone has one choice only, it is soon discovered how often mutual choices occur, how often there are chains of choices: A choosing B, who chooses C, who chooses D. Triangles may also form: A choosing B, who chooses C, who chooses A. By allowing more than one choice to each person it is possible to get a clearer picture of the likes and dislikes and particularly to discover who is the most popular in the group and who is isolated. Other observations may show which members of the group are the most active, which the least active, who initiates action, who agrees, and who opposes. Various questions about other people may give an indication of the role each member assumes in the group. 'Who do you like best?' may reveal the most popular group member. 'Whose opinion would you ask?' might show up the person with most prestige. 'Who do you think would be most useful in an emergency?' might indicate the leader of the group. From the number of mutual choices in the group, the way in which people are connected with others, some valid conclusions can be drawn about the morale of the group.

Group morale

Morale is a psychological phenomenon closely related to group functioning and leadership. It refers to the atmosphere which exists between people and which affects their attitude to the place of work, their job satisfaction, their acceptance of change or even commitment to it.

Morale cannot be measured directly; when morale is high everything at work goes well, when it is low there are many indications of disturbance. The group may resort to a variety of defence mechanisms (see p. 22) which may be successful in keeping it intact but interfere with its productive functioning. In an attempt to increase cohesion between members the group often behaves as if it were attacked by an outside enemy. It feels under attack and reacts by finding a scapegoat. This may be one of the members who is gradually made to leave the group, or more often the group unites in some warfare against another group. Preoccupation with enforcement of rules and preservation of group standards makes it very difficult for change to take place. The normal process of internal argument is suspended and consequently the group becomes resistant to change. Misunderstandings often occur where members of the group are uneasy with each other. This makes the group wide open to rumours. Members of the group believe rumours about each other and about people outside the group and, in turn, contribute to the spread of rumours. Discussion is often avoided and people feel uneasy with each other. They cannot safely reveal their feelings and consequently hide them and avoid all topics which might arouse strong emotion. The result often is that the group is unable to deal with its business. Instead it chooses neutral topics, resorts to lengthy small talk or explores important topics by indirect reference. This is sometimes seen in meetings in hospital where the most important item on the agenda is never discussed at all or dealt with very briefly while some unimportant point is dealt with at length. Some committees spend an excessive amount of time in discussing food problems. This serves the purpose of testing out the feeling among the members and making it possible to reach agreement on a neutral topic rather than risk disagreement. It is interesting to note how a group settles on some apparently irrelevant topic of discussion and uses it to examine feelings within the group. Someone may, for example, relate the difficulties of a friend of hers in another hospital. The whole group may show great interest and concern and explore at length relationships at that other hospital. All the arguments and anxieties which are relevant to their own group are used in reference to the other situation. When morale is good in industry, productivity rises. In hospitals, Revans (1964) has shown that the recovery rate of patients is related to other indicators of morale. In hospitals where evidence pointed to high morale, patients were discharged more rapidly and mortality rate was lower than in hospitals where morale was low. Staff turnover and absenteeism are other indicators of morale.

Much of the knowledge about groups is derived either from the therapeutic groups with mentally ill patients or from detailed study of industrial relations. Some applications to hospital are obvious. The extensive study of morale carried out by Revans (1964) and his team in Manchester has shown that the same forces are present in hospital as in industry. Unlike industry, however, the main problems and conflicts among hospital staff are not those of policy or value systems. The disagreements arise over the way in which each member of the staff evaluates his own and the other members' contributions. If the ward sisters, for example, feel that the doctors do not pay enough attention to their advice, student nurses tend to feel that the ward sisters similarly do not pay enough attention to their contributions. Equally if the sister feels that the nursing officer will not listen to her or take an interest in her problems, junior nurses tend to feel the same way about the sister and even the patients feel the same about the staff.

This process of 'information blockage', created by low morale and resulting in increased anxiety, tends to pervade the whole hospital structure and can only be remedied when the problem is faced by the entire staff. Anxiety among nurses is frequently very high. As discussed earlier, Menzies (1961) draws the conclusion that it is in the nature of the situation that nurses bear the full impact of the stress arising from patient care. The system of work-assignments rather than patient-assignment and the hierarchical structure among nursing staff serve an important function in delegating responsibility and removing it from any one person.

While one can understand the traditional nursing structure better if one sees it in relation to the problem of anxiety, the recent studies have shown that it does not really work efficiently and that communication difficulties arising from anxiety are central to any attempt to introduce change.

Group therapy

Much importance has been attached in recent years to the powerful effect of groups on the ability of members to cope with change.

Patients with psychiatric problems were the first to benefit from organized group therapy. In such groups, patients experience support from each other, develop awareness of the reasons for their problems and learn new and successful patterns of adaptation (Walton, 1971).

Therapeutic groups can take many forms and no one technique can necessarily benefit everyone. Some patients may need to belong to a group which emphasizes rehabilitation and re-education. Others need groups which deal with the exploration of unconscious motivation and the analysis of personality problems.

Some patients' needs are highly specific, and selection for membership to some therapeutic group may be related to the therapeutic skills available to deal with such needs. Special groups for people suffering from alcoholism is one example. Family groups are convened sometimes to help the family of a patient, with or without the patient's presence, to solve some of the problems created by illness. Other family groups are convened in order to ascertain where the problems in relationships really reside and who has the strength to promote healthier interaction.

The success of group therapy in psychiatry has led to the adaptation of the techniques and the principles involved by many other groups of patients and clients. It is now, for example, very common to develop a group approach to the rehabilitation of patients who have suffered a stroke. Expectant mothers participate in group work to prepare for their new role. Groups with patients who have diabetes or other chronic conditions may be very helpful in encouraging patients to deal with the limitations imposed on them by their illness.

Many patients benefit from self-help groups in which they join fellow sufferers committed to mutual support such as Alcoholics Anonymous, the Multiple Sclerosis Society, the Epilepsy Society. It may be that patients in hospital need the support of nurses to take the first step in joining such groups, as they are often afraid that the company of others who may be worse off than themselves could increase their distress rather than alleviate it. There is, however, ample evidence that, for many patients, group membership results in increased self-esteem, diminished isolation and the development of a new and positive outlook on life.

One type of self-help group with a puzzling degree of success is the weight-reducing group, of which Weight-Watchers is one example. Overweight people may have psychological problems similar to those of, for example, people with drug dependency problems. Weight-reducing groups are often successful without attempting to resolve any deep-seated psychological problem which may be the cause. It would appear that they operate by fostering competition, and by using reward and punishment in an atmosphere of cooperation and support. Health visitors are often successful in getting such groups going.

Methods of monitoring group processes have been developing since the 1950s. Bales (1950), for example, devised a category system which allows an observer over a period of time to establish which group member is active, positive and constructive and who might have the opposite effect on the group. Bales studied verbal and non-verbal contributions. From this work many other studies have evolved.

It is not easy to be, simultaneously, a participant and an observer in a group. Attempts have been made to help people become more sensitive to the processes occurring within groups of which they are members. Groups created for the purpose of learning about group processes are sometimes referred to as 'T' groups, meaning 'training groups' (Cooper and Mangham, 1971).

GROUP LEADERSHIP

Whenever a group of people embark on a joint project some form of leadership is required. Even in groups which meet without any specific purpose, other than perhaps to play or to converse, it soon becomes evident that one person assumes leadership. Sometimes a leader is specifically appointed. Discussion groups, for example, may have a leader appointed for them before the meeting is convened. Football teams or cricket teams have a leader before the team is selected. Appointment to the position of ward sister in hospital or to the unit general manager's job is an appointment to leadership. Officers in the forces are chosen to lead. In industry the foreman, the shop steward, the directors, all have positions of leadership, each of a different kind. The question arises whether certain people have special personality characteristics which give them the ability to lead.

It is well known that some animals adopt a hierarchical order within the herd or flock. Experiments with chickens have shown that the more dominant animals peck the more submissive ones until a definite pecking order emerges. The term 'pecking order' is at times jocularly applied to relationships in human society.

It would appear that leadership qualities do exist in human beings and that suitable education can help people to acquire skills in leadership (Gibb, 1969). To a large extent, however, the characteristics of the group determine the kind of leadership which is required. Every group arranges itself into leaders and followers and adopts the leaders who serve its purpose best. In industry, foremen are often chosen because of their superior skill and knowledge of production. The people so chosen have proved their ability to understand the goal of the management and are able to make a substantial personal contribution. It is assumed that their greater skill gives them the necessary prestige and enables them to lead the workers. This often proves to be a fallacy. If the workers were all primarily concerned with the goal of the organization, the foreman so chosen would have greater success. Very frequently, however, the individuals and the various subgroups of individuals have objectives and goals far removed from the overall purpose of the industry. A successful leader takes the changing needs of the small groups into account and aims to make the small groups integrated parts of the entire organization.

Just as members of a committee should have shared

aims, so should hospital employees if problems are to be successfully resolved. However, there are many problems specific to small subsections of personnel. Student nurses have problems of their own not shared by trained staff. Nurses have problems and needs which are special to their work and different from the problems of doctors. Electricians in hospital have special concerns of their own; kitchen staff meet difficulties that other groups fail to notice or understand. Each of these groups and all other subgroups within a hospital require leaders who understand the effect they have on each other. Excellence in nursing or electrical engineering or cooking is not sufficient to make a person acceptable to the group as a leader.

In different situations people may require different leaders. A particular person may satisfy the group while they are all engaged on learning a new technique in their job. His knowledge and teaching skills may render him particularly suitable for leadership. If a fire were to break out, an entirely different member of the group might take the initiative to lead people to safety and to avoid panic. If the group decided to form a dramatic society another member would emerge as leader; if they decided to form a cricket team yet another man would be appointed. Where the organization is sufficiently flexible to allow different people to adopt new roles as the need arises, leadership is usually determined by the group itself. This is referred to as 'emergent leadership'.

In most employment situations leaders have to be chosen, trained and appointed, although this does not have to preclude the emergence of spontaneous leaders. It is the practice for ward sisters to be appointed and not left to the group to select someone to lead a nursing team. A good ward sister makes it possible to allow individual nurses to assume leadership for a special purpose, e.g. in planning a particular nursing project or in organizing the Christmas activities. Good leadership on the part of management entails discovering the people who can take the initiative in leadership in a large variety of nursing activities. Delegation of responsibility, which is part of good leadership, is the ability to utilize leadership qualities wherever they are found and to give those who are able to take responsibility the greatest possible scope for independent action and decisions on behalf of their group. Appointed leaders derive their legitimacy from holding office. They use influence rather than power to motivate their followers.

There is a type of leadership called 'charismatic leadership'. Charismatic leaders have some special personal characteristics which inspire their followers. Such leaders are more likely to bring about organizational change than others because their followers identify with the objectives presented to them. Followers develop an intense loyalty to the leader who demands the change.

When a charismatic leader leaves, the group often loses impetus and disintegrates. Martin Luther King has been cited as an example of a charismatic leader of the Civil Rights Movement (Hollander, 1981).

AUTOCRATIC, DEMOCRATIC AND LAISSEZ-FAIRE LEADERSHIP

People appointed to leadership can use their position in a variety of ways. These have been described as autocratic, democratic and laissez-faire. The word democratic is not used in a political sense. Broadly speaking, autocratic leadership has all authority vested in the leader himself. In democratic leadership responsibility is delegated. In laissez-faire leadership, if it can be called leadership, channels of authority and the areas of responsibility are ill-defined.

An investigation of different types of leadership in youth groups was carried out in America by Lippitt and White (1947). Each group in turn was organized under each of the three forms of leadership. It was found that under what was described as laissez-faire leadership there was the smallest amount of constructive or enjoyable activity. Under autocratic leadership the young people functioned well while the leader was there, but all activity ceased when the leader left the room. In the absence of the leader the group became totally disorganized. With democratic leadership the group was most productive, morale was highest and activity continued in the absence of the leader.

Democratic leadership seems to be most desirable to some psychologists, although in some organizations it may be less appropriate. The army, for example, functions well on an autocratic organization. Industry may do better with democratic leadership and hospitals may be very similar to industry. In small groups democratic leadership often produces the best results, though some people feel safer with a more authoritarian approach. Leadership itself depends for its success on the channels of communication made available.

In some autocratic organizations communication only takes place in a downward direction. The directors give instruction to top management. The top management passes it on to the intermediate management, which in turn passes it on to the foremen who instruct the workers. There is no official opportunity for people at the same level to discuss with each other or to make their views known to people above them.

In democratic leadership there is a provision for communication between people at each level and for 'feedback'. Each group informs the person who has given the instructions of the outcome of discussions. Difficulties that are anticipated or have occurred as a result of new instructions are discussed and the management is informed of the way in which their plans are received. Upward communication also makes it possible for workers to make suggestions and to take an active part in initiating change.

Some organizations have the necessary machinery for democratic functioning, but it is used in an autocratic manner. There may be meetings of workers, but these are used only for grumbles about unimportant matters. Meetings between workers and management are called but abandoned for want of agenda. Suggestion boxes are available but not used. In such organizations it appears that people in leadership positions are unwilling to try a democratic organization. Their reluctance may be due to the fact that a change from autocratic to democratic leadership is often accompanied by a period of relative disorganization. The belief that democratic leadership is desirable has been gaining ground but it can be shown that the sudden removal of autocratic leadership may create tremendous anxiety. The transition to democratic organization can take some time and may not immediately appear to be successful. If a change from autocratic to democratic leadership is to be tried out in industry or in a hospital it may be necessary to prepare for a period of difficulty. It may take a few weeks before meetings and other channels of communication can be used constructively and everybody can be convinced of the benefits of such change.

It is in small groups that the various forms of leadership can be most clearly observed (Shaw, 1964). Many nurses have had experience of participating at meetings or conferences, for example, where different group leaders have adopted different techniques. Some group leaders act in such a way that the members of the group feel free to discuss anything they like. This leader summarizes, clarifies or helps the group to return to an important point without too many side issues being pursued, shows interest in the contributions of each member and encourages shy and retiring people to speak. Silence is allowed while people are thinking or trying to cope with their feelings. Most of the discussion takes place between members of the group and the leaders' remarks are addressed to the group as a whole; the members' remarks are addressed to each other. Such leadership qualities are often found in a good chairperson.

Another group leader may take a much more active part. She decides on the choice of the subject, decides what is and what is not relevant. She addresses people individually, calling on them to speak. All remarks are addressed to her.

It is interesting to note the effect of seating on the type of leadership. Some leaders feel that they need a table in front of them or that they like to be seated in a raised position. This clearly marks them off from the group. A barrier is set up between the leader and the group which is symbolic of the relationship he wishes to create for the successful performance of his role. Where the leader wishes to be a member of the group a barrier would be an obstacle to his function. The kind of group in which members communicate with each other is more successful where the room is small, seating informal, preferably in armchairs, and where coffee or tea is provided (Figure 13, Group I).

There are advantages and disadvantages in both types of leadership. Most committee procedure is formal, all remarks addressed to the chair (Figure 13, Group II). Committees are meant to settle issues efficiently and

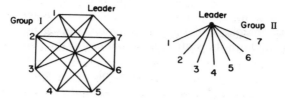

Channels of communication

Figure 13. In Group I, members communicate with other members of the group as well as with the leader. In Group II, the leader communicates with everyone, but the members of the group do not communicate with each other.

fairly rapidly after preliminary discussion has already taken place. During the preliminary discussion, where all issues should be raised and where it is not yet clear who has the greatest contribution to make a more informal setting is appropriate. Hospitals, with their large staffs and complex problems, may need both types of leadership on different occasions. Both need practice for successful use.

We have seen that there are two aspects to the question of leadership, one which is concerned with the characteristics of the person who is recognized as a leader, the other with the skills and knowledge required to assume power and exert influence in a group. The first is sometimes thought to be an aspect of personality, perhaps enhanced by a specific situation. The second can be learnt.

Leadership skills have traditionally been taught in management courses for nurses, but it is becoming increasingly clear that such skills should be introduced as part of the nurses' basic curriculum. Nurses rarely work alone. Even the care of a single patient in hospital requires the coordinated effort of a number of members of staff. One person, for example one nurse, is assigned the planning of care which may then be carried out by several members of the team. Leadership is needed in involving both the staff and the patient in the planning of his care.

Understanding the leadership role is as much a part of the nursing process as understanding the patient's needs. Leadership involves responsibility. The power and influence of leadership carries with it the duty to ensure that it is used to the benefit of those who are led and not to the personal enhancement of the leader.

References

Bales, R.F. (1950) *Interaction Process Analysis: A Method for the Study of Small Groups*. Cambridge, Massachusetts: Addison-Wesley.

Cooper, C.L. & Mangham (1971) *T-groups: A Survey of Research*. London: Wiley.

Gibb, C.A. (ed.) (1969) *Leadership*. Harmondsworth: Penguin.

Hoffman, L.R. & Clark, M.M. (1976) Participation and influence in problem solving groups. In Hollander, E.P. (ed.) *Social Psychology*, 4th edition, p. 442. New York: Oxford University Press.

Hollander, E.P. (ed.) (1981) *Social Psychology*, 4th edition. New York: Oxford University Press.

Lewin, K. (1947) Frontiers in group dynamics. *Human Relations* 1, 5–42.

Lippitt, R. & White, R.K. (1947) An experiment study of leadership and group life. In Newcomb, T.M. & Hartley, E.L. (eds) *Readings in Social Psychology*. New York: Holt.

Menzies, I.E.P. (1961) *The Functioning of Social Systems of Defence Against Anxiety*. London: Tavistock.

Milgram, S. & Toch, H. (1968) Collective behaviour: crowds and social movement. In Lindzey, G. & Aronson, E. (eds) *The Handbook of Social Psychology*, Vol. 4. Reading, Massachusetts: Addison-Wesley.

Moreno, J.L. (ed.) (1960) *The Sociometry Reader*. Glencoe, Illinois: Free Press.

Revans, R.W. (1964) *Standards of Morale: Cause and Effect in Hospital*. London: Oxford University Press (Nuffield Provincial Hospital Trust).

Shaw, M.E. (1964) Communication networks. In Berkowitz, L. *Advances in Experimental Social Psychology*, pp. 111–147. New York: Academic Press.

Sherif, M. (1936) *The Psychology of Social Norms*. New York: Harper.

Walton, H.J. (ed.) (1971) *Small Group Therapy*. Harmondsworth: Penguin.

Further reading

Argyle, M. (1989) *Social Psychology of Work*. London: Penguin.

Kagen, C.M. (ed.) (1985) *Interpersonal Skill in Nursing*. London: Chapman and Hall.

Marson, S., Hartlebury, N., Johnston, R. & Scammel, B. (1990) *Managing People*. London: Macmillan.

McCormick, E.J. & Ilgend, D.R. (1989) *Industrial and Organisational Psychology*. London: Unwin Hyman.

14 Illness, chronicity and disability

DEPENDENCE, INDEPENDENCE, CONTROL

The aim of providing nursing care can be thought of as 'assisting the patient to attain the highest possible level of independence'. This, in terms of the activities of daily living, means aiming for self-care—undoubtedly a desirable goal. For those who are healthy, self-care is, however, only a necessary prerequisite for the more important aspects of living, e.g. for the achievement of satisfactory relationships in the family or with friends. Love, companionship and emotional closeness are important to most people. Along with these go autonomy in decision making and the knowledge that one is in control over many of the events which affect one's life. As an adult, one also has a certain amount of influence and control over others; one has duties, obligations and responsibilities. Sickness interferes with all of these, particularly if admission to hospital is necessary, but to some extent also if one is ill at home. Relinquishing some of the duties and obligations in illness has been described by sociologists as adopting the 'sick role' (Parsons, 1951). This means not only relinquishing some of one's usual role, but also that other people must adjust their role correspondingly. Inevitably, illness results in disturbance in family and other social relationships.

There is a loss of prestige, for example, if a breadwinner has to stop work, or when the head of the family must leave to the spouse decisions over important matters of child care or finance. Because this may only be a temporary change there is often uncertainty about what is expected of each person involved.

There may be considerable emotional disturbance among relatives who may feel guilty about not having observed symptoms of illness earlier, or about not having taken complaints seriously. There may be anger about overwork, the hazards of the occupation, and about a dangerous lifestyle which may be held responsible for the illness. If the illness is serious and the prognosis is poor, the relatives' fear for the patient's life is accompanied by anxiety about impending bereavement and doubt about their own ability to cope.

Frequently there are problems about communication because relatives may not know how much to discuss with the patient. Neither patient nor relatives may know how well informed the other is. The difficulty is often aggravated by the fact that the doctors, or nurses, may not be entirely frank with the patient or the relatives or both. This raises the issue of honesty and truth telling.

Even when the patient's illness has been openly discussed with all the people concerned, problems in communication may arise from lack of understanding or because communication about a painful subject is inherently difficult. Discussion between the patient and his relatives about all important aspects of the illness, about the way people feel and about practical organizational aspects, requires a lot of time, repeated contact, privacy and intimacy; all of these are difficult to obtain in a hospital ward.

All these difficulties may combine to make visiting time for family and friends embarrassing and painful instead of the enjoyable experience it should be.

When the patient first falls ill, his relatives often obtain a lot of interest, help and support, but this can tend to be short-lived. Because there may be little they can do and little to talk about which is new, visitors and phone calls from friends soon diminish and the patient's close relatives may be left unsupported just at the time when difficult decisions may have to be made or when drastic changes in their lifestyles become imperative.

For patients in hospital, visiting can become an ordeal. Not only can it be very tiring if they feel obliged to converse politely for a long period with successive arrivals, but it can become almost impossible to pay attention simultaneously to visitors who are sitting on both sides of the bed. Conversation can become like observing a tennis match. Visitors too may find conversation with the patient difficult. They tend to ask a lot of questions and often forget that they have more news to give to the patient than he has for them. Patients need the stimulation of news about current events and of people in the outside world, and visitors should be encouraged to give news, rather than ask for it. The greatest difficulty which faces the hospital patient in relation to visitors is that so much control has been taken away from him. We do not normally entertain visitors in the bedroom, but the patient in hospital usually has no other territory at his disposal. Normally visitors come in response to the specific invitation of their host, but while the patient is in hospital visitors have the right to turn up uninvited. It is the nursing staff rather than the patient himself who exercise control, if any restriction is placed on visiting. When people normally invite visitors they take care to ensure their compatibility. In hospital the most ill-matched visitors often arrive together.

The problems of visiting patients in hospital illustrate that some of the most important human needs are difficult to satisfy by nursing staff.

Patients have needs for affiliation and friendship; they have the need to retain important emotional relationships with family members and friends. Psychologists use the term 'significant others' for the people who matter a great deal in people's lives.

Patients have a need for autonomous decision making and for exercising control over certain aspects of their lives. People need a certain amount of territory of their own. Within that territory they can normally rely on privacy; they can control who may enter. They can prevent crowding within that space. None of these needs can easily be met in hospital. It may be one of the functions of the nurse to attempt to ensure that they are not too drastically violated. It may be possible, for example, to help the patient exercise control over the movement of visitors, perhaps by writing and sending invitations to visit on specific days or at a specific time.

Normally there is a well-defined role relationship between host and guests. Hosts tend to offer some refreshments to their guests, even if only on a token basis; guests tend to bring some present as a token of their esteem. The patient's role as host is nearly always ignored by the hospital. There are occasions when patients are served with meals while visitors look on—a complete reversal of normal role behaviour.

Visitors often bring presents, especially some items of food. These gifts from visitors are of great importance to patients, not least for their symbolic significance. The exchange of such gifts is one way of ensuring the patient that he continues to be remembered and valued.

While food or flowers are gifts which most readily spring to mind, they may not always be the gifts the patient needs most and nurses may be able to help relatives make more appropriate choices by, for example, mentioning how much the patient enjoys games, puzzles, magazines or books. Visitors may not always appreciate that the patient may enjoy things to do, in order to regain interest and self-confidence.

The need to maintain family relationships and friendships during illness may be particularly important when small children are concerned. Separation of children from their parents can cause great anxiety. If the child is the patient, the importance of visits by the parents is well recognized, and is discussed in another chapter. When one of the parents is ill in hospital, it is equally important that children should be allowed to visit.

The mother often worries about the welfare of children during her absence and may be reassured by seeing them. Children are anxious about the absent parent. They may find it difficult to imagine what hospital is like. They may not believe that the mother is ill and have fantasies about her having died, unless they can see her for themselves. It is usually not as difficult as some people fear to distract children from unpleasant sights and to prevent them making a disturbing noise.

Relatives may have serious difficulties when they visit a patient who is critically ill and when visiting time is therefore unrestricted. A feeling that it is their duty not to leave the patient, combined with a sense of helplessness and uselessness makes visiting very painful. Relatives can be made to feel of value if in some way they can contribute to the care of their loved one and indeed, in this way, help the nursing staff. It is not necessary that all nursing care for the patient should be completed before the arrival of visitors. On the contrary, it may be easier for visitors to appreciate how well the patient is cared for when they are allowed to witness care being given or even lend a helping hand.

Caring for patients at home

Patients who remain in their own home during illness retain a greater amount of autonomy and control than do patients admitted to hospital. The change of role relationship between the patient and his family and friends is less dramatic and he is able to retain greater independence. This may render nursing care more challenging as the patient may more readily exercise his right to deny care and forgoe advice. For a relative to enforce a therapeutic regimen would require that she steps out of the usual relationship within the family and adopts a role in which she gives orders, and the patient submits— a role change which, for example, a daughter may feel unable to accept towards a parent and which a patient who is a parent may find embarrassing. Patients may be quite unwilling to let a close relative carry out intimate care, such as washing or bathing, attention to toilet, sputum or vomit. In spite of the best intentions the care given by close relatives is sometimes inadequate because relatives cannot overcome their repugnance for certain tasks, but at the same time cannot ask for help as they don't like to admit such sentiments.

Because of their professional status, nurses are often preferred to relatives in the giving of many aspects of personal care. Relatives sometimes cannot give the most effective care because of the emotional involvement in the patient and his well-being. Anxiety about his condition, concern about deterioration and excessive worry about his response to care make it difficult for relatives to bring sufficient objectivity to care.

Prolonged illness in the home often results in isolation of the family as a whole. People find illness distressing. The family who is busy nursing an invalid may lose contact and find they have little in common with others. The additional expense of entertaining a lot of visitors exerts a restraining influence on the welcome visitors receive.

The contribution a nurse can make to care of a patient in his own home goes beyond the giving of physical care and includes supporting and assisting the family as a whole. They may be able to offer respite by arranging for short-term admission to hospital or for someone to stay in the home. Home care may be entirely possible if the carer can feel confident that the help and support of a community nurse is available.

CHRONIC SICKNESS AND DISABILITY

In the course of growing up people develop ideas about themselves which determine how they behave in different situations. They get to know their capabilities. They undertake only those activities of which they know themselves to be competent. Interests develop according to an individual's ability to understand the subject and take an active part. People, for example, compete in sports only when they can approximately equal the performance of others; they study only those subjects which are within their competence and present themselves for examinations only if there is at least a chance of passing. Choice of friends is often determined by mutual interests. Friends are made at work or amongst those who play the same games, share a particular interest, or are equally energetic in climbing mountains.

People's estimate of their own ability usually becomes surprisingly accurate. They form an image of themselves by identifying with what is referred to as a 'reference group'. The individual sets standards for himself by comparison with members of the group to which he belongs or to which he would like to belong (Hyman and Singer, 1968).

Some may have been so profoundly discouraged during childhood that they consistently underestimate their ability and lack confidence. Some people who grow up with a handicap devote most of their energy to overcoming it and excel in the use of precisely those skills which they have found hardest to acquire. Others cope with their disability by ignoring it and concentrating on excelling in some other sphere of activity. These methods of compensating for some real or imagined inferiority are part of the driving force in people's way of life. Gradual changes in ability, as it increases during growth and declines in old age, are incorporated into people's ideas of themselves. Illness is regarded as a temporary interference in the normal process of life and does not, at first, lead to a change in outlook.

Prolonged and chronic illness and permanent disablement, however, may necessitate a reconstruction of the patient's ideas of himself and a complete reorganization of relationships. The ordinary expectations of the family and of society as a whole must be changed. This process can be slow and painful and requires considerable assistance from those who are caring for the patient.

Stigma

Often the patient who realizes that he is permanently disabled becomes angry with himself and with everyone whom he feels he can blame for his predicament. He may express his feeling in his criticism of the treatment and care he is receiving in the hospital, possibly even in litigation against the hospital or those he thinks are responsible for his condition, or he may accuse his family or people in general of being hard-hearted, of disliking him because he is a burden to them, of looking down on invalids. At some stage of the illness most disabled people project their anger on to other people. They refuse to meet people, refuse to be seen or to go out. This phase of self-consciousness increases the difficulties because, while originally people may not have harboured any of the feelings ascribed to them, the patient's attitude creates in them embarrassment, discomfort and eventually rejection. The expectation of being rejected becomes a self-fulfilling prophecy (Merton, 1957). Goffman (1968) discusses situations which render people socially abnormal, e.g. situations of disfigurement, blindness, mental illness. He refers to this as 'stigma'.

When the patient first realizes that he cannot completely regain his physical health he may become depressed. He may feel that in such circumstances life is not worth living. He may lose interest in himself, his treatment and the conditions surrounding him. When the patient is in this frame of mind it is difficult to care for him because he himself does nothing to help. He may refuse to take sufficient nourishment, neglect his personal hygiene, lose all interest in any activity. The will to live is essential to recovery and nurses must help the patient to see that in spite of his handicap he is needed by those who love him and that he can be useful to the community. It will be necessary for the patient to find a new 'reference group' and restore his mental well-being if not his physical.

DISABILITY AND COMMUNICATION

It is inevitable that a disabled person must lose some of his former friends. For example if he can no longer play golf he loses interest in the conversation of his golfing friends; if he can no longer work he loses interest in discussion about his former job. After an initial attempt to keep in touch he becomes increasingly isolated from all those whose interests he can no longer share.

The greatest isolation occurs in those who lose sight, hearing or speech. We rely, in our social contacts, on communication by speech and we keep informed about our environment mainly by sight and hearing. It is important for the nurse to learn how to communicate with the deaf by gesture, mime, writing and demonstration and to learn how to help the friends and relatives to continue their efforts to communicate in spite of deafness. Partially deaf people may be even more handicapped because they may be less conscious of defective hearing and more inclined to blame others for failing to make themselves clear. Conversely, they may be aware of their inability to fully participate in conversation and may therefore withdraw completely.

People who have become partially sighted or blinded need constant interpretation of their environment while they are learning to use their other senses. It is possible for the nurse to pay attention to noises and movement and to explain their meaning to the blind person before he becomes startled by someone's presence. The total isolation of those who cannot see may lead to a period of confusion, disorientation and a terrifying feeling of being lost which may result in uncontrolled, sometimes aggressive, behaviour.

Patients who cannot speak can make their wishes known by signs and non-articulate noises. It is a great effort for them, however, to attract attention and, having done so, to make themselves clear. It is easy to become impatient with the person who is aphasic but very necessary to take all the time needed to understand. However, in the long run the patient's speech difficulty may lead other people to stop speaking to him and thus deprive him of intellectual stimulation and social contact. To avoid this, every effort is made to teach the patient new methods of communication. Speech therapists have developed various systems of sign language to help aphasic people.

The nursing care and rehabilitation of the disabled must aim at helping the patient to acknowledge his disability so that he can create a new idea of himself which includes his handicap. Often, in a well-meaning attempt to spare the patient suffering, the likelihood of permanent disability is not mentioned for a long time. By then the patient has already begun to realize that all is not well and, sensing other people's reluctance to face facts, he keeps his worry to himself and begins to see himself as an object of pity and despair. Sensitive assessment of the patient may result in the decision that it is wiser to encourage talk of the future as early as possible, and to help the patient to get to know himself as a different, but in no way inferior, person to the one he used to be.

REHABILITATION

This can best be done by emphasizing what the patient can do rather than what is no longer possible for him. If he has lost the power of his legs he can work with his hands, he can paint, or learn a new craft. He can use artificial limbs to perform skills he may never have realized he possessed. It may not be very wise to over-emphasize progress in the use of the disabled part of the body. Improved use of the muscles is at the same time a reminder of the deficiency of movement. However helpful physiotherapy, for example, may be, it is a constant reminder of disablement. The creation of new interests, new skills in no way connected with the disabled part of the body, gives purposive direction to life and helps to create a positive self-image.

Many patients are able first to accept the fact that they may be useful to other sufferers of their own kind. Associations for sufferers from paraplegia or epilepsy may, for example, offer the opportunity of doing useful work and of developing the ability to meet people again. Help is more easily accepted from those who are fellow sufferers because there is no need to feel that help is given only out of pity.

There are opportunities for working with other disabled people in special workshops and clubs. Competition in sports can be encouraged. Many paraplegic patients, for example, excel in archery and participate in national or international competitions. Many disabled people gain fulfillment by collecting funds for research and for treatment of their particular handicap for the benefit of future patients. What matters most to the disabled person and those around him is that he feels equal to, though different from, other people—able to hold his own in a newly-formed circle of friends and fellow workers.

The process of becoming used to the idea of a new and different self must be accompanied by parallel changes in the expectations and attitudes of the family. During the patient's illness it is easy to make allowances for his deficiencies and excuse all he says or does by reference to his condition. This cannot be done for ever, and gradually the family realizes that changes in the patient may be permanent. They have to learn when to stop considering the patient as the focus of all attention and begin to expect from him a certain amount of consideration.

People behave differently in different settings. Hospitals tend to encourage dependence all to easily. In his own home the setting may be right for reinforcing independence. The size of a hospital ward may be frightening for patients who are unsure of their ability in locomotion. On the other hand, crowding may prevent the patient from obtaining a large enough personal territory (Goffman, 1971) but in the privacy of their own home, surrounded by relatives or personal friends, attempts at independence, without loss of face, can be made.

When the family begins to treat him as a responsible person he may respond by accepting responsibility and becoming interested in living once more as full a life as possible. Some families, of course, find it difficult to readjust themselves to the patient's resumption of his position. The patient's illness may have served as a convenient excuse for them to explain their failure to reach acceptable standards of living. For the patient, disablement may be a respectable way of explaining his inability to cope with the stresses of life. When illness is used by the family in this way the whole family is in need of help, support and encouragement.

Many disabled people can be helped to return to work but sometimes it is necessary for them to change their occupation and undergo a course of training. Some patients may be able to return to their former type of occupation provided they find work in suitable premises, e.g. where there is a lift or the work is on the ground floor. Adjustment may have to be made in working hours to allow for rest breaks, or in working conditions to enable work to be carried out from a wheelchair or with specially designed equipment. It may be necessary to register for employment under the Disablement Resettlement Acts. Sympathetic employers may considerably assist rehabilitation.

Legislation ensures that public places, such as theatres and libraries, are now accessible to disabled people. These facilities are not, however, always made use of because disabled people may be reluctant to accept the label of 'handicapped person'. A determined education effort is necessary if the disabled are to participate fully in society.

Some disabled people find it impossible to live entirely

without the help of nurses. For many, regular help from the community nurse may be enough, but some people need to return periodically to hospital. Some paraplegic patients, for example, may need repeated readmission to hospital in order to help them to cope with urinary control or with the occasional occurrence of pressure sores. During a period of hospitalization. It is important that they do not lose whatever coping skills they have acquired at home (Atkinson and Sklaroff, 1984).

PROGRESSIVE DISABLING CONDITIONS

It is not always possible to achieve improvement. Some conditions are progressive, causing increasing dependence, disablement and suffering. Patients and their relatives are often aware of the unfavourable prognosis before anyone has actually discussed it with them. Considerable unhappiness and anxiety occur if this happens. The patient may feel obliged to pretend that he feels optimistic in order not to cause pain to his relatives. Relatives and friends may believe that a pretence of cheerfulness on their part will spare suffering for the patient.

It is usually easier for all concerned to bear the sorrow involved, knowing of the poor prognosis, if they can freely talk to each other, comfort and support each other. The patient may wish to make realistic plans. He will want to have some say in any decisions which are made about him. Where he is to spend the rest of his life may be of great concern to him. Hospital wards are not considered the most desirable environment for prolonged disablement. Young people suffering from chronic illness are particularly unhappy in the chronic, often geriatric, wards of long-stay hospitals. A cooperative effort of friends and family can sometimes enable a patient to spend the remainder of his life in his own home if help can be provided.

Financial assistance may be necessary to provide such aids as wheelchairs or lifting hoists. Structural alterations in the home may be necessary if the stairs are an obstacle to movement or if the doors are too narrow to allow the passage of wheelchairs. Gadgets may have to be bought to help the patient to retain some independence. Special clothing, which can be put on and taken off in spite of the patient's difficulties in movement or posture, may be needed and laundry facilities and transport may have to be provided.

All these arrangements can only be set in motion if the patient and his relatives can freely discuss the problem with each other. If the prognosis is that of a long-drawn-out, gradually deteriorating condition the patient may need to prepare himself for a life in which, increasingly, he will be dependent on others. One of the hardest things to accept may be that even total dependence on others does not lessen his value as a person. Despite this he may have thoughts about suicide, or a wish for euthanasia, which he may need to discuss with someone. He may have plans for the completion of some work and need urgent assistance, he may have some wishes which remain unfulfilled and may want to tell his relatives about this.

Relatives, too, may need to discuss their feelings when they learn of the adverse prognosis for the patient. Guilt feelings almost inevitably occur. Sometimes a relative may feel the patient's illness could have been prevented if only he had paid attention earlier to the complaints. Relatives might reproach themselves for real or imaginary neglect of the patient. Many relatives become irritable with the patient at times and then regret their behaviour. The emotional and financial strain of chronic illness often results in a secret wish for a speedy death. Such a wish is then followed by immediate regret and by attempts to compensate for the guilt feelings. Relatives need someone who can help them to see that such thoughts are normal and understandable. When relatives can talk about their feelings they can often continue to shoulder the burden of care. When they cannot talk about their feelings their only remedy may be to detach themselves prematurely. For many the pain of witnessing deterioration in their loved one may be too much to bear. They mourn the loss of the perfect image of the person they loved. By the time the patient dies, their grief may already be spent.

LOSS AND GRIEF

Patients who are terminally ill are often aware of the approach of death before anyone has thought of discussing the subject with them. Glaser and Strauss (1965) have described three states of awareness that may surround the dying person and his family. These are closed awareness, mutual pretence and open awareness. In *closed awareness* the patient and his family may be unaware of the impending death and may even lack a full appreciation of the illness. It may be that the relatives know but have decided that the patient should not be told. Conversely, the patient may know the truth but does not know if his closest relatives do. This creates problems for both the patient and his family and a dilemma for the nursing staff who may feel that the patient's trust in them may be threatened by less than honest communications. In *mutual pretence* the patient, his family and the carers know that the prognosis is mortal but choose not to discuss the subject. Such mutual pretence is often motivated by concern to protect against distress but in reality may lead to a sense of discomfort and burden created by the absence of anyone in whom to confide. In *open awareness* all concerned know the truth and feel able to acknowledge and discuss the impending death. By so doing, the patient, in particular, is able to express his needs and desires and feel a continuing sense of belonging and participating. It must be said, however, that open awareness is not an easy option and many still avoid it; some may feel able to discuss practical arrangements but need support and understanding to come to terms with their emotional responses.

Some patients are afraid of death but more often the fear is of pain and the disintegration of their lifestyle. They seek reassurance that they will be helped to a pain-free, dignified, 'good' death. The hospice movement has come into being to ensure that the care of the terminally ill deals effectively with these fears (Lamerton, 1973). Hospice care is based on holistic concepts and focuses not on cure but on symptom control, in particular the management of pain (see p. 336). It is still the case, however, that 70% of patients die in a hospital (Centre for Policy on Ageing, 1983) and 74% of such patients may die alone (Bowling and Cartwright, 1982). Nurses, especially within the acute hospital setting, are learning much from the experience of the hospices. Pain, nausea and other distressing symptoms can be controlled effectively and a good quality of both remaining life and death achieved.

Kubler-Ross (1969) described five stages through which a patient may pass as he approaches death. Such stages may accompany a loss of any kind, for example, loss of a parent, loss of a limb or loss of a breast. In the first stage there may be denial. The patient refuses to believe that his illness is fatal and may make quite un-realistic plans for his future. In this stage he may not wish to discuss his illness at all, will not ask for inform-ation and will ignore it when given. He may appear inappropriately cheerful but in reality may feel isolated and misunderstood. At the next stage there may be anger—anger with the nurses and doctors, with his family, with himself and sometimes with God. This may give way to what Kubler-Ross describes as 'bargaining'. The patient tries to bargain for time, to hang on a little longer. He may seek advice from different sources, hoping to get a more favourable prognosis. Equally he may change his lifestyle or go away on a holiday, hoping to put off death for a little longer. He may experience a religious conversion as a means of obtaining a promise of life. For some, depression may follow with the feeling that too little has been achieved in life. The final stage reflects coming to terms with impending death and is described as acceptance. There is no fear and the patient feels able to enjoy to the full what life is still left. In this stage the patient no longer strives for self-preservation. Rather he may seek self-fulfillment. Salter (1982) sug-gests that care, therefore, should be focused not on the end but on living each day to the full. Recognizing the gradual decline, Salter describes a process of care that moves from enjoying pleasurable activities while that is possible, to quiet relaxation and finally to letting go and allowing others to meet both physical and psychological needs.

It is important to recognize that not all patients nec-essarily go through all these stages. For each patient the last experiences of life have unique significance. It is generally believed, however, that it is desirable to help a patient to reach a state of acceptance, rather than for him to die in anger or depression. It may be necessary to help the patient work through earlier stages and this may be achieved by allowing the patient to talk about his feelings to an attentive listener. Of great value to all is for the patient and the relatives to listen to each other, but it may often be the case that overt distress of one or other may prevent this. Both the patient and the relatives may look to the nurse to help them come to terms with their own emotions before they can support each other's grief. It is not easy, however, for the nurse to cope with the emotions of dying patients and their relatives and to accept whatever feelings they express. Quint (1975) has shown that nurses find the care of dying patients both demanding and upsetting. Particularly distressing can be the death of a patient whom the nurse has got to know well or when a life is cut short and death unexpected. For nurses to be able to offer patients the support they need, the nurses, in turn, must feel able to talk to someone about their feelings. A counselling service for staff can provide such support (see p. 350).

MOURNING

When death eventually occurs, friends and relatives go through a period of mourning which follows stages that may closely resemble those experienced in the process of dying in that the grieving process has also been described as going through a series of separate stages or phases before full resolution and restitution can occur (Engel, 1986; Parkes, 1972; Murgatroyd and Woolfe, 1982). Parkes identified four phases of mourning. Initially there may be a numbness that gives way to yearning and protest at the loss. The realization that reunion is impossible can lead to a phase of apathy, loss of identity and disorganization. Parkes saw this as a necessary phase if successful readjustment was to be achieved and a new identity established and that full readjustment could take many months, long after the visible tears may have ceased.

Worden (1983) sees the grieving less in terms of stages or phases, which he sees as implying passivity, and more in terms of tasks that can be seen to involve activity on the part of the bereaved. He describes four tasks: accepting the reality; accepting the pain that grief engenders; adjusting to a life without the loved one; and lastly being able to reinvest emotions in other relationships. As with the process of dying, these theoretical approaches must never be considered rigid entities. An individual may move between stages or tasks or it may be that no one stage or task can ever be definitively identified. What is stressed, and appropriately so, is that the process of grieving is never easy and in many ways Western society does not encourage grieving. Indeed, for many, another's grief is a source of embarrassment to be avoided. Grieving relatives may feel, at times, an obligation to suppress their tears, appear stoical, calm and unaffected. Adult mourners sometimes feel that children should be protected from discussions about death but evidence has shown that children can accept the reality of death and should not be excluded from family grieving (Bluebond-Langer, 1977).

Following the death of a patient, hospital nurses are available to support the bereaved only during the early phases of mourning. General practitioners and community nurses are increasingly aware of the duration of the grieving process, and that if prolonged and unresolved it may result in both physical and psychological problems. Some bereaved persons never establish a satisfactory life for themselves after the death of a spouse, parent or child. They continue a life that becomes progressively more isolated and depressed such that relationships with other relatives and friends deteriorate and may even be lost. Some may develop extreme hostility and resentment towards those with whom they were formerly associated through the deceased person. In some instances, especially in the elderly, the death of the remaining spouse may occur soon after bereavement. An awareness is developing within the caring professions that bereaved people are a group 'at risk' and that professional support should be available. In addition volunteer support groups such as CRUSE—a widows' self-help group—can provide valuable counselling.

The hospital nurse must give support to fellow patients of the deceased, who often experience grief and bereavement. For such patients to have witnessed the support the staff are able to give and to observe the dignified and caring behaviour that has led to a peaceful death, can make the prospect of dying less distressing for them. The old notion of secrecy surrounding the death of a patient has been replaced, for the most part, by gentle and honest explanation and discussion.

References

Atkinson, F.I. & Sklaroff, S.A. (1984) *Acute Hospital Wards and the Disabled Patient: A Survey of the Experiences of Patients and Nurses.* Nurses Studies Research Unit, University of Edinburgh.

Bowling, A. & Cartwright, A. (1982) *A Life after Death: a Study of the Elderly Widowed.* Tavistock, London.

Bluebond-Langer, M. (1977) Meanings of death to children. In Feifel, H. (ed.) *New Meanings of Death.* New York: McGraw-Hill.

Centre for Policy in Ageing (1983) *The Hospital Movement in Britain: its Role and its Future.* London: Centre for Policy in Ageing.

Engel, G. (1964) Grief and grieving. *American Journal of Nursing* **64**, 93–98.

Glaser, B.G. & Strauss, B. (1965) *Awareness of Dying.* Chicago: Aldine Publishing.

Goffman, E. (1968) *Stigma* Harmondsworth: Penguin.

Goffman, E. (1971) *The Presentation of Self in Everyday Life.* Harmondsworth: Penguin Books.

Hyman, H.H. & Singer, E. (1968) *Readings in Reference Group Theory and Research*. New York: Free Press.

Kubler-Ross, E. (1969) *On Death and Dying*. New York: Macmillan.

Lamerton, R. (1973) *Care of the Dying*. Harmondsworth: Penguin.

Merton, R.K. (1957) *Social Theory and Social Structure*. Glencoe, Illinois: Free Press.

Murgatroyd, S. & Woolfe, R. (1982) *Coping with Crisis*. London: Harper & Row.

Parkes, C.M. (1972) *Bereavement*. London: Tavistock.

Quint, J.C. (1975) *The Nurse and the Dying Patient*. New York: Macmillan.

Parsons, T. (1951) *The Social Systems*. London: Routledge & Kegan Paul.

Salter, R. (1982) The art of dying. *Canadian Nurse* **78**, 20–21.

Worden, J.W. (1983) *Grief Counselling and Grief Therapy*. London: Tavistock.

15 Stress

As human beings we are innately equipped to adapt to changes in our environment. We have the necessary reserves of energy to deal with environmental demands and still maintain the homeostasis of the body. Stress has been considered as the body's reactions to environmental changes and challenges and therefore is part of our normal functioning and integral to life. In moderate and appropriate degree, stress arouses and alerts us, improving and enhancing mental and physical activity. Therefore, despite the popular connotations, stress is not necessarily a bad thing. Optimal stress has been described as *eustress* (Selye, 1980). When we suffer from stress it is because we are trying to cope with either too little or too much stress (Welford, 1973). Either extreme will disrupt equilibrium, but most commonly stress is described as resulting when too intense and prolonged a demand is put on an individual—be it physical, psychological or social. The finite capacity to cope is exceeded and this may result in both emotional and physical disorder. Stress can be manifested in many ways but of most significance is the emotion anxiety, and often the two terms are used interchangeably. Spielberger (1972) describes anxiety as:

> a transitory emotional state or condition that varies in intensity and fluctuates over time and is characterised by feelings of tension, apprehension and heightened autonomic nervous activity.

Understanding the concept of stress is important because it reveals how people perceive and respond to all the demands of everyday life. Nurses, like many others, tend to consider stress holistically, seeing it as both cause and consequence, but it is considered more useful to look at the causes of stress as stimuli known as stressors and to see stress itself as the reaction or response to such stimuli. Indeed, one can only really determine that an event or experience is stressful by observing the reaction of the individual. Perhaps more crucial to the current ethos of nursing which aims to provide more personal and responsive care, is the appreciation that how events and experiences are perceived in terms of their stressfulness is highly individual. Equally individual is how perceived stress will be coped with. Although, of course, there is some degree of consensus as to situations that may cause stress, no two patients will necessarily respond in the same way to a similar experience. Sources of stress, the stress response and individual differences will now be considered in more detail.

SOURCES OF STRESS

In everyday life we can easily identify stressful events and experiences, but stress has a complexity of origins. It can be caused by physical stimuli such as excessive heat, cold, pain, strenuous exercise or bacterial contamination. Psychological sources are such things as fear, frustration or the cognitive dissonance discussed in Chapter 13. Social sources of stress can be found in such things as bereavement, unemployment or role ambiguity. It should not be forgotten that the stress response can be evoked also by intense pleasure or happy events such as marriage and Christmas. The work of Holmes and Rahe (1967) demonstrated this clearly. They developed a scale to measure stress in terms of life changes ranking events in order from the most stressful to the least. Like many others, they were concerned with the psychological and social causes of stress; those aspects of everyday life that can disrupt well-being and appear to be linked with physical and emotional disorders.

THE STRESS RESPONSE

Research into stress owes much to the work of Hans Selye and it was he who coined the term 'stressor' in order to distinguish cause and effect. Selye, a philosopher and physiologist, was essentially interested in the stress response. During his research into hormonal function he became side-tracked when he observed that whatever form of distress his experimental animals experienced, the reaction followed a characteristic pattern. He described this as a general alarm to whatever stressor was inflicted. Also, he consistently found that these animals developed enlargement of the adrenal cortex, atrophy of the lymph nodes and thymus and peptic ulceration. He concluded that organisms not only react in a generalized way to any stressor but also developed anatomical and physiological alteration if stress persisted. He described what he called a general adaptation syndrome (GAS)— 'the non-specific response of the body to any demand made on it' (Selye, 1974; see Figure 14).

Three stages were identified:

1. The alarm stage.
2. The stage of resistance.
3. The stage of exhaustion.

The initial alarm reaction brings about the 'fight–flight' response. The individual becomes aroused and there is a surge of sympathetic nervous activity. Adrenaline and

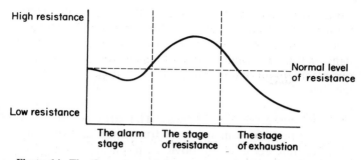

Figure 14. The three states of the general adaptation syndrome.

noradrenaline are released from the adrenal medulla and glucocorticoid hormones from the adrenal cortex. Physiologically the individual is prepared for action: cardiovascular and respiratory activity increase, blood pressure rises and blood flow is diverted from skin and viscera to vital organs and skeletal muscles; muscles are toned, pupils dilated and nutrients mobilized; gut mobility decreases, sphincters contract and the inflammatory response is suppressed. Psychologically the individual experiences anxiety. This can vary from anxiety which alerts, arouses and motivates to that which results in paralysing panic. Selye's second stage is of resistance which occurs as all the homeostatic and adaptive mechanisms come into play to restore equilibrium. However, if there is prolonged and excessive stress the reserves of energy for adaptation become depleted and the third stage of exhaustion occurs. If the stressor has been physiological in origin, such as injury or disease, the stage of exhaustion may result in death. According to Selye, psychological stress rarely leads to terminal exhaustion, but may well result in various physical manifestations of ill health.

Further detail on the physiological basis of the stress response can be found in Montague (1980). What emerges is that the stress response is highly appropriate when fight or flight is required and was probably necessary for our primitive ancestors. It would seem that the response has become established in our genetic make-up. However, twentieth century stressors less commonly require such physiological preparedness. The stressors of today are identified more in terms of frustration and tensions that do not require an obvious physical outlet. The constant inhibition of the 'natural' reaction may actually do us harm and has been implicated in such disorders as heart disease, peptic ulceration and autoimmune impairment. Disorders and physical symptoms where the origins are attributed in part to psychological stress are known as psychosomatic.

INDIVIDUAL DIFFERENCES

Extending Selye's physiological theories to psychological factors is not always easy. The latter are less easy to define and measure. Ethical considerations occur when research is on human beings. One of the major criticisms of Selye's work is that he gives a stereotyped response and ignores both individual variation in response and how any one response may be interpreted. Psychological studies of stress have been pursued in order to understand human behaviour in relation to stress and to how variations in response to stress occur. Lazarus (1966) contributed much to our understanding with his transactional theory of stress. He was less concerned with the stressful stimuli *per se* but more with how the individual actually perceived the stimuli. Only if it was interpreted as stressful would a stress response be triggered and the response itself would be modified according to the appraisal made of the situation. In this context stress is perceived as an 'imbalance between demand and resources' (Monat and Lazarus, 1977). How the stressor is perceived depends on individual predispositions, personality, values and attitudes, self-concept and what may have been learnt from past experience. These cognitive, affective and adaptive processes will influence how the individual actually copes with environmental demands. Many attempts have been made to identify those who might be more vulnerable to stress than others. Levi (1974) argues that, not only do individuals have predispositions to experience stress and stress-related disorders, but also predispositions to develop a specific stress disorder. Some may develop gastric problems, some migraine and some back pain. Others may experience all these things. Individuals have also been described as Type A or Type B (Friedman and Rosenman, 1974). The former are considered to be competitive, ambitious and conscientious, the latter more relaxed and easy-going. Type A people are thought to experience more stress and stress-related disorders than Type B people. Cherniss (1980) suggests that many who work in health care are Type A. Research has also revealed that there are some who experience frequent high levels of anxiety and who perceive as dangerous many situations which others do not regard as dangerous. Such people are said to have 'trait' anxiety. Others respond with acute anxiety only to specific situations. This is referred to as 'state' anxiety. It is thought that psychosomatic disorders are associated with trait anxiety whereas panic attacks and phobias are, perhaps, serious examples of state anxiety.

Levine (1969) suggests that optimal human growth and development incorporates learning the ability to cope with stress. It could be argued that younger patients in hospital, who appear to experience excessive stress and pain, may have had, as yet, limited exposure to environmental stress. This may not be the case for the older patients who may have experienced childhood illness, injury and hardships and lived through the years of war. Seligman (1975) argues that successfully coping with stress, which he describes as 'mastery of the past' can 'inoculate' people against subsequent stress and facilitate effective coping. This supports the notion that older people may be less vulnerable to stress than younger people. It is a debatable point as many other factors must be considered, but when considering the stress in nurses it has been suggested that the older nurse appears to experience less stress (Livingstone and Livingstone, 1984; McCarthy, 1985).

COPING WITH STRESS

Lazarus (1966) proposes that once primary appraisal of a situation has deemed it to be stressful, then a secondary appraisal is made to determine the coping strategy to be adopted. Coping mechanisms can be divided into two categories: direct action and indirect palliative action. In direct action, active steps are taken to demolish, avoid or flee from the threatening stimuli or advance action is taken to meet the threat. Often direct action can involve aggression whether or not it is entirely appropriate. Indirect or palliative mechanisms may be used if direct action is too difficult or has failed. Indirect methods tend to be concerned with reducing the unpleasant emotions experienced, even though the actual source of stress is not addressed. The emotion-focused mechanisms may take the form of tranquillizers, alcohol or smoking or involve the use of the defence mechanisms described in Chapter 2. By these means the ego is protected and in the short term such palliative methods may serve a purpose. By reducing the emotional disturbance the individual may feel able to tackle the problem more directly. Dewe (1989) thinks that the emotion-focused mechanisms are not given enough status and that coping with emotional discomfort is especially legitimate where little else can be done. However, as a long-term strategy, palliative mechanisms are considered maladaptive as reality may be ignored and normal interactive processes hindered.

Coping may not always be appropriate, but it is always purposeful. Mechanisms adopted are not fixed and can vary according to the stress perceived. They can also vary over time as the individual has the capacity to learn from experience and adopt more effective coping strategies. Based on his research with patients suffering from cancer, Weisman (1979) identified individual coping strategies. He suggests that those who cope well with the stress of cancer are those who adopt 'active problem-solving' coping styles, confronting the issues, seeking help and advice, discussing fears and anxieties and taking a positive approach to life. Those most vulnerable appeared to adopt a 'passive defending' coping style, withdrawing from people, suppressing emotions, and passively and pessimistically accepting anything that is to happen to them. Seligman (1975) has described this latter way of coping in terms of learned helplessness. If a stressor is seen as inescapable, and one over which the individual believes he has no control, then the motivation to cope is lost. Having perhaps tried and failed to cope, he has learnt that it is pointless and he becomes helpless and hopeless. Similar reactions can occur in people after such stressful events as major disasters. Equally it can be found in elderly hospitalized patients, to whom things may seem to just happen without any choice or control on their part (Robertson, 1986). The antidote to learned helplessness must be a relearning process to restore a feeling of control and purpose. This can be achieved by reinforcing behaviour that allows for both individual control and positive coping.

STRESS IN PATIENTS

Clearly illness and hospitalization are potentially and even inevitably stressful events, but when stress is so great that it hinders recovery and detrimentally affects the patient's whole view of his life, then the coping strategies have been ineffective. More importantly, the sources of stress must be examined to distinguish unavoidable from avoidable stress. There have been many aspects of hospital life which patients find anxiety-provoking or stressful. Among the stressful events are admission and discharge procedures, doctors' visits, visiting hours, using bedpans, surgical dressings and, of course, painful treatments, discomfort, lack of privacy and loneliness (Munday, 1973; Franklin, 1974; Wilson-Barnett, 1979; Davies and Peters, 1983). Volicer, Isenberg and Burns (1977) designed a Hospital Stress Rating Scale to assess the stress experienced by medical and surgical patients and they, like many others (Cartwright, 1964; Hayward, 1975; Wilson-Barnett, 1976; Boore, 1978), found that the most stressful experiences related to failures in communication. Both Hayward (1975) and Boore (1978) were able to demonstrate how improved communication had a notably positive effect on physical recovery and psychological well-being (see Chapter 14). However, it is not only information *per se*, but the quality of interaction between nurse and patient that is important. Just being there with a patient may be as valuable in many circumstances.

This may be particularly so for patients in intensive care units where the normal environment is necessarily so disrupted. The importance of communication in intensive care units owes much to the work of Ashworth (1980), who recognized that not only is the patient exposed to a strange and alien environment, but is also deprived of all the normal orientations of daily life. Both can be sources of great stress.

STRESS IN NURSES

Many occupations and lifestyles can be described as stressful, but those working in the caring professions continually exposed to human suffering are, arguably, at greater risk from stress-related problems (Bailey, 1985). Marshall (1980) believes that nurses experience stress because in their work such importance is attached to success; failure of nursing care is clearly visible. Sources of stress must arise, in large part, from the contact with patients who may be in pain or afraid, but stress also arises from the demands of the organization in which nurses work. Some form of stress can be found in all specialities. Intensive care units (ICUs) have often been identified as particularly stressful for both the patient and the nurse. However, Claus and Bailey (1980) point out that the very same sources of stress in ICUs are also sources of great satisfaction. Likewise, although there must be some consensus as to the sources of stress—the perception of potentially stressful events will vary – one man's meat is another man's poison. A nurse may well find that being the only trained nurse on a busy geriatric ward to be far more stressful than being one of many such nurses on a highly mechanized intensive care unit.

Whatever the source of stress, nurses often feel that

any sign of anxiety will meet with professional disapproval and that the ideal nurse is one who has the emotional maturity to cope with frustrations and sadness, is able to subjugate her own needs to the needs of others and always puts on a 'good front'. Such an ideal is unrealistic and can often serve as yet a further source of stress as nurses strive to achieve this ideal. As the stressful nature of their work has been increasingly recognized, the coping strategies adopted by nurses have received considerable attention. How much do nurses adopt direct problem-solving techniques and how much are palliative, emotion-focused techniques the only means of coping available? One might assume that problem-solving approaches must be the most appropriate, but indirect and palliative methods are often the only means available if the nurse perceives her ability to alter the source of stress as limited. Avoidance mechanisms have been much cited. Menzies (1960) described how nurses avoid prolonged contact with patients in order to limit their own stress levels. Organising nursing care on a task basis, where care is fragmented and responsibility diffused allows only for limited involvement with patients. McGrath et al. (1989) argue cogently that with the current nursing philosophy of holistic care, which seeks to give a more personalized and less fragmented care that is responsive to patients' needs and problems, the demands made upon the emotional resources of nurses must be even greater. The effects of stress must militate against the provision of good nursing care. The nurse may become 'moody' and depressed, her concentration and judgement may be impaired such that decision-making may be avoided (Firth et al., 1987). In addition, she may experience distressing psychosomatic symptoms that may further impair nursing care and lead to absence from work. Concern over such stress has led to the recognition of the phenomenon of 'burn-out'. First identified by Freudenberger (1974), burn-out in nursing describes a state of 'professional depression' (Firth *et al.*, 1987) whereby, as a result of persistent stress and disequilibrium, the nurse becomes physically, emotionally and intellectually exhausted. Cherniss (1980) describes 'burn-out' as a disease of over-commitment—a constantly frustrated desire to achieve only the best. Eventually there is a progressive loss of idealism which is replaced by feelings of hopelessness (cf. Seligman, 1975). In behavioural terms, Maslach (1976) describes the resulting nursing care as lacking in concern, detached, impersonal and even dehumanized.

STRATEGIES FOR STRESS

If stress is an inescapable part of life, 'a by-product of the transaction between the individual and the environment' (Meichenbaum, 1983), then the understanding of stress and how we can both harness it and cope with it, should also be part of life. This is especially so for those whose role it is to help prevent and alleviate stress in others. By understanding the causes and individual manifestations of stress, nurses can go a long way in their assessment of patients to recognize when a patient is experiencing distress and when the balance between stress and the ability to cope is lost. By understanding the coping strategies adopted by patients, nurses can usefully re-inforce effective and adaptive mechanisms. It has been repeatedly shown that one of the most important ways of preventing and alleviating stress is via good communication. Just by being allowed to talk about their stress, people may be able to come to terms with their situation and cope with any feelings of fear and despair.

To cope with their own stress, nurses must also be

allowed to express their anxieties and have the support of their colleagues. Counselling, stress management techniques, assertiveness training and even 'stress inoculation' programmes have been used to good effect to enable nurses to master their own stress. Ceolowitz (1989) argues that 'planful problem solving' approaches to managing stress can significantly reduce the burn-out level in trained nurses. Many individual techniques such as relaxation and biofeedback can also prove helpful, but if the sources of stress in nursing are also within the organization of nursing, then organizational strategies to alleviate stress must also be addressed. Handy (1986) suggests that more energy should be expended in tackling sources of stress inherent in bureaucratic rules and regulations, rather than placing the onus for change entirely on the individual.

Whatever strategies are adopted, it serves only to conclude that a nurse who is able to recognize and cope with the demanding stimuli of her chosen career will then be well equipped to prevent and alleviate stress in her patients.

References

Ashworth, P. (1980) *Care to Communicate*. London: Royal College of Nursing.

Bailey, R.D. (1985) *Coping with Stress in Caring*. Oxford: Blackwell Scientific.

Boore, J.R.P. (1978) *Prescription for Recovery*. London: Royal College of Nursing.

Cartwright, A. (1964) *Human Relations and Hospital Care*. London: Routledge and Kegan Paul.

Ceolowitz, S. (1989) Burn-out and coping strategies among staff nurses. *Journal of Advanced Nursing* **14**, 553–557.

Cherniss, C. (1980) *Staff Burn-out: Job Stress in the Human Services*. London: Sage Publications.

Claus, K.E. & Bailey, J.T. (1980) *Living with Stress and Promoting Well-being*. St Louis, Missouri: C.V. Mosby.

Davies, A.D.M. & Peters, M. (1983) *Stress of hospitalisation in the elderly: nurses' and patients' perceptions. Journal of Advanced Nursing* **8**, 99–105.

Dewe, P.J. (1989) Stressor frequency, tension, tiredness and coping: some measurement issues and comparisons across nursing groups. *Journal of Advanced Nursing* **14**, 308–320.

Firth, H., McKeown, P., McIntee, J. & Britton, O. (1987) Professional depression, 'burn-out' and personality in long-stay nursing. *International Journal of Nursing Studies* **24**, 227–237.

Franklin, B.L. (1974) *Patient Anxiety on Admission to Hospital*. London: Royal College of Nursing.

Freudenberger, J. (1974) Staff burn-out. *Journal of Social Issues* **30**, 159–165.

Friedman, M. & Rosenman, R.H. (1974) *Type A Behaviour and Your Heart*. New York: Knopf.

Handy, J.A. (1986) Considering organisations in organisational stress research: a rejoinder to Glowinkowski and Cooper to Duckworth. *Bulletin of the British Psychological Society* **39**, 205–210.

Hayward, J.C. (1975) *Information: A Prescription against Pain*. London: Royal College of Nursing.

Holmes, T.H. & Rahe, R.H. (1967) The social readjustment rating scale, *Journal of Psychosomatic Research* **2**, 213–218.

Lazarus, R.S. (1966) *Psychological Stress and the Coping Process*. New York: McGraw Hill.

Lazarus, R.S. & Folkman, S. (1984) *Stress Appraisal and Coping*. New York: Springer.

Levi, L. (1974) Psychological stress and disease: a conceptual model. In Gunderson, E.K. and Rake, R.H. (eds) *Life Stress and Illness*. Sprinfield, Illinois: Thomas.

Levine, S. (1969) An endocrine theory of infantile stimulation. In Ambrose, A. (ed.) *Stimulation in Early Infancy*. London: Academic Press.

Livingstone, M. & Livingstone, H. (1984) Emotional distress in nurses at work. *British Journal of Medical Psychology* **57**, 291–294.

Marshall, J. (1980) Stress amongst nurses. In Cooper, C.L. and Marshall, J. (eds) *White Collar and Professional Stress*. Chichester: John Wiley.

Maslach, C.C. (1976) Burned out. *Human Behaviour* **5**, 16–22.

McCarthy, P. (1985) Burn-out in psychiatric nursing. *Journal of Advanced Nursing* **10**, 305–310.

McGrath, A., Reid, N. & Boore, J.R.P. (1989) Occupational stress in nursing. *International Journal of Nursing Studies* **26**, 343–358.

Meichenbaum, D. (1983) *Coping with Stress.*, Amsterdam. Multimedia Publications.

Menzies, I. (1960) A case study of functions of social systems as a defence against anxiety. *Human Relations* **13**, 95–123.

Monat, A. & Lazarus, R.S. (1977) *Stress and Coping: An Anthology.* New York: Columbia University Press.

Montague, S. (1980) The physiological basis of the stress reaction. *Nursing, Series 1* (10), 422–425.

Munday, A. (1973) *Physiological Measures of Anxiety in Hospital.* London: Royal College of Nursing.

Robertson, I. (1986) Learned helplessness. *Nursing Times* **82**, 28–30.

Seligman, M. (1975) *Helplessness: On Depression, Development and Death.* San Francisco: Freeman Co.

Selye, H. (1974) *Stress Without Distress.* London: Hodder and Stoughton.

Selye, H. (1980) Stress and a holistic view of health for the nurse. In Claus, K.E. and Bailey, J.T. (eds) *Living with Stress and Promoting Well Being.* St Louis, Missouri: C.V. Mosby.

Spielberger, C.D. (1972) *Anxiety: Current Trends in Theory and Research.* London: Academic Press.

Volicer, B.J., Isenberg, M.A. & Burns, M.W. (1977) Medical–surgical differences in hospital stress functions. *Journal of Human Stress* **3**, 3–13.

Weisman, A. (1979) *Coping with Cancer.* New York: McGraw Hill.

Welford, A. (1973) Stress and performance. *Ergonomics* **16**, 567.

Wilson-Barnett, J. (1976) Patients' emotional reactions to hospitalization: an exploratory study. *Journal of Advanced Nursing* **1**, 351–358.

Wilson-Barnett, J. (1979) *Stress in Hospital: Patients' Psychological Reactions to Illness and Health Care.* Edinburgh: Churchill Livingstone.

16 Pain

Although we all accept that pain is an unpleasant experience causing distress and suffering, and although all of us have experienced some degree of pain over the years, none of us can really know how pain feels to another person. This highly subjective feeling cannot be seen or measured directly. The pain of another can only be appreciated by its reflection in what the individual says, how he looks and what he does.

Current understanding of the complexity of pain recognizes that it cannot be explained by purely physical means. Physiological theorists now acknowledge the crucial role played by other disciplines, particularly the contribution of psychology. Few would deny that, for nurses, the care of patients in pain is an integral part of their role. Despite this, their knowledge and understanding of the mechanisms of pain and its relief is often somewhat lacking. As a result the assessment and relief of pain is often sadly influenced by misconceptions, stereotyping and a somewhat simplistic analysis of cause and effect. McCaffery (1983) has said that pain is 'whatever the experiencing person says it is, existing when he says it does'. In many ways this is both an ideal starting point and end point for the understanding that is necessary if nurses are to contribute effectively to the relief of pain.

It must not be forgotten, however, that pain does have a positive survival function, warning the individual of actual or potential harm. By so doing it enables defensive measures to be taken. One has only to consider conditions where pain perception is impaired or absent to recognize how important the protective function of pain can be. Unfortunately, many harmful conditions such as malignant tumour development or exposure to damaging X-rays may not give warning pain. Equally the experience of pain may far exceed its beneficial value or even occur when no cause for the pain can be identified. In such cases the pain can only be perceived as an unqualified evil and its alleviation becomes the main preoccupation.

UNDERSTANDING PAIN MECHANISMS

Despite the fact that pain is a universal experience, no anatomical location for pain can be identified. There is certainly no discrete pain centre in the brain. Rather it is felt that pain constitutes a complex interaction of many peripheral and central neural structures and that most of the brain plays some part in the experience (Melzack, 1973) and current research pursues this holistic line of thinking.

Before considering the various theories of pain that have been proffered over time, the physiological pathways shall be briefly outlined. Further specific detail can be usefully found in Boore *et al.* (1987).

The principal pain receptors, known as nociceptors, are the free nerve endings of small myelinated A-delta fibres and the unmyelinated C-fibres. These nociceptors are found abundantly throughout the body. Somatic pain describes that originating in the skin, muscles and joints and visceral pain describes that originating in the thorax or abdominal cavity. Qualitatively the pain experience differs according to source. A-delta fibres are essentially somatic, and transmit impulses rapidly and the pain is localized and sharp or pricking in nature. C-fibres can be both deep somatic or visceral and transmit impulses more slowly. The pain is diffuse and burning or aching in nature; a pain that is inclined to persist. These sensory fibres, sensitive to mechanical, thermal or chemical noxious stimuli, travel from their site of origin and enter the spinal cord and synapse with neurones in the substantia gelatinosa of the dorsal horns. Pain impulse result in the release of substance P, considered the main neurotransmitter of pain. This neurotransmission allows the pain impulses to cross over the spinal cord and connect with ascending pathways. Although there are thought to be several ascending pathways for pain, two main tracts have been identified whereby impulses ascend to the thalamus and relay on the cerebral cortex. It is via these specific tracts plus other non-specific tracts that impulses, both rapid and not so rapid, form multiconnections within the structures of the brain stem, thalamus hypothalamus and cerebral cortex. The result of such activity is that the individual is able to make perceptual discrimination as to the nature of the pain, become necessarily aroused in order to respond to the pain and make both cognitive and emotional evaluations of the pain. It is on the basis of these processes that the particular degree of pain is perceived and physiological and behavioural responses made.

THEORIES OF PAIN

It was until relatively recently that it was assumed that the mechanism of pain was quite simple. In the seventeenth century the philosopher, Descartes, proposed that the pain system was a straight through channel from the source to the brain. This specificity theory was taken up by von Frey (1895) who argued that every sensation had its own receptor which responded to a particular stimulus and that impulses were carried to a specific pain centre which he located in the thalamus. Would that it was that simple! The theory failed to account for so many individual responses, for example, the pain experienced in the absence of stimulation and the absence of pain that can occur despite noxious stimuli. Such responses deny a direct relationship between stimulus intensity and pain. In addition, pain fibres have also been shown to carry pressure and temperature impulses.

In contrast to the specificity theory, intensity or pattern theories of pain were developed that denied the existence of specialized receptors and pathways arguing instead that, as long as sensation of any sort exceeded a critical level, a pattern for pain would be produced. Thus sheer intensity of non-specific stimulation resulted in pain. In support of this theory, Livingstone (1943) suggested such stimulation could trigger off reverberating circuits that continued sending impulses to the brain after the stimulation has ceased, explaining, perhaps, the experience of pain with no identifiable source.

However, neither specificity nor pattern theories have adequately explained the experience of pain and it was not until the work of Melzack and Wall in the 1960s that a fuller and more satisfactory explanation of pain mechanisms was proposed.

THE 'GATE CONTROL' THEORY OF PAIN

The contribution of Melzack and Wall took the understanding of pain beyond that of mere sensations. Not only were they able to advance neurophysiological thinking, but were also able to demonstrate the importance of psychological influences on the neurophysiological mechanisms. Melzach (1973) has developed a three-dimensional model of pain: sensory, motivational/affective and cognitive/evaluative. The two latter dimensions are directly concerned with psychological processes that can modify the pain experience.

The original theory put forward by Melzack and Wall was quite simple in concept (Melzack and Wall, 1965). They argued that the transmission of painful stimuli could be controlled by a gating mechanism which they located in the substantia gelatinosa of the dorsal horns. They hypothesized that when there are a great number of impulses along the large nerve fibres that carry heat, cold and touch, then the transmission of pain impulses along the small A-delta and C-fibres is blocked by a synaptic gate. Only when these proposed gates are open, as when pain impulses predominate, does the individual experience pain. Further exploration of the gate control theory reveals more precise detail. It would seem that the overall effect of large fibre impulses is to activate the substantia gelatinosa. Small fibre activity has the opposite effect. The activation of the substantia gelatinosa inhibits transmission cell activity and it is this latter which is responsible for the central transmission of pain impulses to the brain. Hence massage, touch and warmth can cause the 'gate' to be closed to pain. However, it is important to note that adaptation of large fibre stimulation can occur quite quickly so that, unless the stimulation is sufficiently varied, its effect on the gate will gradually diminish. Pain impulses, on the other hand, do not adapt and in fact receptors may become more sensitive with repeated noxious stimulation.

The modulation of pain impulses does not only occur at the level of the spinal cord. With increasing theoretical refinement the 'gate control' model now incorporates the role of pain-inhibiting impulses that descend from the cerebral cortex and thalamus. It is thought that these inhibitory impulses may be directly under cognitive and emotional control in 'deciding' how much pain the individual will feel.

ENDORPHINS AND ENKEPHALINS

The discovery in the 1970s that the body has its own natural opiate analgesics served to support and build on the theoretical thinking of Melzack and Wall. Receptor sites for these natural opiates, polypeptides known as endorphins and enkephalins, are found, not only in the brain and spinal cord, but also peripherally in the neuronal synapses of the dorsal horns (Hughes *et al.*, 1975). It is thought that endorphins exert a central influence, modifying the painful experience via inhibitory descending pathways. In contrast, enkephalins play a role peripherally at the neuronal synapses of the dorsal horn. Here, under the influence of large fibre activity, enkephalin is released which inhibits substance P. By so doing, the transmission of painful impulses is also inhibited. Although the understanding of these natural opiates is as yet tentative, the recognition that psychological factors can increase or decrease their level in the body adds yet further credence to the importance of these psychological factors in the experience of pain.

PSYCHOLOGICAL FACTORS

Clearly, higher level processes influence the perception of pain. It may be that, in some circumstances, descending impulses inhibit the transmission of all pain impulses. However, even those impulses that are transmitted to the brain must undergo interpretation to determine the nature, quality and intensity of the sensation. It is this central interpretation that may result in the intensity of the noxious stimulation having little relationship to the actual pain experienced. The question has to be that of what the sensation means to the individual.

The American psychologist, Beecher, was one of the first to make the distinction between the purely physical sensations of pain and the actual perception and response which involved psychological processes. Beecher observed that people who had suffered the same degree of injury but under very different circumstances experienced very different levels of pain. He looked at soldiers who had suffered severe wounds in combat and compared their need for opiate analgesia with civilians who had similar injuries. For the soldiers for whom severe injury also meant withdrawal from the risk of further injury and who were, perhaps, just glad to be alive, the need for analgesia was minimal. However, this was not the case for the civilians for whom the similar injuries, having no positive connotations, were viewed entirely negatively (Beecher, 1959).

The work of Beecher led to a burgeoning of similar investigations that were to conclude that actual physical damage is only one aspect contributing to the experience of pain (Melzack, 1973). Yet the meaning of the pain is not only influenced by the actual circumstances in which the noxious stimuli occurs (Beecher, 1959), but also by the personality, cultural, upbringing and past experience of each individual. Nurses who understand this will realize that in aiming for relief of pain, they are caring for whole people not just a physiological symptom.

PAIN THRESHOLDS AND TOLERANCE

Before considering psychological influences in detail, two important and dependent concepts need to be identified. They are pain threshold and pain tolerance. Unlike other sensations, pain thresholds and tolerance can vary widely. Threshold refers to the intensity of the stimulus necessary before the person perceives pain. Such thresholds may be very high or even seemingly absent, for example, in situations of intense emotion. By contrast, chronic anxiety can lower the pain threshold. Physical destruction of nerve endings that can occur in the severely burned individual will also cause the loss of pain perception. Less easy to understand are those individuals who suffer from the rare clinical disorder of 'congenital insensitivity to pain'. Such people have never experienced pain and yet their sensory system is intact. Psychobiological theories developed by those such as Melzack (1973) may help provide some answers. Pain tolerance refers to the amount of pain an individual is willing to endure before seeking relief. Such things as religious faith, distraction, alcohol and drugs can increase tolerance whereas fear, anger and boredom can reduce tolerance. Western society tends to look more favourably on those whose tolerance is high, who will 'grin and bear it', but such value judgments may only impair the capacity to help someone in pain.

In the light of the above, the psychological factors referred to will be looked at more closely.

CULTURAL FACTORS

Increasingly we live in a multicultural society and must be aware of cultural variations in values, attitudes and behaviour. Cultural influences on the experience of pain has been widely examined. One of the key studies was by Zborowski (1969), who was able to show significant differences in the behavioural expression of pain among different ethnic groups. Not only did the expression of pain vary, but also the purpose of their expression. One group sought only relief of pain, whereas another sought understanding of the cause. Two important points should be raised from such findings. Firstly, as indicated above, there is a tendency to judge others from the standpoint of one's own cultural values and, secondly, there is an equal tendency to stereotype individuals and assess and predict their pain accordingly. Davitz and Davitz (1985) suggest that generalization are hard to avoid and therefore should be used in a constructive rather than prejudicial manner.

PERSONALITY AND PAIN

The belief that one's personality can influence the experience of pain is not new. The relationship between specific traits and pain responses as measured on personality inventories has led to interesting and controversial findings. Eysenck's Personality Inventory (E.P.I.), which looks specifically at degrees of neuroticism and extraversion, has been usefully correlated with pain responses. Perhaps the most important outcome from these and similar studies is the realization that anxiety—be it part of the individual's unique personality structure or purely situationally determined—can have a considerable and negative effect on the pain experience (Sternbach, 1974; Weisenberg, 1980). Bond (1971) used the E.P.I. to study the pain experience of women with cervical cancer. It appeared that the sociable, but less emotional women were less likely to experience pain than their more emotional but less sociable counterparts. However, the latter seemed less likely to complain of their pain. Those women identified as both sociable and emotional were more likely both to experience pain and voice their distress. Further research suggested that introverts were more sensitive to pain, but that, when in pain, extroverts were far more expressive. Other work on personality factors have looked to categorize 'types' in terms of how they react to pain. Petrie (1967), for example, identifies the reducer, the augmentor and the moderate. The disadvantage of such approaches is that it could result in inappropriate labelling of patients in pain. Indeed, Engel (1959) describes a 'pain prone personality' which he associates with a particular family and personal background.

Of course, the experiences of childhood may significantly affect how pain will be perceived and responded to as an adult. Children can quickly model their behaviour on that observed in significant adults. The small child at the dentist who observes anxiety and fear in his accompanying mother, will quickly learn to associate the dentist with fear and have a high expectation of pain. McCaffery (1983) argues that excessively anxious parents of ill children, determined to prevent further harm, may sometimes only increase the child's fear of pain. Consider also the gender of a child. A small boy tends to be encouraged to be stoical whilst a small girl is allowed much greater expression of her emotions (Shultz, 1971). In this way values are transmitted from one generation to the next and the observation that women tend to be more responsive to pain than men is not so surprising. However, it should be noted that the actual experience of pain in an individual's past can have positive effects. If such pain had been intense it may make any subsequent pain appear relatively mild. Equally, having perhaps coped successfully with the stress of previous pain, the individual feels less threatened or fearful of an unknown such that pain tolerance is increased. Such arguments may support the notion that older people tolerate pain better than the young (cf. Chapter 19).

ENVIRONMENTAL AND SITUATIONAL FACTORS

The observations of Beecher show just how significant other situational factors are in the interpretation of painful stimuli. Anecdotal evidence of sportsmen ignoring severe injury in the 'heat' of competition and of individuals equally unaware of physical trauma in their need to escape from mortal danger demonstrate how such things as attention, distraction and emotional preoccupation can vastly modify pain thresholds and tolerance. Central mechanisms filter out extraneous 'disadvantageous' information in order that the individual can focus completely on perceived priorities in a situation. Interestingly, both pain and the absence of pain, in response to physical injury, may be seen as having positive survival value. Environmental factors also include the interpersonal environment. Pain is often better tolerated in an atmosphere of trust and support, for example, the presence or touch of a friend or relative. Sometimes pain tolerance is enhanced, not by diversion of attention, but by actually being able to focus on and feel some control over the pain, for example the patient removing his own adhesive dressing.

TYPES OF PAIN

The most crucial aspect of caring for someone in pain is believing their pain. The pain is what the individual says it is. However, in order to assess the pain experience and plan relief, it is important to understand the differing qualities and types of pain. Pain can be described as either acute or chronic. Acute pain is usually sharp in nature, of short duration and ends when the source has been removed. This is not the case for chronic pain which may be throbbing, burning or aching in nature and last months or even years, long after the original source has ceased to exist. Moreover, chronic pain may not have an identifiable source and may carry with it the associated miseries of insomnia, irritability and depression. Sometimes the pain is described as intractable, dominating a person's life and reducing horizons to a total preoccupation with the pain and means of relief. It can be argued that the use of the term intractable is unhelpful, as it has such negative connotations. Dolan (1982) describes intractable pain as stubborn but not invincible.

Pain is sometimes described as referred. The pain experience is actually located away from its source. Commonly the origin of the pain is visceral but the experience may be somatic. Explanations of referred pain suggest that pain impulses from the viscera share the same neural pathways as somatic impulses and that the latter predominates in terms of pain experience. Referred pain can be especially distressing to the individual as it would seem to defy logic thereby causing misconceptions and even fear. Even more distressing may be the experience of phantom pain associated with amputation. Many explanations have been put forward to try and increase the understanding of this phenomenon, but none fully account for the experience of pain from a source that is no more.

A false dichotomy has often been made between pain for which an organic cause is found and pain for which there appears to be no organic base; organic versus psychogenic pain. This dualism owes its origin to Descartes, who saw body and mind as two separate entities. However, following this line of thinking only impedes fully understanding people in pain. As has been shown, diagnosing organically based pain does not rule out psychogenic factors and whether the source of the pain is organic or psychogenic, for the individual there is no discernible difference. Both organic and psychogenic pain hurt. Fortunately with the ever increasing appreciation of the complex nature of pain, the latter can no longer be dismissed as 'all in the mind'.

ASSESSING PAIN

In the introduction it was stated that no one can really know another's pain. The only 'expert' as to the pain experience is the patient himself. By increasing her knowledge and understanding of pain, the nurse can develop skills that will enable her, not only to assess the nature of the pain, but also to plan appropriate and individualized ways of relieving or at least minimizing the pain. As has been discussed, it is very easy to bring one's own values and attitudes to the assessment of pain, but very hard to actually accurately measure the seemingly immeasurable. To this end great effort has gone in to developing imaginative ways whereby the patient can communicate his pain—both verbally and non-verbally. Many scales, charts and 'painometers' have been developed which allow patients to rate his pain or describe it in orthodox and unorthodox terms, but probably the most sensitive assessment is achieved by skilled communication which allows the patient to fully express his feelings in an atmosphere of empathy and trust. A useful model of pain assessment has been developed by Loeser (1982). It reflects the psychobiological basis of pain and is sensitive enough as a measure to allow appropriate individualized nursing intervention. The model looks at four factors: nociception, pain, suffering and pain behaviour. Nociception concerns the identification of actual tissue damage and sources of pain initiation. Pain looks for both subjective descriptions of pain and objective physiological measures of such things as blood pressure, heart rate and respiration indicative of a response to the stress of pain. Suffering, which is not synonomous with pain, concerns how the pain affects the patient emotionally. Emotions are often harder to verbalize than descriptions of the pain. The last aspect of assessment looks at pain behaviours such as facial expression, limitation of movement, withdrawal from social interaction and need for analgesic medication. All the factors assessed build on each other and provide the data from which a plan of care can be developed to meet physical and psychosocial needs.

RELIEVING PAIN

In the real world of nursing it is often found to be all too easy to give analgesic medication in response to expressed pain and ignore the many other valuable therapeutic measures. Often the patient himself is deprived from exploiting his own psychological capacities that may enable him to cope with pain. This is not to deny the vital part analgesic medication plays in pain relief, but the use must be judicious, discriminate and personal, never administered or withheld without thought and feeling. McCaffery (1983) encapsulates, succinctly and soundly, the nurses' duties and responsibilities required.

The many alternative strategies to relieve pain point up the increased understanding of the psychology of pain. Liebeskind and Paul (1977) state that man has powerful endogenous mechanisms that enable him to inhibit or modify pain experiences and that these mechanisms must be harnessed and employed. To this end, techniques and measures that enhance the body's natural opiates by, for example, minimizing anxiety or facilitating 'gate closure' are used to the full. Techniques may be quite sophisticated but often research serves only to reinforce the efficacy of simple comfort measures, such as rearranging pillows, repositioning limbs or simply being with a patient in pain. Other effective measures have been the use of massage, warmth, acupuncture and transcutaneous electric nerve stimulation (TENS), all of which are believed to relieve pain by stimulating large nerve fibre activity thus, mediated by enkephalins, closing the 'gate' to pain transmission. Strategies that are thought to act more centrally and increase the level of endorphins, are such techniques as relaxation, distraction therapy, biofeedback and guided imagery. By so doing the perception of pain is modified. It should be recognized that often these techniques do no more than build on and enhance an individual's natural capacities. Enhancing the patient's confidence in his own ability to reduce pain is an essential part of positive coping. For some patients the use of hypnosis can prove effective (Barber and Adrian, 1982). Its success is thought to relate to the suggestability of the individual such that he expects not to feel pain afterwards. A similar explanation is given for the placebo effect whereby a patient is given a physiologically inert substance and yet experiences relief of pain. The patient believes and expects it to work. In no way was the original pain unreal (a common and foolish misconception). On the contrary, it is believed that in response to the psychological state of high expectation endorphins are released and, as with the other measures described, 'natural' analgesia is obtained.

The reduction of anxiety can be achieved by all the above measures but, arguably, it is the nurse's ability to communicate effectively that will reduce anxiety and thereby facilitate the efficacy of the techniques used (cf. Chapter 14). Good communication, be it verbal, such as information-giving and explanations (Hayward, 1975), or non-verbal, such as the use of touch and eye contact, is fundamental to the relief of suffering (Sofaer, 1983).

The successful management of chronic pain, whether the cause is known or not, still poses the greatest challenge for those who care for or live with the sufferers. By viewing pain holistically the hospice movement and the development of pain clinics have done much to help in the alleviation of such pain. As indicated earlier, chronic pain can go so far as to alter an individual's very existence, making him anxious, depressed and even angry. Booker (1982) argues that many of these changes are due to biochemical imbalances, not least the depletion of endorphins caused by the pain. For some the experience of chronic pain can lead to the development of distorted associations. The pain becomes associated with the gaining of love and attention, escape from reality or total dependence on medication for relief. The behavioural problems that can result may be helped by behaviour therapy whereby using the principles of operant conditioning, inappropriate pain related behaviour patterns are gradually extinguished and replaced by behaviour that enables positive coping. The work of those such as Fordyce (1978) and Seres and Newman (1976) has shown how effective behaviour therapy can be.

In conclusion, it can only be said that if nurses will

recognize and seek to understand the complexities of pain and use this understanding to enrich their skills necessary for relieving pain, the challenge pain poses will bring its own rewards.

References

Barber, J. & Adrian, C. (1982) *Psychological Approaches to the Management of Pain*. New York: Bruner-Mazel.

Beecher, H.K. (1959) *Measurement of Subjective Responses: Qualitative Effects of Drugs*. New York: Oxford University Press.

Bond, J.R. (1971) The relation to pain to the Eysenck Personality Index, Cornell Medical Index and the Whitley Index of Hypochondriasis. *British Journal of Psychiatry* **119**, 671–678.

Booker, J. (1982) Pain: it's all in your patient's head (or is it?) *Nursing 82* **12**, 47–51.

Boore, J.R.B., Champion, R. & Ferguson, N.C. (1987) *Nursing the Physically Ill Adult*. Edinburgh: Churchill Livingstone.

Davitz, L.L. & Davitz, J.R. (1985) Culture and nurses' inferences of suffering. In Copp, L.A. (ed.) *Perspectives on Pain*. Edinburgh: Churchill Livingstone.

Dolan, M.B. (1982) Controlling pain in a personal way. *Nursing 82* **12**, 68.

Engel, G.L. (1959) 'Psychogenic Pain' and the pain prone patient. *American Journal of Medicine* **270**, 825–827.

Fordyce, W.E. *et al.* (1976) *Behavioural Methods for Chronic Pain and Illness*. St Louis, Missouri: C.V. Mosby.

Fordyce, W.C. (1978) Learning processes in pain: In Sternbach R.A. *et al.* (eds) *The Psychology of Pain*. New York: Raven Press.

Hayward, J.C. (1975) *Information: A Prescription against Pain*. London: Royal College of Nursing.

Hughes, J., Smith, T.W., Kosterlitz, H.W., Fothergill, L.A., Morgan, B.A. & Morris, H.R. (1975) Identification of two related pentapeptides from the brain with potent opiate activity. *Nature* **258**, 577–579.

Liebeskind, J.C. & Paul, L.A. (1977) Psychological and physiological mechanisms of pain. *Annual Review of Psychology* **28**, 41–60.

Livingstone, W.K. (1943) *Pain Mechanisms*. London: Macmillan.

Loeser, J. (1982) Concepts of pain. In Stanton Hicks, and Boas, R. (eds) *Chronic Low Back Pain*. New York: Raven Press.

McCaffery, M. (1983) *Nursing the Patient in Pain*. London: Harper & Row.

Melzack, R. (1973) *The Puzzle of Pain*. Harmondsworth: Penguin.

Melzack, R. & Wall, P.D. (1965) Pain mechanisms: a new theory. *Science* **150**, 971–979.

Newman, R.I. *et al.* (1978) Multidisciplinary treatment of chronic pain: long term follow up of low back pain patients. *Pain* **4**, 283–292.

Petrie, A. (1967) *Individuality in Pain and Suffering*. Chicago: University of Chicago Press.

Seres, J.L. & Newman, R.I. (1976) Results of treatment of chronic low back pain at the Portland Pain Centre. *Journal of Neurosurgery* **45**, 32–36.

Shultz, N. (1971) How children perceive pain. *Nursing Outlook* **19**, 670–671.

Sofaer, B. (1983) Pain relief—the importance of communication. *Nursing Times* **79**, 32–35.

Sternbach, R.A. (1974) *Pain Patients: Traits and Treatment*. New York: Academic Press.

Von Frey, M. (1895) Cited in Melzach, R. and Wall, P.D. (1982) *The Challenge of Pain*. Harmondsworth: Penguin.

Weisenberg, M. (1980) Understanding pain phenomena. In Rackman, S. (ed.) *Contributions to Medical Psychology* Vol. **2**, pp. 79–111. Oxford: Pergamon Press.

Zborowski, M. (1969) *People in Pain*. San Francisco: Jossey Bass.

Index